D0443913

# SEAN CONNERY

Michael Feeney Callan

This revised and updated edition first published in
Great Britain in 2002 by
Virgin Books Ltd
Thames Wharf Studios
Rainville Road
London
W6 9HA

First revised edition first published in Great Britain as *Sean
Connery: The Untouchable Hero* in 1993 by Virgin Publishing
Ltd

First published in Great Britain as *Sean Connery: His Life and
Films* in 1983 by WH Allen & Co Ltd

A catalogue record for this book is available from the British
Library.

ISBN 1 85227 992 3

Typeset by Phoenix Photosetting, Chatham, Kent
Printed and bound in Great Britain by CPD, Wales

*To Corey Callan
the next James Bond*

# CONTENTS

# LIST OF ILLUSTRATIONS

# PREFACE

Celebrity is a murder weapon. Its advantages are obvious but it is also easy to see its facility for social abuses and its destructive power both for the celebrated and the celebrators. Reading the tabloids, it appears more a pathology than a state of grace. Given that, it seems strange why so many pursue it. The superficial attractions, perhaps, are obvious: power, wealth, and the salve for vanity. But there are different kinds of celebrity with different mechanisms supplying them. On the face of it Sean Connery falls into the classic variety of fame seeker. Born into abject poverty in the slums of Edinburgh, his early and only dream was escape. Before he was 14, the potential of the body beautiful showed him the way. As an instrument of accomplishment it could, seemingly, achieve anything. With it, he could win sex, friendship, money, esteem. Ergo, he worked it, honed it like Michelangelo perfecting David, and it brought him to the movies and the celebrity that generates this book.

But that's the pat and facile reading of Sean Connery's character that explains more his contempt for fame than the *raison d'être*. In short, Connery doesn't fit the standard pattern of fame seekers. He is of that sub-genre that finds its way into the history books with descriptive superlatives like 'inspired' and (usually too generously) 'genius' garnering their flanks. Certainly – and obviously – Connery was driven. It is impossible to look at the contemporary photographs or documents of inner city Edinburgh of the depressed 1930s and not be awed, humbled even, by the ravages of rabbit-warren housing and visibly absent social services; it is also impossible for anyone with a little imagination and half a heart not to feel the same sense of agitation Connery found overpowering and, fundamentally, motivational. Poverty got Sean Connery moving. It started his upward climb, first of all to economic independence at any cost, thence to a malleable career, thence the adventures in creativity that yielded cinematic James Bond and much beyond. It also fuelled his acute social conscience, his antipathy towards institutional tyranny – be it the empire ethics of Great Britain as they related to Scotland the beloved heartland or Hollywood big biz – and the scourge of an untiringly nomadic spirit. Along the way, though, something happened.

To pose Connery as mystic-minded, as a questing artist hungry for spiritual meaning in self-realisation, appears, on the face of it, absurd: the body of philosophy discernible from his scant exchanges with the press amounts to a laundry list of self-protecting (self-effacing) one-liners that would have bored Freud or Jung. But there is revelation in the omissions. Connery, more than virtually any star actor – Brando included – has walked the walk in place of talking the talk. His reclusiveness is authentic, not arrogant, and there is evidence, both in the objective analyses of those close to him and in the pattern of his artistic choices, of important forces at work. He is not a jobbing actor – despite the apparent indulgence of pap like *Meteor* or *Sword of the Valiant*. Michael Caine is a jobbing actor. Michael Caine is also a sensitive, unselfconscious and finely gifted man capable of the truly trans-porting inventions – as in *Hannah and her Sisters* – that won him Oscars and BAFTAs. But Connery's awards, be they Oscars or knighthoods, seem secondary to the undercurrents we sense in a career that stands before us with the monolithic bulk of great architecture.

The evidence of a scheme – of inspiration beyond instinct – is there from the start of his professional life. One has to remember the world he emerged from. In 1957, when he started in movies, aged 27, British film was culturally lumpish and non-representative. Intelligent actors like Dirk Bogarde would sense the collapse of potential and quickly turn tail, but the prevailing production spirit was class-riven and, in hindsight, almost offensively anachronistic and the favoured acting style all but Elizabethan. Connery would have none of it. When his muscle-man body earned him access to treading the boards in *South Pacific* he immediately armoured himself with self-education. There was nothing saintly about him. He accepted with vigour the prizes of the spotlight: the women, the travel, the money-for-jam. But the greater part of his energies was

PREFACE

applied to understanding the mythologising of human experience in the classics. Robert Henderson, his acting guru, insisted till his death that he had never, in more than fifty years' performing and directing, encountered a raw talent like Connery's so focused on the discipline of understanding human behaviour in the course of establishing an acting compass. 'He approached Joyce and Ibsen,' Henderson recalled, 'as if they possessed the keys to the kingdom.' Contracted early on to Fox – in its dying throes in British production – Connery would have nothing to do with the status quo. In one or two movies where he had bit parts he seemingly toed the line; but this, he admits, was about 'finding the furniture' of the movie set. In a subsequent one or two he drifted. Thereafter, when finally cast prominently in (for its time and place) an edgy British thriller, *The Frightened City*, he upended the furniture. *The Frightened City*, all about sub-Krays racketeering in Macmillan's Britain, *should* have felt cosy. British thrillers of the era featured elegant Jaguars, plane-tree lined squares and toffs in cashmere coats shooting guns that went *bang-bang*. Connery entered stage left spitting rocket fuel. In *The Frightened City* he is borderline frightening, an utterly appropriate depiction of a half-cocked thug that seemed to borrow the goods – inappropriately in context of the norm – from the contemporaneous manic flux of the Theatre of the Angry Young Man. *The Frightened City* was the laboratory for James Bond – at least in part. The other experimental borrowings came courtesy of Hollywood, from the previously headlined *Darby O'Gill and the Little People* where Connery first breathed the catalytic air of hardcore Hollywood (Walt Disney, for heaven's sake), and sang, danced and romanced with a sexy girl. The extrapolations of both movies gave flesh to James Bond, renewed domestic cinema and briefly, brilliantly, paralleled the Beatles in bringing a British voice into the cultural civil rights movement that was the pop 60s.

Bond and the Beatles equally asserted the sanctity of 'the original'. Both, in their mint form, railed against the homogeneity of the conveyor belt. Each had a respectful, even curatorial, respect for the past, counterbalanced by courageous and healthy iconoclasm. Each was the product of team playing: in the case of the Beatles John Lennon led the quartet of talents, while in Bond

3

Connery led a not dissimilar symbiotic foursome. Cubby Broccoli and Harry Saltzman were the producer talents while director Terence Young brought an anthropological accuracy to the sophisticated updating of the blue-chip MI6 man, but Connery lent nuance. Some of it was basic: the leonine walk, voyeuristically observed by Broccoli and Saltzman as Connery left their audition rooms at South Audley Street in London, presented ready-wrapped the unevolved animal in the trained killer. The rest came from Connery's impressive autodidacticism and pure giftedness. Connery was quoted in 1965 as saying that he felt not so much 'sympathy' for Ian Fleming's literary Bond, the source reference, rather that he felt 'like a medium' for Fleming. It is hard, here, to overstate his achievement. Connery's James Bond was much more than a rethreaded adventure/spy formula: it was a new genre, a place of transgressed boundaries and fused polarities, where sadomasochistic sexuality was made palatable by virtue of the subtlest wit, where pyrotechnics muscled in on the Aristotelean principles of drama – and it was universally alluring most of all for the virtuosity of its core character, a sole actor: Connery. Unarguably, the most manifest measure of the success of Bond was financial. No British franchise before or since has generated anything comparable at the box office and the quirky international mega successes of the 80s and 90s – movies like *Chariots of Fire* and *Four Weddings and a Funeral* – just touched the coat-tails of the individual early Bonds in terms of net profits.

Ironically, for many tragically, it was the very issue of profits, of filthy lucre, that antagonised Connery and made him quit Bond at the apogee. Connery's oft-reported 'reputation' as a penurious individual owes its origins to the squabbles with the Bond producers – especially Harry Saltzman – at this time. But given his own origins, and his personal contribution to Bondmania, his focus on a fair share of the kitty seems no less than reasonable. By the time he first quit in 1967, after the fifth Bond, *You Only Live Twice*, the movies had grossed more than $150 million (ten times that amount in today's values); it is unlikely he had seen more than a hundredth of that sum, and indeed had only been cut in on profit-sharing after the third movie. What Connery wanted in 1967 was a three-way equitable partnership with Broccoli and Saltzman that would allow them, in his words, 'to own United Artists'. A lesser actor, a lesser spirit, might be called to account for this greed. But Connery's artistry with Bond, and his concurrent role-seeking in ambitious movies, indicated the territory he was navigating. Sure, there's no debating the commercial acumen of Broccoli (Saltzman was another matter: he amortised his Bond earnings and ended up a potentially serious bankrupt); and there is clearly no debating the popular success of the franchise when it moved into the hands of other directors and other actors. But there is a strong argument for the inestimable loss to the British film industry in the missed moment. Connery was never just an actor. Everyone close to him attests to his authorial hand in almost everything he has done in movies; on top of that, he is, as evidenced by his charity work and promotion of an autonomous Scotland, a visionary businessman. In the mid-60s, at the height of the game, it seems certain that Connery would have parlayed his Bond success into an inventive broad-basing that committed UA to heavier investment in varied projects, thereby securing a more resonant and lasting triumph for British film production. As it was, the honeymoon of critical Brit relevance in the international pop culture scene ended with the disintegration of the Beatles and Connery's falling-out with Broccoli and Saltzman.

More than any other actor, Connery was set up at the end of the 60s with a licence to print money by rethreading pop spies. Michael Caine, Rod Taylor and Dean Martin were hard at it, but apart from two shoot-from-the-hip forays into resurrecting Bond (one savvy, one stupid), Connery chose another course. Reading the scant press files (in comparison with any equal star, and apart from Bond floss, his lengthy interview-features are negligible), it appears that Hollywood, plain and simple, was the choice and covenant. As early as 1964 he was actively hunting a casting by Hitchcock – and got it, in *Marnie* – and 23 years later the crown of Oscar was granted, for *The Untouchables*. But any study of his life, or careful evaluation of his work, turns up the kind of quixotic idealism that distinguishes the mystic and the fool. He is certainly no fool, so it's interesting, in light of his enduring and apparently inviolable iconography, to pay attention to those who know him and speak earnestly of his 'still vastly underrated genius' (so says his friend Michael Caine), to contemplate the elusive forces that feed him.

By his own frequent admission Bondmania traumatised him, as Beatlemania traumatised the Beatles. But its force was also – in both cases – epiphanic, and propelled him inward to greater introspection than most would allow. Mixed with the anthropological groundwork of his actor training, this frantic self-seeking produced the motley collection of superbly realised alter ego roles from the middle 60s to the 90s. The media cavalcade of Bondmania drowned the finer points, but a revisit to such important movies as Irvin Kershner's *A Fine Madness*, made when Connery was 36, demonstrates the intensity of the emotional journey he was embarked on even then, and the riches effortlessly mined there. The cursory glance shows Connery as the cowboy, the king, the unstable police officer, the Berber pirate, the buffoon, the pious, the lecher, the triumph and disaster. Only on secondary closer inspection does one see the uniqueness of the journey. The greatest living movie actors, from Brando to De Niro, have the courage and integrity to shave their heads and play the villain; but few have ventured, shaven or bewigged, through quite so many ranks of the human parade.

None of which is to say that Connery, even in his 70s, has offered us any significant mystical insights. But what he has done, often by default it seems, is gain our attention in a way no contemporary British actor has. The constantly regurgitated reports that he is regularly rated among 'the world's sexiest men' are really pointers only to the architecture of his massive career and the signposts onward. 'There comes a moment,' Michael Caine told me, 'when you reach a sense of the boundary of an actor. You know what he is, and what he can do, and you know he cannot surprise you. I defy anyone to say that about Sean. It just isn't credible. We are way, way past James Bond now. James Bond was just a moment when Sean tapped into a kind of universal unconscious – where the whole world was comatose in the drabness of the postwar years, and then he woke them up. That's long past. But his power isn't. He's like a tiger. He can lie there. He can rest. But there is always the *suspicion* that he'll jump up any minute and shock you.'

The body of the text of this book was researched and written in the 1980s, coinciding with Connery's ill-judged reactivation of Bond in the execrable *Never Say Never Again*. Then, it benefited hugely from the guiding contributions of his younger brother Neil, and from lovers and friends, as well as his major movie associates like Fred Zinnemann, Richard Lester, John Boorman and the Bond directors. It also took advantage of that untypical period of Connery's media-friendliness as he heavily promoted a Bond movie (developed with producer Kevin McClory) that, finally, he had significant partnership points in. In the early 90s the book was re-researched and updated, this time invigorated by Connery's landmark concession to a substantial film biography – the only one he has ever allowed – which was made for STV by producer–director Ross Wilson and to which this author contributed. Since the screening of that documentary and the reissue of this book in 1993, Connery has been unavailable for media self-analysis but has continued to make movies, many in the negotiated 'control role' of executive producer, many for his own production company, Fountainbridge Films. Five of the ten he has made are notable; five seem whimsical. What unifies them is the undercurrent of relentless ambition, a disposition manifestly unaltered since the pre-Bond years. The notorious bomb, *The Avengers*, illustrates the unyielding spirit. Connery accepted the role with Swiftian wit. In the 60s, as Bond ruled the big screen, ABC television's *The Avengers* paced him for sophistication and surreal inventiveness, all credit to its writer/producer team, Brian Clemens and Albert Fennell. *The Avengers'* icon John Steed was James Bond's television mirror-image. In tackling a movie of *The Avengers*, Connery explored his own iconography with irony by aligning himself with the ranks of the opposition. Perversely, he would not be Steed, but Steed's evil nemesis. Those close to Connery attest to his intellectual glee at the prospect; but he hadn't, he later moaned, accounted for the director. The movie was a mess and, true to his 'call a spade a spade' legend, Connery openly threatened 'to kill' the makers if he could lay hands on them. Nonetheless, the movie indicated the subtlety of his modus. In the 80s, before his tragic death by drug overdose, Jay Maloney at CAA agented Connery and fought regularly with him over hefty proposed scripts that Connery threw aside. Money was important, but it was, as Maloney learned, far from everything. Successive established producer-directors – from Neil Jordan to Richard Lester – failed to win him to dreamy scenarios offering top dollar. Instead, Connery followed his muse towards some self-resolution. In movies like *Just Cause* and *Rising Sun* there are signs of intellectual stretch. *The Rock* and *First Knight* show his Dylanesque determination to 'rage, rage, against the dying of the light'. But the recent thoughtful movies like the provocative romance *Playing by Heart* and *Finding Forrester* attest to consolidated growth. Each could have been apt vehicles for James Mason, Richard Burton or Laurence Olivier at their best; each postulates a master class in cinema art, where less is more and the mesmerising power of the actor is his nano-second facility to affect and afflict.

So Connery has grown through the silence of the 90s, but he has also hugely changed. As the autumnal awards were heaped on him – the BAFTA Lifetime Achievement, the Cecil B DeMille, the Lincoln Center Film Award, even the belated knighthood – he was eloquent in his humility, often softened to tears. He seemed, again, the strokable, somnolent big cat. But the triumph of occasion was illusory. As the awards heaped up, so the scars of his personal past and the impatience of his social conscience roused him. Empowered by honours – by 'the seat at the top table', as he once called it – Connery lashed out at the moral definitions of his status as a Scotsman. Always a supporter of Scotland's underprivileged and, ultimately, of the SNP, he spoke out for Scottish independence in an affiliated partnership with Britain and Europe and upset many. The press portrayal was of a regressive, aggressive oddity, a political anachronism who ill understood the economic values of globalisation. Connery has employed bodyguards and publicists, but he should have engaged a speech-writer. Eloquent sporadically, but victim of moods, his true position, his friends agree, was not fully articulated. Born to the slum, he is a convert to compassionate socialism. But he is also, in the simple sense, a capitalist who believes that every man should have his chance. Individualism, he contends, is what has driven human evolution and attained the great goals of civilisation; and individualism must be cherished and encouraged at all costs. Though the anti-SNP press would pretend otherwise, he is, as a humanitarian, the perfect model of the social activist: he allows for the inevitability of the global village whilst demanding the preservation of cultural and tribal integrity. He is a realist, perceiving the survivable world in only one way: as a pluralist community.

But, as the millennium turned, there were other changes in Sean Connery that called a revision and reconsideration of this book back into being. In 1998 he quit his longtime home near Marbella in Spain for a nomadic life, drifting between apartments in New York and LA and a small white bungalow with a forty-foot front garden at Lyford Cay near Nassau in the Bahamas. For almost forty years the game of golf had been his anchor, as staunch a part of his life as the John-and-Yoko closeness with Micheline, his wife since 1975. But in an interview with the *Daily Telegraph* in 2001 he stated that he'd had enough. To those who know Connery, the declaration of a future without golf was tantamount to a hint of surrender. Perhaps, despite the spirit of the big cat, retirement to gentle pastures was finally in view. But before the curt *Telegraph* interview was dispensed with, Connery was pledging an alternative: from henceforth his extra curricular time would be spent in competitive tennis foursomes.

In the spring of 2002, after the usual months of square-dance negotiations, Connery and his agents agreed a new multi-picture deal with Fox, the studio which had first contracted him more than forty years previously. Connery's most recent movie had been *Finding Forrester*, his second powerhouse rendering (after *A Fine Madness*) of the surreal life of an author. Fox's new arrangement, initially committing him to a movie called *The League of Extraordinary Gentlemen*, to be followed by sequels, seems to return him to the territory of James Bond. Producer Don Murphy described the new movie as 'a period-piece *X-Men* type', based on the comic art novels of Alan Moore, in which Connery will play a kind of heroic composite who sounds nothing less than Homeric. To some, there seemed on the face of it a jaded surrender in this apparent return to sources, to Fox and action-cartoons. But the fury of *The Avengers* debacle and what Michael Caine insists remains a no-compromise determination for growth, speak more of a creative surge comparable with the focus of the early 60s. It is revealing that, throughout the late 90s, the unshakeable Kevin McClory, he who sued Fleming for a share in Bond and won the rights to remake *Thunderball* ad infinitum, constantly pressed Connery to return to Bondage; all sorts of borderline reinterpretations of the original movie were posited, but Connery always went no further than maybe. Now, with *The League of Extraordinary Gentlemen*, Connery enthusiastically embraces once again the spoof world of hero-myth.

It is possible – probable even – that *The League of Extraordinary Gentlemen* and its successors will deliver the bacon in terms of conclusively defining the value, scope and durability of Connery the artist, and allow us the deepest insights into his character and his vision of himself. Robert Hardy, Robert Henderson, Ian Bannen and Michael Caine all attest to the warmth and sensitivity of Connery, while immediately reminding you that he remains, beyond most, in Caine's words, 'somehow private and unknowable'. With the new Fox contract Connery is brazenly taking us back to the creative well, to his apparent best self. Henderson spoke incessantly of Connery's 'fixation' with the classics and his quest for discovery. It is beyond argument that Connery is now, in his 70s, a serious man who values what time he has and refuses to suffer fools. The corollary is inevitable: with *The League of Extraordinary Gentlemen* he has the appetite and skill to present the magnum opus.

James Bond, now in the hands of genre actors, writers and producers, is today a separate entity from the glorious original created by Sean Connery. Part of the purpose of this book is to recall the uniqueness of the process whereby a great entertainment institution was founded, and celebrate its titan architect. But the bigger part is the humble story – Homeric in itself – of the disadvantaged slum kid who took on the challenges of life to grow and contribute by enhancing others' lives. In the following chapter, I have retained the core elements of the 1993 preface, recorded at the time of the STV documentary that remains the sole 'autobiography' Connery has ever offered. These 'opening statements' – and the information extrapolated at the time which is dispersed throughout the text – represent the knowable Connery. It is my belief – what joy for a biographer to write these words! – that there is more – the best – to come.

Michael Feeney Callan
Dublin, April 2002

# 1. EDINBURGH FOREVER

It was the summer of 1991. Ross Wilson, an accomplished documentary director for Scottish TV, was looking forward to this foreign film assignment. 'It crept up on me,' he said. 'Like everyone else, I grew up with this implacable vision of heroism, of what men should be, called James Bond. And being Scottish – though from west of the promised land of Edinburgh – I took a special interest in Sean Connery. So I was keen to meet him.' Karen Cook, Wilson's researcher, was even more eager. 'I mean, for women everywhere he has become this dream figure. Still. Even twenty years after Bond. He was Adonis arisen, the Perfection of Man.' Andrew Fyall, who was to be the Connery insider on the production team, and who has known him for twenty years, was equally enthusiastic – but a little wary. 'Sean is very straight,' he said phlegmatically. 'That's the way his Scottishness works. We had been friends for a while. He'd made an important Edinburgh promotional film for me ten years before. He calls me whenever he's coming home, to say: Do this for me, or check out that. So I felt I would have his cooperation in this film documentary, and it was vital we had it because it was all about celebrating his coming home. You see, he had been given the keys of the city, he was to be a Freeman of Edinburgh. It was the crowning moment, I believe, maybe even beyond that Academy Award. This was where Sean Connery *arrived*. This was where he made history.'

Connery himself echoed the sentiment. He said, 'When I was first approached I didn't realise the significance of the gesture. It was started in 1495. [The honour has been given] to people like admirals, kings, queens, princes. Names like David Livingstone, Ben Franklin, Ben Jonson, an amazing list.'

Connery called Fyall from Mexico to outline his agreement to do the programme and suggested that he, Wilson and the film crew flew directly to Spain. This access to the inner sanctum was, in effect, the breakthrough. It was popular knowledge that the

Connerys – Sean and second wife Micheline – carefully guarded the privacy of the Casa Malibu, their retreat on the coast near Marbella. Only twice before had film crews been given the run of the Connery homestead – and then just fleetingly, reluctantly, for movie promotions.

After weeks of transatlantic negotiations Fyall and Cook had the deal done. Wilson was triumphant, the tight budget was tweaked, and all departed in high spirits.

Momentarily there was disillusion. Though Connery's secretary, Maha, had arranged the accommodation at a local hotel, Wilson and the production team found themselves adrift in the bars and bistros of trendy Puerto Banus, kicking their heels. 'There was a lot of procrastinating and not a little anxiety,' said Wilson. 'It was evident that we were victims of the celebrity stand-off but with Sean – and despite Andrew's intimacy – there was also the suggestion of angst and withdrawal, that on reconsidering what we'd proposed, which was nothing short of a mini bio-pic, he might fall back to form and pull up the drawbridge. We endured many grim days awaiting the court summons.' When finally it came, Wilson encountered a Connery he hadn't expected. 'He was very rough and real. He'd just returned from this horrendous foreign shoot on *Medicine Man* in the jungles of Central America, and accordingly looked exhausted. He had a cold sore on his lip, his hair was long and tousled and, while he greeted us cordially enough, our Scottishness won no favours. He had a distinct attitude of *I couldn't give a damn*.' Wilson was alarmed, but Fyall understood: 'Sean never really compromised, that's the great secret. He never changed. I can't think of anyone who has had this kind of fame and been so separated from their humble beginnings and yet remained so in touch and grounded. We approached him with the deference one would offer any accomplished individual. He responded like Joe Average – a tired man coping with a posse of eager beavers with high, perhaps unreal expectations.'

Given Connery's mood, the shoot was frantic and fast. For the main part, Connery sat on the plump white settee in his Malibu-white lounge, under an elegant, Modigliani-like portrait of him by Micheline, which depicted tufted, near-naked masculinity beneath a delicate intellectual face. 'Another hairpin,' said Wilson, 'because it was all extraordinarily frank. He didn't censor us in any way. One had preconceptions of the prima donna, the inevitably difficult interview. But Sean bowled us over. This time he was ready for it.' Wilson's concerns were real concerns. Tom Carlisle, one of the key Bond publicists, famously described Connery as 'the best three-second interview in the business'. Fyall said, 'Though I knew him and knew I could trust him, I knew too that he wasn't a pushover. I knew that you don't get from Sean anything other than what he wants to give. I had a suspicion – no, call it hope – that the occasion of this particular Edinburgh homecoming would elicit a new candour, but I think we were all surprised by the degree of openness.'

As the story unfolded – Connery's life from Connery's lips – paradoxes abounded. He was effusive about politics and art but seemed, oddly, broadly conservative. He had, he said, Micheline's homemaker skills to thank for his easy domesticity and it was evident that the comforts were enjoyed not with pride of achievement, but with a childlike sense of wonder. Micheline's on camera contribution was to highlight the humility and innocence at the heart of this complex man. Her retelling of the Christmas door story captured the heart of it. In the winter of 1987, as he wrapped *The Untouchables* in Chicago, Micheline planned a quirky holiday gift for him: a room extension on his favourite haven, the bathroom. This, Micheline said, would be, for Sean, a happening: 'So when he arrived from the airport and I brought him to the bedroom, I had the door [to the extension] covered with ribbons. I said, "There's your present …"' Connery's reaction, said Micheline, was one of gushing praise for the gift of a door. When she told him to open it, he was, she said, 'like a child'.

The secret sanctum of the bathroom – where he keeps his two BAFTAs and the Oscar he won for *The Untouchables* – was, in Fyall's view, symbolic of the measure of distance he had travelled in his sixty-plus years. 'He spends hours in there,' Micheline revealed and Fyall wasn't surprised: 'The luxury of it, and the awards littered around with his favourite golf manuals, were a far cry from Edinburgh, where the bathroom was a cast iron tub by the stove. Imagine it through his eyes. Many celebrated people who endure the fan worship Sean has experienced regard their bedroom and bathroom as their only escape haven. For Sean it had a completely different resonance: as a place of escape, but also of inevitable reflection.'

Shortly before, in a more conventionally brief interview with film critic Marjorie Bilbow, Connery defined his sense of fulfilment in terms of financial independence: 'I mean, one certainly has to strive for it, one really has to fight. Coming from my background I was always very conscious of the fact that I could never lift the phone, there was nobody at the other end of the line to help.' Here, with Wilson and Fyall, the conclusion was restated: inner calm and sound finance were all one, and all that really mattered to him. Still, Wilson noted, there was the contradiction of indifference towards material possessions. Bathroom apart, Connery seemed positively disdainful of the concept of ownership. 'Jackie Collins asked me what I did with those original Bond scripts and I told her I didn't have them. I never keep any of those things.' Right through the Bond years the automobiles he'd owned were secondhand – the best, a two-year-old Jensen which he awarded himself in the late 60s, after partnering Brigitte Bardot in *Shalako*. In Marbella, Wilson saw, his usual mode of transport was a Renault mini-van – 'adequate for a set of golf clubs and a change of shoes, and that was all that was needed.'

As a result of his stressed childhood, Connery told Wilson, 'I find it hard to ask anyone for anything.' This tone of proud-loner individualism explained for Wilson the conundrum of contradictions and the chronically regurgitated media misconceptions of Connery the Hard Man, Connery the Aggressor, Connery the Bigot, Connery the Litigant: 'It struck me that there were some wounds from the severity of his past experience, that he had learned to cope with alone, to overcome obstacles and *make it work*. The downside was this "personality terminus", where the interviewer or analyst gets just so far, and then hits the wall of the shell. I didn't doubt that he had some answers he could have given us, but shied away from. But I didn't doubt either that there were unresolved issues in his personality that might be mutually tempting to explore. But he wasn't going to go there. Like he said, he doesn't ask for anything from anybody – so he is not about to beg for understanding. What he projects is: *This is me. Take it or leave it. That is all I want to give to you.*'

Psychological wrangling apart, Wilson found Connery true to reputed form and tending to unpredictable moodiness. 'You certainly wouldn't call him a pussycat. When the interviews were over and we did the walking-about stuff – showing him in his work studio at the end of the garden, going through scripts on offer, going off to play golf – I was nervous about directing him. At one point I asked him to walk from the house across the garden to the studio den. I didn't think the shot worked well so I asked him to do it again. I expected a growl, but he just said a very cheerful, "Oh, right-o," and was very accommodating. So I assumed he was an easy collaborator. Later in the day I thought it would be good to film him doing what he likes best when he's in Spain: getting geared up for some golf. That was my downfall. As soon as I mentioned the subject of golf he went into another mind set and seemed to be thinking *only* of the golf. I could see what was going on behind those eyes. He was thinking, What the hell am I doing with these jerks, opening up my diary, as it were? So we managed to get one shot set up, with him loading the van and driving off. The plan was, we'd do one angle, then reposition the camera to get a cutaway shot of him driving out the gates of the Casa Malibu. But it didn't work out like that. I gave him a rundown of the plan, and of course film language is his second tongue, so he knew precisely what I wanted. But that's as far as we got. When I set up the first shot and called "Action!" he hit the gas and disappeared in that little Renault van, and that was the last we saw of him.'

But back in Scotland some weeks later, Wilson saw a totally different man whose sentimentality belied even the grating turmoil of the Marbella movie star at his confessional best. This, for Wilson, was the core of his film: physically returning the prodigal son to the backrooms of the alma mater to illustrate the metaphorical all-points-access of the Freeman award. 'I had a suspicion that Scotland truly meant a lot to him, that this was far from a photo-opportunity, but I didn't really comprehend the bonds of his connection till we went out in those mean streets together.' At Bruntsfield Primary School Connery appeared at his happiest, mixing with the children of a gentler, socially softer place than the Edinburgh he had known. 'It was a real eye-opener because he did a Q&A with the kids and he cooperated fully, answering questions he has, to my knowledge, never answered – even for us in Marbella.' Wilson was amused to see that he drew the line just once: when a daring boy asked how much he earned per year. 'Since nobody had any interest in my yearly earnings when I was on the brew here,' Connery responded wryly, 'I never discuss it with anybody now.' Later, as a camera followed him and Micheline through the suburbs and he saw, for the first time in years, the revision of his old home town, he was smiling but subdued. Later still, at the grand reception at the Usher Hall when the formal presentation of the Freeman award was made, he was, said Wilson, overcome. Andrew Fyall said, 'I hadn't seen him like that since the BAFTA tribute two years before.' There, at the BAFTAs in the presence of Princess Anne, he became very emotional when he spoke of the gaps in his life, and all he had missed out on in friendships by burying himself away in Spain. His son Jason said he needs the seclusion, that he overworks and burns out and then scurries off for the peace of Marbella to repair himself. And Michael Caine also said he cuts himself off geographically to his detriment, that it isn't good for him emotionally. 'That night [at the BAFTAs] he was emotional and he lost his voice for a full minute. It was very moving and revealing. But at the Freedom of Edinburgh ceremony he was positively fazed. You saw it all in an instant in his eyes. The crowd gave him a colossal ovation after he made his speech. His eyes ran round the galleries, recognising many, many old Edinburgh faces, faces from his childhood. It was heartbreaking and heartwarming ... and for Sean it was a sensory overload. For a moment you looked at him and he wasn't a mythic hero figure or a movie star. He was a child, with a child's appreciative, awestruck eyes.'

Ross Wilson too was moved. 'One is a filmmaker and one makes documentaries and hopes they have some lasting value. In Sean's case, I had no idea what to expect from the Freedom of

Edinburgh film other than a kind of celebration. But it was obvious, taking him back to Scotland, that we hit some critical keys. Sean Connery played a major part in the creation of a modern myth of Jungian proportions. He came out of provincial Britain at a time of austerity to create a cornerstone of the hedonism of the 60s and help change the fortunes of British cinema. He was a dynamic force, seemingly self-made, at the centre of a cultural hurricane. Historically that kind of energy can be corrosive to many and I wondered, while we were filming in Marbella, what psychological price Sean had truly paid for his part in this great invention. In Edinburgh I saw that his great asset was his spiritual strength. The Freedom of Edinburgh ceremony marked something special for him, but it did for us, too, because it showed us the poet beneath all the marketing and media. Sean's cooperation [with the film] showed that he has genuinely distanced himself from the tedious Bond fallout. He has earned his rewards, and he knows it, and he has spiritually moved on. But it is obviously nurturing for him to come home, to remember what he did and why he did it and just how tough the road was; to define himself against the passage of time and of people and places. Bond is a fighter – and so is Sean. You understand it all, all the harmony between Sean and his creations, by looking back. Sean was moved by the Freedom of the City because it was more than just revisiting roots. It was an exercise in revisiting dreams. Everything Sean is, all his motivations and creative goals, began in the challenge of Edinburgh at a time of turmoil.'

# 2. FOUNTAINBRIDGE, FIFE AND A FEELING FOR FREEDOM

Auld Reekie – Old Smoke – the nickname given to Edinburgh during the eighteenth century, remained particularly appropriate to Fountainbridge, an unprepossessing slab of industrial red rock that lay in the valley fringing the south-western slopes of the old town. Then, in the 1920s and 30s, Fountainbridge lived up to the nickname, giving refuge to the factories and steam-driven businesses the town proper didn't want.

Developed through the eighteenth century and blackened in the Industrial Revolution, Fountainbridge was a residential-factoryised anomaly in a city which prided itself on being professional-orientated, rather than industrial, where even the railways are conscientiously hidden away. High-living Edinburgh folk adverted to the city's auspicious past – the links with Allan Ramsay, David Hume, Oliver Goldsmith, Sir Walter Scott and Robert Louis Stevenson; but the resilient folk of Fountainbridge just spat out the black dust of the district's innumerable chimneys, knuckled down and coursed on with survival. Underprivileged they may have been, but they didn't, and with hindsight, still don't, recognise that. For the dwellers of the cramped tenement blocks life had an isolated tribal closeness that separated them from Brit-Scots and burned in a pride of autonomy that was vivid and lifelong. Children of Fountainbridge, the slogan went, were Fountainbridgers for ever.

Today the area which took its name from the main, thirty-yard-wide thoroughfare is a saw-spined semi-wilderness, its pell-mell destruction in the 80s checked by Edinburgh's Housing Action Programme. But pointers to the past still stand, and it remains possible to cross a busy cobbled street, walk through the close of a reconditioned tenement, and imagine what it was like 75 years ago when Joe Connery took his 20-year-old bride across the threshold of number 176 Fountainbridge (now demolished) and set up home. Then, the view from the ground-floor entrance of 176 was serried tenement windows, the sprawl of McEwan's

Brewery and the friendly face of the Fountain Bar opposite. All of this topography is either prettified, or lost. The sweetie shop is gone; the great rubber works that gave so much employment to the locals is gone; the Clanhouse Dance Hall now sells fancy goods to tourists on the Connery trail.

Joseph Connery's settling in Fountainbridge in the 20s was a shrewd and necessary move, because the kind of work he needed, unskilled labouring, was most readily available in an area of concentrated industry. His father, a first-generation Scotsman called Thomas, remembered only as Baldy by grandsons Sean and Neil, was the son of an Irish Catholic peddler from County Wexford, who grew up in Glasgow through the turn of the century, married an East End cloth mill worker called Jeannie McNab and found employment as an arithmetically unreliable bookie's runner. More often than not Joe totted the bookie's accounts. Neither Joe nor his father were the kind of men given to poetic whimsicality about remembering the past but Joe took some small rebel pride in his Irish ancestry. Had he delved into parish and civic records (something Neil has been threatening to do on behalf of himself and his brother for many years) he might have found an ancestral link with the prestigious O Conraoi or Mac Conraoi clans of County Galway, of which the most famous modern writer in the Irish language, Padraic O Conaire, is a descendant; though more probably he would have unearthed an association with a quite separate group, the O Conaires (specifically anglicised as Connery) of Munster. Smith's *History of County Waterford* records the O'Connerys as principal inhabitants of Waterford and Wexford around the end of the sixteenth century.

Joe was a simple, straight-from-the-shoulder man with a gravelly singing voice he chose to air loud and often. He liked beer first, whisky second and hard toil third and was engaged, and valued, by the North British Rubber Works as a £2-a-week labourer. The rubber mill had good working conditions and such small security afforded Joe the opportunity to contemplate marriage. He proposed to his first and lifelong love, Euphemia (Effie) Maclean, an Edinburgh lass six years his junior, and married her the same year. The ceremony and ensuing boozy, Christmassy celebrations on 28 December 1928 were attended by the roisterous Macleans and the less outgoing Connerys in full numbers and, in the way of these affairs, a fine time was had by all. Joe took Effie home to a two-room Fountainbridge tenement with a lightless, damp-smelling hallway and outside toilet. He bought some sturdy ship's linoleum for the floor from the Forces Surplus Store round the corner in Grove Street and geared himself to carve out a comfortable life for a future growing family in the smoky tranquillity of factory-land.

The encroaching Depression, recognised and gloomily discussed every night in the Grove or the Fountain Bar, didn't affect the young couple: 26 years old, 5 foot 8 inches tall, Joe was 180 pounds of taut, bursting muscle, fit as a fiddle and work-hungry, like his father; they had a roof over their heads and rent for the landlord and, as soon as Effie got her hands on the rubber mill's pay-packet, the makings of a savings account. Physical stamina was Joe's forte, thriftiness Effie's. Together they made a formidable pair, close and resilient as the stained red brickwork of No. 176, and much admired by their neighbours in 'the stairs', as the tenements were known.

A neighbour from nearby Brandfield Street which boasted a different type of stair, but of identical proportions (twelve to fourteen families per house), remembers: 'The Connerys were "poor" for a time, that's to say they had no children. Big families were usual round Fountainbridge. It was the sort of place where the sounds of children, with the paper-thin walls and all the rest, kept fair pace with the noise of industry.'

But by Christmas 1929 Effie was pregnant. Joe, in his enthusiastic, responsible way, took whatever overtime he could find – so much in fact that he was more often out of the stair than in, setting a domestic routine that was to stretch into the war years. On a muggy, late summer's day, 25 August 1930, with Joe standing by for once to mark the occasion with a whisky at the Fountain, Effie gave birth at the Royal Maternity Hospital to a ten-and-a-half-pound child whose name she had already decided upon: Thomas (after Joe's father), later to become Sean.

Thomas Connery was a child of the Depression, arriving on the scene just as purse strings all over the country tightened and unemployment soared. Joe, like a thousand other unskilled workers in Fountainbridge, clung to his job tenaciously, accepted cutbacks where he had to and, for the first time, considered contingency options of work outside Edinburgh, even abroad. But Effie, less practical perhaps but just as obdurate, was not about to give in. 'I had wonderful neighbours and good times in Fountainbridge,' she later declared, explaining pithily her reluctance to bolt for greener pastures.

In spite of Joe's energies and Effie's care with money, young Tommy's first awareness was of a grimly restricted world. The cramped top-floor flat consisted of a bedroom and a combined living room-kitchen called in Scotland a but-and-ben. An alcove off the living area housed the kitchen – a cast-iron coal fireplace with two side ovens and a top-plate, a cold-water stone sink with wooden drain 'bunker' and, above, a pulley arrangement screwed to the ceiling for drying clothes when it was too wet to use the outdoors drying green. Tommy slept in his parents' bedroom, in the bottom drawer of the wardrobe, a popular cot for a newcomer. Later he graduated to the bed-settee in the but-and-ben, a hunk of a kid at five with gypsy-black hair and piercing chocolate eyes. Even then he was, as his mother recalled, 'different from Neil, who came along much later – impulsive, independent, ambitious'. He had Joe's restless energy, a flair for games and a passion for comic strips which quickly led, his childhood friend John Brady remembers, to 'an unusual interest in all kinds of reading matter'.

At five he was quite ready for the strictly disciplined primary school that was his destiny, but at the same time more than a little dismayed at leaving the full freedom of the streets. His playing world was bordered east and west by factories, north and south by a rough-hewn recreation ground and the basins of the Grand Union Canal. The canal was officially out of bounds to the very young, but Tommy was never deterred by threats of authority. He fished for tiddlers with the older kids, using the end of one of his mother's nylon stockings, and boated on the lower basin at some risk. Altogether a safer proposition and far more significant in his young life was the playground behind his stair, popularly called 'the biggie'. Here, with John Brady, Michael O'Sullivan and others he discovered the challenge of soccer for the first time, scoring regular bleeding noses. 'He was football mad from very early,' says Brady, 'and inclined to be a wild player.' Another friend from the biggie insists that Connery, who quickly assumed the nickname of Big Tam on account of his size, was not a brilliant player, more a useful one.

Bruntsfield Primary School, an imposing red Victorian building that even today exudes a finger-wagging earnestness, swallowed up most of the five-to-eleven-year-olds from Fountainbridge and attempted to displace that endemic braggart street-wisdom with academic ABCs. Here, surprisingly, young Connery was somewhat out of place. By five he could read and write and was proficient at mental arithmetic, a knack handed down from Joe. He was in trouble often for totting sums too fast, or lapsing into loud-mouthed boredom when half the class was fumbling over A-is-for-Apple. Effie scolded him in the evenings, just as she did every other weekend when he slunk off adventurously to the canal, or tackled shins relentlessly in the biggie; Joe, fighting for family survival as job lay-offs shadowed every factory in the area, was seldom around long enough to observe or object.

'My background was harsh,' Connery has said. 'We were poor, but I never knew how poor till years after.' It was impossible for a youngster to be objective about the situation but Tommy sensed Joe's deepening inability to cope, despite Effie's efforts. The birth of Neil in 1938, when the home financial situation was at its worst, complicated matters. So at nine Tommy decided, fully on his own account, to stop off at 'the store' – St Cuthbert's (then Kennedy's) Dairy Stables in Grove Street – on his way home from school and ask for a job. He was articulate and impressively built and, in spite of the jobs pinch, a place was found for him on a delivery dray. Thus began an eight-year on-off spell with St Cuthbert's. The early days, for sure, were the most strenuous. 'I was up at dawn,' Connery recollected, 'then through a milk round before school.' There followed the long, dull school day then, after a while – an almost unbelievable self-inflicted punishment for a sporty, freedom-loving boy – an evening shift as a butcher's helper. Effie, naturally, was proud of him. 'With two jobs he was bringing me home £3 a week,' she glowed, 'and that was before the war. He gave me every penny he earned and I banked savings for him.'

The main reason Tommy chose the milk round, Neil insists, rested in his love for horses. 'He was horse daft in those days,' Effie recalled for the Scottish *Sunday Express* in 1964. 'Always taking my dusters to rub down the milk horse. And he loved driving that cart.' Connery's own memories broadly concur but over the years in varied interviews a barb of deeper insight has revealed itself. He told *Playboy* magazine: 'One's parents left one free to make one's own way. When I was nine my mother caught me smoking and she said, "Don't let your father find out, because if he does he'll beat you so hard he'll break your bottom." From the time I started working I always paid my share of the rent, and the attitude at home was the prevalent one in Scotland – you make your own bed and so you have to lie in it. I didn't ask for advice and I didn't get it. I had to make it on my own or not at all.' The implication, borne out in many later interviews, was that Tommy learned to take care of himself because he had no choice. There was only so much family could provide: a good work ethic and a relatively stable home; after that Tommy had to find his own niche, and pay his way.

Others have spoken of young Tommy's topsy-turvy relationship with both parents. A respectful and generally dutiful son, he was also, according to some, wary of his mother and obsessed with pleasing her. 'I wouldn't go so far as to say he was afraid of Effie,' says a friend from Fountainbridge, 'but she was the undisputed binding force in the family and she subtly dominated everyone and everything. In the rocky tough times Joe did what he could, but it was Effie's strength that held the family together. She was the glue and Tommy – and Joe and Neil – were never allowed to forget it. I believe that all his life Sean lived under Effie's influence. The hardness in him is her.'

There followed a period of educational disruption. As the economic and social upheavals of the Second World War reached Edinburgh school buildings were requisitioned and temporarily closed. For many months, the children of working-class families like the Connerys were farmed out to the spacious suburban homes of the wealthy for alternative daytime 'grinds'. Connery reflects sourly on this experience: 'It was an eye-opener. These people wanted us to deliver coal and what have you – but they didn't want us in their homes. We were too lowly for them.' As Neil remembers it, this period of 'outside schooling' didn't last long and Sean quickly returned to Bruntsfield where he sat the customary qualifying examination and graduated – in Neil's wry words – 'after a fashion'. By now the war in Europe was raging, rationing was in full force and Joe was pursuing the tack he always guessed lay before him – working for Rolls-Royce in Glasgow, travelling home at weekends only. Tommy seems to have taken ominous warning from his father's experience and clenched his hold on his part-time job even though the obligatory two-year course of secondary education now confronted him. A contemporary of that time, Craigie Veitch, remembers facing the prospect of second level, career-orientated education: 'Fountainbridge children had two main avenues open to them. Those who had the aptitude, or won scholarships as a result of their qualifying exams, went to Boroughmuir School. Boroughmuir had commercial ends in mind, and that's where people learnt languages – French and Italian – or economics. The second choice, the second best for many, was Darroch, a school that gave you a good basic technical education, where you learnt science and metalwork and craft. In some ways, I suppose, the measure of a man's learning capacity was which school he ended up in. Sean, of course, ended up – with me – at Darroch.'

Connery entered Darroch Secondary determined, by his own account, to fail. What is more likely, in perspective, is that his exhausting extracurricular activities did not allow him the chance to succeed. At any rate, John Brady said, Connery proved himself 'adaptable and a fair scholar'. Craigie Veitch painted a compelling picture in an article he published in the 70s in the *Edinburgh Evening News*, a paper that Connery himself would work for:

*A gaunt, grey building, Darroch was staffed by no-nonsense teachers with strong right arms, the better to belt you with, and attended by plus-12 girls in print dresses and rough-and-ready boys whose school uniform was a woolly pullover and short trousers with a shirt tail peeping through, topped off in winter with a balaclava helmet. Pop Hendry, our English teacher, always insisted that the well-rounded man must be accurate in his spelling and he kept to hand a largish Chambers Dictionary, which he would bounce on the head of any boy thick enough to think that sieze was 'seize' . . .*

*We were versed in poetry too, but I cannot recall Connery ever being called to the front of the class to recite lines from three epic poems which happened to be in vogue in the Forties: 'Splendour Falls on Castle Walls' . . . 'A Wet Sheet and a Flowing Sea' . . . and something about a slave having a dream with his matted hair buried in sand . . .*

*There was nothing of the long-haired poet about schoolboy Connery. He was big and he was as hard as nails in an easygoing way and anyone at school who messed him about got a thick ear and a black eye; one torrid encounter, Connery v. Anderson, going the best part of 12 bloody rounds in the playground before the janitor and two teachers managed to break it up . . .*

Though Neil says Tommy was inclined to be 'oversensitive' in some regards, it is apparent he was also quite tough and ready for whatever trouble came his way – a by-product of his already well-developed physique and the fitness forced on him by early-morning rising and, now, in place of the butcher's shop, a strenuous evening newspaper round. Neil remembers Tommy had little sense of his own strength – 'which was unfortunate because he had a precocious talent for melodrama'. Once, unthinkingly, Tommy squeezed the fancy glass handle of his parents' bedroom door so fiercely that it shattered in his grip. In shock, he danced round the room, screaming so shrilly that Joe was convinced he was clowning. When he calmed down and everyone saw the blood pouring from his hand, they were at last stirred to first-aid action. 'They had quite a job digging all the glass splinters out of him,' Neil says. Later there was a sledging accident in the snows of a particularly bad winter. Tommy hammered up a makeshift contraption in the walled back drying green and christened it 'The

Coffin'. He crossed Tollcross to the Meadows, a huge public park half a mile from 176. The park was full of snow-crazed kids playing recklessly safe but Tommy wanted to test real risk. He found the steepest slope, padded up, mounted his rickety sledge against all advice and hurtled down. Flushed with success and the admiration of the weaker-spined after a first go, he tried again. This time mischance befell. The sledge went out of control and hit a tree. Tommy met the bole head first, but recovered enough to fling the sledge on his back and stagger home. In shock, he sat silent at 176 while Effie raged about the boys' lateness for tea-time. 'Then,' said Neil, 'she noticed the blood spilling down his neck. The wound was huge and very obviously serious. Dad was in Glasgow at the time, so my mother called the next-door neighbours for help. It was one instance where Tommy was too traumatised to be melodramatic. He was concussed and in a daze and they rushed him off to the hospital, where he was kept in for five days, then spent another ten days in bed at home convalescing.' Two days after he got out of bed, Tommy was back at the Meadows with the same sledge. 'Once he recovered he made the most of the drama,' says Neil, 'because I think he quite liked the mixture of the attention and adventure.'

Whatever histrionic facility Connery developed during his early teens found plenty to feed on around Fountainbridge. As the accelerating war effort injected life back into factories that had been foundering, vacated stairs filled up again, dormant businesses awoke to churn out dirt and smoke and draw in rowdy newcomers. A neighbour who lived on Freer Street, down the road from the Connerys, says: 'Everything was dominated by the smell, which was a heady blend. You had the sweetie factory, MacKay's, just fifty yards up from the Connerys, gushing out a sickly odour round the clock, then the acrid rubber smell and, on top of that, the yeasty smell from the brewery opposite. On warm days the mixture was overpowering, especially to the newcomers who weren't acclimatised. But people kept flocking into Fountainbridge, looking for work. The men's lodging house in Grove Street began doing great business, and the bars thrived as never before. There was plenty of high entertainment created by all this movement, a lot of it with the Saturday night brawls, but a lot in the character of the people as well.' Wherever immigrant workers – most Irish, some Welsh and English – came to swell the slums, tricksters and troubadours followed, begging for the scraps. A noisy busker from nowhere, weighed down with instruments he could barely coordinate, was a favourite with the stair children. He would park outside the men's lodging house or Sammy's Ice Cream Parlour, right next door to 176, and rattle off free rubbish daily. A crooning drifter called, inevitably, 'Bing' was another new Fountainbridge staple. His repertoire included 'South of the Border down Texaco Way'. Bing's inability to remember five lines of any song, combined with his entrancing habit of muffling one ear, closing his eyes and singing into a bean can, won him the adoration of the children especially. Asa Wass, a wizened Jew with a huckster shop in a close beside Freer Street, was another local hero. By dint of turning unneeded clothing and household ornaments into hard cash, Asa became Fountainbridge's uncrowned king. He was gruff but good with kids and on many occasions Tommy was despatched with the bounties of a spring-cleaning to make a deal with Asa. Sixpence for Joe's cast-off winter jersey was luxury money and Tommy had the kind of hulking inscrutability that clinched six when fivepence-ha'penny was more to Asa's thinking. Tommy was, says Neil, the popular choice to send on all such bargaining errands.

Outside school and work, Tommy's main and increasingly important interest was football. In an overpopulated district where space was at a premium, games that could comfortably accommodate two twenty-man sides, with a ref thrown in, obviously thrived. Connery had been determinedly ball-playing since he could walk, and was at home on the football field. He was unusually fast ('nimble,' says John Brady) and also sensible enough to recognise the fringe advantages of the game's huge popularity. 'We didn't carry coshes or bicycle chains or knives,' Connery now says appreciatively. 'We spent all our energy on the football field. I was football mad. That's why I left school when I was thirteen, because they played rugger at the grammar school. I set out to fail the qualifying examination, and I made it.'

There are varying stories about the abrupt conclusion of Connery's academic life. The precise facts, as Craigie Veitch says, 'went down with the ship'. No school rolls or records of Darroch for the period survive, probably mercifully. The lingering, symbolically significant memory of those who served with Connery in that unpretentious throng is of morning assembly in the big hall. 'Hail Darroch!' was the school song, drilled out pitilessly every day at nine sharp. One line rang 'Darroch ways are honest ways' – ironic, Veitch suggests, because quite a few of their numbers were residing in Borstal at the time. But Connery took particular pleasure in that song. 'He was nothing as a scholar,' John Brady said, 'but he was straight as the day's long. That plain-talking honesty won him friends easier than most.'

Survival, with the hard work it entailed, was Tommy Connery's preoccupation. Schooling, he judged, offered him no rung on any worthwhile ladder. Fitness and football, on the other hand, offered benefits – if not in the direction of self-improvement and success, then at least in terms of fun. 'His appetites were always big,' says Neil. 'Whether it was appetite for grub, or hard work or fun and freedom, the big measure was his way.'

Football apart, fun and freedom for young teenage Tommy were largely connected with life away from Fountainbridge. In this, he and his brother, comparatively, were privileged. Neil and Helen Maclean, the maternal grandparents, were in their 60s; worldwise, clever, fun-loving people, utterly at ease with children and passionate in particular about their grandsons. Grandfather Neil was a plasterer who rose to public works' foreman before retiring to a peaceful house in Gorgie, Edinburgh. But Gorgie satisfied this open-air fanatic's needs for only a short time.

Upping roots, the Macleans moved to a country cottage north of Kirkcaldy, Fife, where they bred pigs and kept chickens. It was here, on summer holidays during and after the war, that the Connery youngsters came and Tommy found a slice of heaven larger than the biggie. The shock of pleasure he experienced on first encountering 'wild' farm animals and wide, open skies would, Neil hints, have been worth witnessing. 'There was no running water and we washed at the spring. First thing each morning

Granny would give us a pitcher and Sean and I would go down the road to the next farm for milk, still fresh and warm from the cow. There was a pond where we fished for tadpoles, newts and frogs, and a huge Clydesdale horse on the farm, a real whopper.' In contrast to jam-packed Fountainbridge, the country life assumed a magical aura. Here were the true luxuries of space and free time. There was room to kick a ball any which way, with no concern for close-ranked neighbours' windows, and time to idle, wander and think. For Tommy, temporarily relieved of the responsibilities of wage-earning, the chance to play at being a kid again was precious. In Fife he discovered things about himself that had been buried under the rush to grow up. He found he liked his own company, liked to indulge his fantasies about being a cowboy riding the range. The big Clydesdale horse came in useful, far better, wilder, than anything back at St Cuthbert's. It was actually possible to mount the Clydesdale and romp over prairie-like meadows – without fear of admonition – day in, day out, almost as if freedom had no boundaries.

Neil Maclean was an inspiration too. He was big, tough, a whisky-loving, Scottish John Wayne who could lift the kitchen table single-handed and down raw eggs for breakfast without the blink of an eye. His purpose, in a nutshell, was to get the best out of life by living bravely and uncompromisingly. Tommy spun boyish fantasies around him, and cherished them into adulthood. As late as 1963 he was talking about 'this 86-year-old grandfather who drinks a bottle of Scotch a day, and he's in great shape because he always eats with it'. Neil Maclean's recipe for a long life, Connery claimed, centred on cold food and plenty of alcohol. In a newspaper interview in 1964 the old man laughingly dismissed his grandson's remarks. Exercise, he insisted, was the secret of a healthy long life. Neil Connery remembers his grandfather's dying request – for 'a drop of the hard stuff', to be snuck secretly into the Edinburgh Infirmary. Neil's greatest regret is that the request was never fulfilled; having checked with nursing staff, Neil himself undertook to bring the whisky, but by the time he arrived with the half-full bottle from the dresser of his grandfather's bedroom, the old man was dead. He was 93.

For Tommy, most important of all, the experience of Fife threw new light on life in Fountainbridge. It represented the unexpected flipside of the coin: the attainable alternative of a sweeter, cleaner lifestyle. All right, one might have to work fifty-odd years to achieve this utopia. But it was remotely possible, Tommy supposed, that such freedom and retirement did not necessarily go hand-in-hand. Some way, some time, there might be a short cut to Fife.

Tommy Connery, the slum kid, just might not be a Fountainbridger for ever.

# 3. 'HE'D NO' HAVE MADE IT AS A MILKMAN ...'

During the Second World War British cinema thrived. British film-making, which had hiccuped with the requisitioning of thirteen out of twenty-two studios and the call-up of two-thirds of its technicians, started an upswing. J Arthur Rank, the future leader of the industry, started his meteoric rise in 1942 with his first major film, a starchy morality tale called *The Great Mr Handel*, but within two years the dam had burst and a flood of pure entertainment movies washed away the quasi-religious and morale-boosting documentaries of early wartime. Annual audience figures were steadily moving towards their 1946 all-time high of 1,635 million ticket sales. Though restrictions continued – film stock was in short supply, individual theatres played limited hours – an estimated 30 million cinema-goers were regularly entertained in more than five thousand theatres. In 1944 in Edinburgh, as across the country, people flocked to see Pressburger and Powell's cheeky *Life and Death of Colonel Blimp*, Carol Reed's *The Way Ahead* and, among the swarm of irresistible Hollywood challengers, Billy Wilder's *Double Indemnity*.

One of Tommy Connery's main local cinemas was called, romantically, the Blue Halls. It stood on the northern border of Fountainbridge and was known to the slum kids as 'the gaff'. 'It was,' John Brady recalls, 'everything fleapits are cracked up to be.' The place was constantly the butt of spiky jokes, few requiring imaginative exaggeration. The standard gospel was 'you go to the gaff with a cardigan and come out with a jumper' – jumpers being fleas. Tommy was not as addicted to movies as his father, but he liked the rainy Saturday afternoons at the gaff, watching a British comedy or a good Hitchcock. In the early war years, admission cost just a jam jar or two, but by the time Tommy was in charge of baby brother Neil the price had risen to tuppence each. Both brothers enjoyed the serial adventures of *Flash Gordon* but Tommy, rich with his memories of Fife and his love for the old milk-cart dobbins, had a particular fondness for Westerns. Tough men living hard lives on the range – men like grandfather Neil – appealed to him. When he first breached the film business in the late 50s Connery expressed an immediate desire to make Westerns. He did eventually make the notable British Western *Shalako*, but Neil is surprised that he tackled no more: 'From our very first movie outings, Westerns were his craze. As he grew up he never lost interest, because at the root of it was his passion for horses, which never wavered.'

With Darroch ingloriously behind him, horses were playing a much larger part in Connery's life. Milk delivery became his first full-time occupation, horses his obsession. For a time he was the helper on Danny Fraser's dray – Connery 14, Fraser the senior at 15. Then he was assigned his own route, the rounds of Cramond and Davidson's Mains, and his own cart. His horse was nicknamed Tich, smallest of the several score at the store, but cosseted like none other. The restlessness that was to mark the later part of his teens might have been more evident now had it not been for the fact that Joe was out of work, having badly broken his wrist and nose in a machinery accident in Glasgow. Effie substituted, char-ring in the rich houses of the West End for thirty shillings a week, but still not quite managing to make ends meet. The pressures of supplementing the income to keep the family together were absorbed by Tommy. He laboured like a Trojan during this time, handing £2 10s to Effie every Thursday but still finding means, through his newspaper round, to maintain his own Post Office Savings account, building on the nest egg Effie had banked for him during his schooldays.

The Fountainbridge vision of a working man's lot was stoical: a man simply works to live. Tommy Connery was unusual in that part of his psyche rejected that standard. Denied the constant bliss of Fife, his independent spirit demanded recompense. One sweated for gain, he decided. So the hundred per cent work effort needed to sustain the family would be augmented by another ten, and in the end he would walk away from his chores with a swag that justified the sweat. Financial targets were set, and met. One Christmas, Neil remembers, Tommy carefully strategised to earn the vast sum of £16 in tips. The following year, with Joe cautiously back at work after an eighteen-month lay-off – this time employed as van driver for Duncan's Removals of Gilmore Place – Tommy's Post Office account was up to £75. The noose of responsibility no longer tight round his neck, Connery decided to reward himself for his labours. Seventy-five pounds wouldn't buy him the horse and stables in Fife he and Neil dreamed about, but it might open a door out of Fountainbridge. The compromise choice, nervously announced to Joe, was a secondhand motorbike.

Joe would have none of it. Always wary of his older son's adventurous nature, Joe suspected the motorbike represented dangerous ulterior motives. Fountainbridge was full of pubescent punk gangs like the Valdors, whose currency was high-power Nortons and tight-skirted tarts. It is likely, too, says Neil, that Joe felt intimidated by his son's precocity: 'He was developing too fast. He was too big for his age, too bold, the bread-earner too early.' In Effie's version published in a Scottish newspaper, Joe entertained no discussion about the motorbike: 'He put down his foot and that was that. No arguments. In those days you could tell a youngster what to do.'

Tommy didn't brood over this impasse. He resumed his milk round, ambled down to the gaff and reconsidered. Within a couple of days he had decided on a next-best option. Without risking consultation with Joe he acted out his decision, and a week later a twenty-year-old upright piano, all of £56 10s' worth, was delivered to 176. The neighbours were impressed and so was Effie, but Joe, said Neil, was speechless. Nobody in the stair could play the piano, least of all Tommy. Tommy reassured his parents that he would pursue lessons, though the likelihood of his finding time for study, Neil said, was next to negligible. As it was, he was spending only an hour before bedtime in the stair: from dawn till three in the afternoon was taken up with the milk round, early evenings went on the newspaper deliveries, later in the evenings was for grooming Tich or football practice with Grove Vale Juveniles, across the Meadows at Tollcross. At first Joe ordered the space-invading piano to be removed, but Tommy outmanoeuvred him. 'That piano was too important,' said Neil. 'I'm sure the idea started life [at the Blue Halls], and it obviously represented some glamorous lifestyle he longed for.' Tommy's trick to appease Joe was his one-fingered mastering of 'Bluebells of Scotland' or 'Annie Laurie', Joe's Saturday night singalong favourites.

Though Connery had, in his own words, 'no sense of the future back then', by early 1947 it was apparent to Neil, Brady and his football friends that he would quit Fountainbridge at the first opportunity. Among casual acquaintances there were boys who had worked as merchant sailors and others who'd served with the forces. Overnight, privately, Connery decided that this was the way out. Neil emphasises that home life pressures didn't drive Tommy's wanderlust, rather the social limitations of Fountainbridge. Connery himself told a newspaper in the 60s that the impetus for escape had nothing at all to do with an unhappy home life: 'Quite the reverse. I suppose I felt that a hard job like my father's or the milk round I was doing would never let me use my body and mind to the fullest. And I think anything less [than a full life] is a waste of a human being.'

Through maturer eyes, the realities of the family's poverty were crushingly depressing. Even in the face of sixty-hour working weeks, minor luxuries were rare. The family diet was a famine diet: porridge, bread, and potato stews. Cakes were unknown, clothes almost always secondhand. In order to acquire money for football boots, or new laces for that matter, a twelve-hour working day must stretch to fourteen, thereby forging the vicious circle: if one laboured so hard for the smallest freedoms, where was the time to enjoy the pleasures earned? At 16, for example, Big Tam Connery was a big hit with the local girls – 'He did better than most of us, without trying,' John Brady said – but the pressures on his time afforded him no more than one night a week scouting for talent. The worst part of being poor and reaching teenhood, Connery later claimed, was that 'Life was completely governed by economics. You didn't leave the light on when you didn't actually need it, because it cost money. You had to count up tram fares. You couldn't have a bath when you felt like it – there was the price of a plunge at the public baths to think of. I wanted to *do* something with my life. I wanted to have pride in it, to feel the joy of it. [In Fountainbridge] there was far too little joy about.'

Effie too was restless in the stair now, speculating openly on the fortunes of those who had left during the Depression and were writing home about the fulfilment of their dreams in the provinces, in England and elsewhere. She began tossing round progressive ideas for Tommy, suggesting jobs beyond Fountainbridge, in Glasgow perhaps, with better prospects. But Tommy had observed Joe's fortunes in Glasgow, and refused to be pushed.

As Connery planned his escape, joining the local Sea Cadets to bone up on his seamanship, the milk round remained a stop-gap – a truth the regimental Mr Marshall, the dairy manager, who liked and encouraged Connery, would not have appreciated. Tich, more than anything, kept Connery faithful to the dairy. A real highlight was entering the horse in the dairy's Best Horse & Cart competition, and winning the embossed 'Highly Commended' card. Marshall saw Connery as a career milkman, but not everyone regarded him as an asset to the dairy. One roundsman called Jimmy, who worked the circuit of Rose Street, Silverknowes, Craigmillar and Corstorphine for forty years, knew Connery as a fitfully enthusiastic worker who stood out in memory 'because he didn't always use his damn brain'. An incident with a fully laden dray in the heart of the city lingered with Jimmy. Connery had just commenced his round, alone with horse and dray when, in the middle of a busy street, the bridle bit broke. Connery couldn't control the dray and panicked. Instead of improvising or summoning help from passers-by – the dairy dictum – he abandoned the cart and ran back to the store. Jimmy – Connery's senior by several years – was appalled when informed that a full cart and lone horse had been deserted in the middle of town. Connery 'stood idly by' as Jimmy was ordered to retrieve the dray immediately, and went running. 'Fortunately most of the contents of the crates were still intact,' said Jimmy, 'which is no small miracle in a town like Edinburgh at that time.' In Jimmy's view, Connery and St Cuthbert's had no future together: 'It's as well he made it as an actor – he'd no' have made it as a milkman.'

John Brady, a keen amateur footballer, was serving his time as a painter-decorator while Connery wound down with St Cuthbert's. 'I knew he'd never stick it out. Tommy always gave the impression he had better things in store and it often felt as if the only thing that kept him in Fountainbridge was the football with Grove Vale.' In fact, Connery's football skills improved dramatically in his mid-teens and his transfer to centre field with Oxgangs Rovers signalled for many the possibility of a professional sports career. 'He was an ideal forward player,' says Brady. 'He smoked a bit and drank a bit when he was out dancing at the Palais or playing snooker, but he was never the boozy type. Tommy's whole image of himself was as an outdoors man and he stood out from the pack because he had real discipline. Others may have had more natural talent, but Tommy's discipline left them in the shade.' Another friend of the Oxgangs era contends that Connery ran everywhere: 'He never ever walked. He gave you the impression that Fountainbridge was a training track, and he was limbering to get out.'

When Connery finally made his decision to move he did so in a characteristic gust of inflexible wilfulness – alone. At the Royal Navy Recruitment office in Bath Street, Glasgow, he signed for seven years' active service, and a further five in the Volunteer Reserve. Returning home, he surprised his friends and shocked not Joe, but Effie. According to Neil, Effie was 'upset by the suddenness' of her son's action. Joe resigned himself quickly: the forces kept a lad out of trouble; the navy was an honourable job, with adequate pay, not as good perhaps as the post office, where all the shrewdest Darroch lads went, but quite acceptable. Conceivably too, Joe was relieved that his biggest boy was safely out of the way: now there would be more room in 176, the but-and-ben need only house Neil; Joe would be the sole man about the house again, his view unchallenged by wit or wiles. Effie's point of view was different. Tommy's departure spelt a smaller weekly purse, less financial input, less to save.

Connery sees his rush to the navy as an elementary case of escapism – and a mistake. Fountainbridge and the workload had exhausted him. 'It was the kind of conditioning that led one to think, "Wow – the navy – abroad – China!"' As it happened, he never saw China, indeed never roamed beyond British coastal waters. Butlaw Camp, next door to Lochinver, was his first unexciting port of call, where he began training. From there he was transferred to HMS Victory Barracks at Portsmouth where, in rapid succession, he was trainee at the gunnery school at Whale Island, boy seaman member of an anti-aircraft squadron, then able seaman assigned, Neil remembers, to HMS *Formidable*. From the start Connery was neither a very active nor interested recruit. Neil cannot recollect any postcards home from exotic ports, nor do his Fountainbridge friends recall much enthusing during the frequent shore leaves. Fountainbridger Tom O'Sullivan says, 'He made no big deal about his uniform or anything like that and anyway, after the war there were uniforms galore in Fountainbridge. The Clanhouse Dancehall [next door to St Cuthbert's] was virtually a forces' dancehall, so Big Tam, when he came home, just blended back into the pack. When you talked with him over a pint, he gave the general impression that the navy was a dull job best not talked about.'

Portsmouth had its moments, though. With his wiry iron build Connery was easily elected on to a naval junior boxing team. He fought a few scraps, enjoyed the release of pent-up energies and earned kudos and bruises. He also awarded himself the traditional naval honour – twin tattoos inked on his right forearm in a dock-side dive. Both bellowed the chauvinistic sentimentality of youth – 'Scotland Forever' inside a bleeding knife-pierced heart and 'Mum & Dad' scrolled in a bird's mouth – but hint also at the sensitivity, unnoticed by even his close friends, that was to inhibit his future as a seaman.

During his second year, Connery fell ill with stomach pains. On the recommendation of his fellow seaman friend Bob McGinty he visited the MO at HMS *Hazler* in Gosport and, after tests, was hospitalised. The diagnosis was peptic ulcers, the prognosis fine – provided that stress and the regular mess diet were avoided. In a word, the MO was giving Able Seaman Connery, aged 19, the passport to a premature pension.

Despite his enthusiasm for the Sea Cadets and his escape dreams, Connery is emphatic about his unsuitability for naval life. Within months of enlisting, he said, he realised sourly that 'the seafaring life wasn't all that one had fantasised it to be. I was a boy seaman, and there was an ordinary seaman above me, and if you reached his status there was a naval seaman and beyond that a leading seaman, and then a petty officer and a chief petty officer – and I was aware that I had not done enough to make this kind of progress.' The dilemma was partly institutional discipline at odds with his own rigid sense of how to do things ('Call it a problem with paternalist authority,' says Neil), partly teenage angst. 'I was conscious of keeping myself emotionally in check, never permitting an outburst,' said Connery. 'And at some point in the navy the steam valve popped.'

Back in Edinburgh he celebrated his discharge – and his 6s 8d disability pension – with a drink with friends at the Fountain Bar and a game of snooker at the Lothian. John Brady says he looked well on discharge. Another acquaintance suggests that he looked too well and mentions he was also 'a resourceful chappie', the inference being that, like so many other immature dreamers who sign their lives away to the Colours and Reserves, Connery's disillusionment inspired the ruse of an ulcer. But against this one must consider the fussiness of the forces' medical personnel, and indeed the fact that ulcers run in the Connery family. Both Joe and Neil suffered stomach ailments. And the late actor Ian Bannen, with whom Connery shared a flat in their early acting days, reckons Sean 'never really shook off that ulcerish uptightness'. As late as the mid-80s, Bannen claimed, he observed that 'flaring ulcer thing whenever Sean gets caught with chit-chatting women or boring people at parties. You see the physical discomfort in his eyes.'

Back in Fountainbridge, it was evident that the man who returned to the stair was considerably different in temperament from the boy who left. Outwardly, to street pals like Michael O'Sullivan and Brady, he was the same humorous, tearaway Big Tam, who loved football, snooker and dancing at the Palais, but privately he was at war with himself. Reclaiming the shakedown bed opposite Neil's settee in the but-and-ben was profoundly demoralising. No matter which way one interpreted his service record it was, in his eyes, a case of abject failure. He had seen no travel, achieved nothing in rank and, despite his brawn, ended up with an invalid's discharge chit. Effie and Neil saw the extent of his unhappiness. The navy had certainly helped hatch him into man-hood, but the maturer Tommy was sharp-tongued and jumpy as a cornered cat. Just as well, Neil said, that Joe was working long-distance lorry runs, and often absent from the stair from nine in the morning till nine at night.

Inertia was against his nature so Connery quickly decided to take whatever work he could find. By Christmas of 1949 he had torn up his medical diet card and flung himself into a routine of physically gruelling, aimless, but reasonably well-paying jobs. He was a coal-delivery man for three weeks, a steelworker for eight, a corporation road worker, an any-hours odd-job man. There was, Neil suggests, almost an element of self-punishment about the fury of effort Connery applied to some of these jobs; but there was, too, something of his old contemptuous wryness: the navy debacle had hurt, not harmed him. 'Money was all that really mattered,' John Brady says. 'He didn't give two hoots about the quality of the work or anything else. He just wanted cash to splash out on recreation, to do things with.' Sneering in the face of a 'twenty per cent dis-ability' stigma, Connery pumped up the power, working constant overtime and often bagging £10–£12, easily twice the weekly takings of the average labourer. This time round priorities had shifted and the overtime money was directed not towards the family funds, but on the pursuit of glamorous West End girl-friends. 'Tommy had no strict preferences in girls,' remembers Brady. 'Basically he went for all women.'

The casual relationships with the opposite sex did not provide enough distraction though, and, in his own words, Connery found himself 'dissatisfied with everything' within a year. Then, out of the blue, the British Legion came to the rescue. Founded in 1921 to lend assistance to ex-servicemen, the Legion was especially active in schemes to help the young disabled. Qualifying with his minor disability, Connery was granted a scholarship to a trades training course. 'You could become a tailor or a barber or a plasterer or a plumber,' Connery said, 'and I chose to be a French polisher. The whole training school practised on one another. You had to go and let some of them cut your hair, and let others make suits for you.'

Connery polished the ramshackle furniture of tenement Edinburgh, a thankless, energy-draining task, before being landed in the Craighouse Gardens cabinet works of Jack Vinestock in the summer of 1951. He was taken on at £7 a week – a sizeable drop in earnings – but then, to Effie's thinking, he was learning a worthwhile trade. His hours were 8 a.m. till 5.30 p.m., five days a week, and the working conditions were good. 'There was a staff of about sixty then and a very jolly atmosphere,' recalled Jack Jr, son of the company's founder. 'We hadn't been allowed to manufacture household furniture during the war, and by 1951 the rush on utility stuff was finished. People were going in for a better class of contemporary designs and we prided ourselves in our craftsmanship. Tommy was an assistant, working up everything from dressers to wardrobes and even coffins. He was a lively fellow who was tremendously popular with many of the workforce, but there wasn't a lot of time for fun-making because we were working fast and under some pressure.' In Vinestock's memory Connery was 'very physical, the kind of kid who laughed a lot ... but he wasn't really a French polisher, he had no talent for it.' Co-workers William Strain and Johnny Wallis found Connery to be a relentless prankster, good company, hard-working but, said Wallis, 'very wild'.

Earlier it was easy to excuse Connery's fickle wit as immaturity. Now, with the failure of the navy behind him, there was a barb in his attitude. In Wallis's judgement he had plans to escape again, to see the world 'but no sense at all of direction in the bigger picture ... He seemed more than anything driven by a kind of anger.'

John Hogg, an experienced cabinet-maker, worked alongside Wallis and Connery and one day, casually, suggested that Connery might enjoy work at the theatre where he himself earned pocket money. Christmas was approaching, and the esteemed King's Theatre in Leven Street needed backstage help for the holiday season. Connery expressed interest, said Wallis, in the easy money and the next day Hogg brought the apprentice to the stage manager of the King's and secured him work as a backstage assistant, tending to wardrobe and sets.

Connery first experienced the greasepaint and glow of theatre fantasyland that Christmas and relished every minute. In Wallis's view, the theatre atmosphere 'quietened and tamed him for some reason'.

He enjoyed the atmosphere and the money in equal measure and for the few weeks of his engagement his wildness and recalcitrance were, in part anyway, curbed. Here at last he had found blood brothers, respected drifters who lived by their wits, moved endlessly, freely, and were, incredibly, related to the lone riders of the gaff range.

# 4. ADRIFT IN *SOUTH PACIFIC*

Despite his height – 6 foot 2 inches at 18 – and broad shoulders, Tommy was, by Neil's reckoning, 'skinny' when he came out of the navy. He was also, after settling at Vinestock's, socially hyperactive and girl-hungry. As a prominent local football hero, he now enjoyed the fan following of Fet-Lor Amateurs, his new team, which was sponsored by wealthy former pupils of Fettes College and Loretto Public School in the old part of the city. The 1950 Fet-Lor victory in a newspaper cup competition won him a silver medal and yet more girl fans. Later, transferring to Bonnyrigg Rose, his speed and strength placed him as a star winger and he was offered a £25 signing fee, which he declined. Neil believes that this unexpected success started Connery thinking for the first time of the possibility of a professional football career as a way out of Fountainbridge. John Brady agrees: 'The word was that even Celtic wanted to give him a trial [but] something kept holding him back, he didn't want to latch on to it as a full-blown career.'

In Connery's version, he turned his physical energies instead towards body-building, 'to look good and get the girls'. 'Jimmy Laurie was the man he idolised,' says Tom O'Sullivan. 'At the end of the Meadows there was a tin shed called the Dunedin Amateur Weightlifting Club and Jimmy was its star member. Jimmy himself was only five foot six and a half, but he was built powerfully and he had been a Mr Scotland. Jimmy became Tommy's coach and friend because he saw in him a great independent determination.' Connery paid his fifteen shillings' entry fee and started on Laurie's three-nights-a-week grind, elbowing football, girls and Vinestock overtime.

The records of Craighouse Cabinet Works were destroyed in the early 80s but there is a pervasive suspicion that Connery got the sack. Jack Vinestock Jr is foggy about the details but Wallis, who was called up for National Service late in 1951, believed it likely. Whichever way, Connery left Vinestock's in the spring of 1952, took a one-penny tram ride down Princes Street and offered himself as a lifeguard at Portobello Pool, one of the largest salt-water public pools in Britain. A strong swimmer since the age of five when Joe taught him at the Dalry Baths, Connery was a well-liked and conscientious guard, only ever distracted, says Brady, 'by the flattering attention of corset-suited sylphs'. His physique, thanks to Laurie's dumb-bells and chest expanders, was spectacular. That hot summer, Brady swears, 'Tommy caught more birds than any man deserves'.

At this popularity peak another former Mr Scotland working out at the Dunedin, Archie Brennan, advised Connery to offer himself for arts modelling. According to Brennan it was money for nothing. Connery warily tested the advice and, to his delight, found extra evening employment at the Edinburgh College of Art, posing in a classical thong, for 6s 8d an hour. Norfolk-based Martin MacKeown, now an established artist, studied at the college and recalled the casual model who brooded over his future: 'I can remember that I felt very sorry for him. He had this dead-end job with no future while I was busy working to become a Great Artist. With hindsight, look how wrong one can be.'

But the big breakthrough, stumbled upon like everything else in this headlong rush to rebuild ego and find purpose to life, was the chance that autumn to return to the theatre – this time flexing muscles as a player on the stage. An advertisement in the *Edinburgh Evening News* caught Connery's attention and Brennan encouraged him: 'spear carriers' were required for backgrounds in the touring version of the London play *The Glorious Years*, starring Anna Neagle, due for a five-week run at the Empire.

Connery won the job, he said, solely because of his height. The show was a hit – not that that affected his career, or his pocket – but it served to highlight the joys of theatre fantasies, the bonhomie, the transience. Neil believes that the experience of *The Glorious Years* was the wake-up call, that here the theatre world impacted on his brother 'like a new home town', a place where there was no need to pretend allegiance in perpetuity, where make-believe was embraced, tomorrow was another day, another problem, perhaps, but – most precious to so many actors – another world.

No efforts were made to persuade friends or family along to the Empire to watch this baptism ritual. 'To me it was just another one of the casual jobs one heard about,' Brady says. 'He didn't talk about it any more than he talked about life-saving at the pool. It just happened, and then he was back playing billiards at the Lothian Hall.'

Connery's days in Edinburgh were numbered. On the face of it he appeared to be content with a weekly ritual divided between French polishing, the Dunedin nights and the modelling nights, with weekends spent at the Palais de Danse. Isa Farmer, a well-brought-up girl from the Grassmarket, behind Edinburgh Castle, became his regular date – was even taken home to meet Effie – but, says Neil, the attractions of the Palais ensured a short-lived affair.

'It was the navy business all over, because suddenly he was eager for a major change,' says Brady. 'Money was not the issue. He stood head and shoulders above all of us in the knack of making money. In fact, it seemed that money-making was a gift he had.' Sure enough, by the measure of his contemporaries, Connery seemed flush. In lieu of a long-term pension he had accepted £90 from the navy and finally acquired the motorbike he'd dreamed of since he was 15 – which he used to motor to Vince Studios in Manchester where he modelled at weekends for arts-photo magazines.

'By then I'd become a wage-earner too,' says Neil. 'I was christened Neil Maclean Connery after my grandfather, and I resolved to follow him into plastering as a career. So money was coming into the home from myself as well as from Sean, and materially things were better than they'd ever been. But that wasn't any inducement for Sean to stay.'

Appeasing Effie, Connery quit the world of furniture-polishing and joined the print room of the *Edinburgh Evening News*, becoming an apprentice machine worker, but the move was clearly a smokescreen. At the Dunedin club Laurie was already scheming to get Connery moving on the competitive body-building circuit, a demi-career that would take him all around Britain, potentially even abroad. 'Tommy was Dunedin's star pupil,' says Tom O'Sullivan, 'and Jimmy looked upon him as a surrogate son. What Jimmy liked to see was initiative, and Tommy was a doer, he was always working out. He got a job as a bouncer at the Palais de

Danse and every traders' holiday, when the factories closed, Ray Ellington, the popular bandleader, would grace the hall. He was into body-building as well and Tommy and himself practised backstage, during shows. The fact that Ray had the best equipment with him was a big asset to Tommy, because that was the kind of chap he was – someone who never missed out on an opportunity.'

When Connery was 22, after three years' working out, Laurie decided he was ready for a major competition. One Friday after a training session, Laurie showed Connery the enrolment forms for the Mister Universe heats, to be held in London. Connery hesitated before agreeing. At the Dunedin and elsewhere he had met plenty of professional musclemen, and most fitted quite a different physical mould: they were short, bulky and bull-necked. In contrast, he had a sinewy frame which, in the words of a girlfriend, 'befitted a champion swimmer'. But Laurie talked him round and arrangements were made for the London trip.

Effie saw the London venture as a bit of a joke, just some act of boyish daftness, like playing Tarzan lifeguards at the baths or at Portobello beach. Neil 'paid no attention at all to it' and Joe missed out because he was absent on a long-haul furniture run when Tommy packed his bags. 'The plan was to stay for a couple of weeks at some bedsit in Chelsea,' says Tom O'Sullivan. 'From there, Jimmy and Tommy would scout out other competitions, but focus mainly on the big one.'

The Mister Universe contest, held at the rundown Scala Theatre in West London, turned into an embarrassing disappointment for Laurie especially. At the last minute, according to O'Sullivan, Laurie himself entered, but failed to win any placing. Connery was more fortunate, coming third in the junior section, winning a bronze. Laurie was disgusted and disgraced but, in his own view, so too was Connery. Years later he told an American magazine, 'I did no good at all. The Americans always won those things. They were much bigger and everybody was impressed by the size of them. It was quite a disillusionment for me to meet them, because at the club I went to we were all very health- and strength-conscious, and we used to run and swim and do many other things. But all the American and the London fellas seemed to be solely intent on acquiring inches and bulk. I was absolutely shattered to discover that somebody wouldn't run for a bus because he might lose some of his bulk. Just to be a bulky physique would be boring to me. Not to run, not to play football, not to swim – just a cul-de-sac, in my opinion.'

The only aspect of the Scala scene that interested Connery was the theatrical one, which was no surprise to people like Neil and the football friends who had seen Connery's enthusiasm for the King's and the Empire, and a whole new breed of casual acquaintances, like Ray Ellington. 'After the navy, or maybe after the Empire,' says O'Sullivan, 'Tommy sought a new kind of companionship. He wasn't exactly your average star-struck stage-door johnny but he went for theatrical-type people, the gypsies, the slightly way-out, if you like.' Another friend recalls Connery raising eyebrows at the West End Cafe by dating Maxine Daniels, sister of the comedian-singer Kenny Lynch and herself a popular singer then appearing at the Empire. 'It wasn't only Maxine,' says O'Sullivan. 'He made new theatrical cronies during *The Glorious Years* and when he went to London that was the community he gravitated to.'

Initially, the London sojourn was about sightseeing. Connery had visited London in his navy days but now took to quartering the city on foot, establishing the cheapest restaurants and the theatre landmarks. Laurie tagged along, though, says O'Sullivan, the popular word in Fountainbridge was that Tommy was 'dragging Jimmy round … He didn't seem to have much enthusiasm for London, or for looking for work, which was really the essence of Tommy's nature.'

On the phone from Edinburgh Effie urged Tommy to return to his job at the *News*, but an alternative proposal took his fancy. Stanley Howlett, another Mister Universe contender whom he'd met at the Scala, detailed for Connery the obvious link between weight-training and theatre: London's West End shows were always on the lookout for muscular young men, either to shift props or dance in the footlights; Howlett himself had auditioned for a chorus Seabee role in the upcoming touring version of *South Pacific*, currently at the Theatre Royal in Drury Lane, and easily landed the job. Connery perked up immediately: he was ahead of the game, with experience already on both sides of the theatrical backcloth.

Connery and Laurie bulldozed into the last days of the *South Pacific* auditions. If there was hesitation for Connery about the negative aspects of a long-term tour commitment they only concerned losing out with the Bonnyrigg Rose football team. Otherwise, the prospect as Howlett described it seemed joyous.

Jerome White was the producer who oversaw the auditions, assessing about twenty-five hopefuls each afternoon. Connery impressed him with shining self-confidence. As Connery later told the story, he spoofed his way through the interrogation by White's casting assistant.

'Are you an actor?'

'Yes.'

'Do you sing?'

'Yes.'

'What experience?'

'Plenty of rep in Scotland.'

'Like?'

'Like *The Glorious Years.*'

'Do you dance?'

'All the time.'

When it came to reading lines, Neil says, Connery's nerves got the better of him. He dropped the script and heard the director call him clumsy. Enraged, Connery threw the script aside – then composed himself, remembered the Empire, relaxed, and rendered a half-dozen American-accented lines.

'I did the best I could,' Connery later said. 'I more or less mouthed one of the songs from the show and did a few fancy steps that were a hangover from my ballroom dancing at the Palais. Not bad, I concluded as I left the stage, but obviously not professional enough for them.'

But White was interested – impressed, Neil said, by Connery's ability to recover from an embarrassment and hoof to his heart's content, and also by his short rendition of 'I Belong to Glasgae'. Two days after the audition a phone call came to the Chelsea bedsit, informing Connery that he'd got the part. Twelve pounds per week was the not inconsiderable fee on offer. Laurie, unfortunately, had failed, but they went out to celebrate anyway, then made a lightning trip back to Edinburgh to break the news.

Neil vividly remembers his brother's excitement on his return from London. Effie and Joe, naturally, were sceptical – 'though Father thought the money was pretty terrific' – but their concerns were assuaged by Connery's declared attitude to the prospect of a formal acting career: 'It was really the idea of travelling round the country and being paid for it that appealed most,' Connery later said. 'I loved the stage, but I didn't seriously consider myself as an actor in [*South Pacific*]. It seemed more like a giggle.'

Jerry White, though, regarded the production as anything but a giggle. Working in the shadow of the celebrated Joshua Logan, who had forged *South Pacific*'s classic status on Broadway, White was determined to keep the quality comparison and commanded what Robert Henderson, one of the actors involved, called, 'a watertight ship'.

Connery embarked on *South Pacific* in high spirits, soaring with White's code of discipline in direct inverse proportion to his fall with the navy's paternalism. Back at the machine room of the *Edinburgh Evening News* there were those who believed Big Tam would get his picture in the paper, earn a few quid, and be back begging off the personnel manager by Christmas. Connery knew otherwise.

# 5. LOVE IN THE STICKS

A conversation about Ibsen transformed Connery the odd-job man into Connery the actor. Robert Henderson, the American actor-director, remembered the occasion well: '*South Pacific* was a quarter-way through its long and extraordinarily successful tour. We'd just done Scotland and we were then in the middle of nine weeks at the Opera House in Manchester. Sean and I were in the same lodging house, a bit away from the theatre, and it just happened we walked home together one night. We were chatting and I mentioned Ibsen and Sean said, "Who's he?" So I told him – he's this famous dramatist, and all the rest. And I suggested he read a few of Ibsen's plays, thinking of course I'd hear nothing about it again. Those musclemen, you see, weren't employed for their brains. In the strict sense it wasn't chorus boys the show's management wanted, just capable big fellows for the "Nothing Like a Dame" routine.'

The plays Henderson loaned Connery were *The Wild Duck*, *When We Dead Awaken* and 'the eternal classic *Hedda Gabler*'. Connery read them, obviously with some difficulty here and there, but surprised Henderson by returning to discuss them intelligently. A voracious student of all theatre but (by his own admission) with no particular eye for new talent, Henderson was flattered and intrigued by the burst of avid interest displayed by the chatty 'muscleman'. Connery, in turn, was grateful for a sympathetic ear, most of all someone who was rooted in the milieu and knew his p's and q's.

A considerable part of Connery's problem in comfortably settling into the show was his accent. 'In the beginning very few of the cast would speak to me,' he said. 'For some reason they thought I was Polish!' The accent certainly jarred with Henderson – 'very awkward', Henderson described it. 'I urged him to get rid of it, and he did soften it down.' (Interestingly, some Edinburgh friends claim Connery has consciously emphasised his dialectal accent. 'There's a scene in *You Only Live Twice*,' Tom O'Sullivan said, 'where Sean and the girl [Mie Hama as Kissy] are about to climb the volcano slope. "We must get *up* there," Sean says. That small sentence, the stress on the demonstrative "up" – that's pure tribal Fountainbridge. Get a Glaswegian, anyone, to say that and it'll sound totally different.' The director John Boorman recalls a dinner party where Connery was queried about his brogue, playing an Arab, in *The Wind and the Lion*. 'Sean's a wonderful mimic, but his response then was, "If I didn't play in my normal voice I wouldn't know who the fuck I was."')

Robert Henderson had come to London in 1947 to study directing, but moved as an actor through fringe theatre to musicals, where he won attention for fine performances in *Damn Yankees* and *West Side Story* in the 50s and 60s. Marriage to the celebrated character actress Estelle Winwood (who would star with Connery in *Darby O'Gill and the Little People*), reinforced his devotion to all things theatrical, and his career was, as he described it, utterly rewarding. Of Connery, he had the fondest, vivid memories: 'That chap had Romany blood in him, no doubts about it. Those features, his eyes – it's there all right.' But if Connery's matinee idol features won over successive future talent scouts, it was his 'divine curiosity' that captivated Henderson: 'It was quite remarkable. After Ibsen he wanted to know more and more, and he seemed deadly serious about it. So, with a twinkle in my eye I listed for him just six books that were worth studying.' There was Proust's *Remembrance of Things Past*; *War and Peace*; James Joyce's *Ulysses* and *Finnegans Wake*; the Bernard Shaw–Ellen Terry letters, and Thomas Wolfe's *Look Homeward Angel*. Henderson considered these books a 'dry choice by any standard, but they all led to endless channels that have been explored and re-explored in theatre. I knew they would stimulate him if he could get his teeth into them but, given his education, I wondered would he have the patience to pursue them.'

Henderson's encouragement apart, Connery was already showing signs of progress in his new job though, objectively, such progress probably had more to do with teen energy than talent. On the tour's first visit to the King's Theatre in Edinburgh Connery was still hand springing with the guys, blaring 'There is Nothing like a Dame!' – but he was also understudying two reasonably important roles and his salary had been upped to £14 10s. When Neil saw him during the first tour visit he found him to be 'as happy as I'd ever known him, and eager to prove his worth to the show'. Michael Medwin, a fellow actor on the tour, commented, 'It was jokey at the start and then, very quickly, he wanted to do well. He had a bit of a chip on his shoulder and figured he could do as well as anyone out front, but that is exactly the kind of thick-neck you need to succeed in theatre and films. Early on I knew he'd stick with it, and try for a proper part.'

Among the men his own age – those who did not mistake him for a Pole – Connery was popular, though considered tetchy. He was a star player at the weekend poker session in endless lodging houses, a cherished wing player with the cast football team and hoarder of rude Scottish jokes. His allegiances, it seems, were confused. 'He loved Scotland for sure,' Robert Henderson said. 'But you got the impression he never wanted to live there again.' Most old Fountainbridge cronies lost touch around this time. 'He changed,' Tom O'Sullivan said. 'In London there had been a blow-up with Jimmy Laurie. Something boyish and crazy to do with the work ethic. Let's say Tommy was a grafter and Jimmy got fed up with work. So the flat they shared came unstuck, and Tommy hit the road. After that Tommy didn't want to look back, he just wanted to get himself on.'

Jerry White, Robert Henderson and the rest of the cast knew Connery only as Sean. The origin of the name-change reaches back to childhood. Connery had a primary-school friend nicknamed 'Shane' and it is likely that George Stevens's Oscar-winning movie, *Shane*, starring Alan Ladd, released in 1953 – about the time Connery restyled himself for Drury Lane – influenced the final choice of the new career name. Connery saw and admired *Shane*, which, in the character of its lone-protector Western hero, had much in common with Connery's eventual cowboy creation *Shalako*.

Meanwhile, Connery's mode of transport was his 150cc motorbike, a post-war relic that reliably took him from town to town in the tracks of the tour. The bike gave him a charge of power and freedom he loved, and the chance to go for country spins, where he could escape alone to the great outdoors beyond theatreland and contemplate *War and Peace*. Henderson's speculation about young Connery's earnestness was resolved just a week after the 'dry book list' had been proposed. 'I suddenly saw that he truly meant it. He was dedicated and everyone on the cast commented on the fact that he always had a Tolstoy or a Proust – which were naturally on loan from the local libraries.'

Henderson's aggressive prompting coincided with an out-of-the-blue offer from the football world that briefly disorientated Connery. 'It was bad timing, or maybe the best timing,' said Henderson. 'A kind of dialogue about the purpose of life had opened between us and Sean was genuinely asking himself if he had what it took for a theatre career. To me, he looked basically like a lorry driver, but I thought suddenly that he could turn this into a great asset. I remember clearly the night we discussed it and I told him, "The work you are doing [with the reading] will get you moving. Tolstoy will lead you on to Dostoevsky and Stanislavsky and so forth. Now, I don't know a lot about stardom, but I have a feeling you could be something big in the States. Here's the trick: if you can *talk* Dostoevsky and *look* like a truck driver, you've got it made. Speak one thing, look another. That's the essence of an artist." And Sean said, "Yes, yes," like he meant it, as though he'd discovered gold. So he had made his decision, in my mind, to really go for it. Then, the very next day, Manchester United comes along and upsets the whole apple cart.'

Always sociable, Connery had been playing on the touring football team, tackling various provincial junior teams. At Manchester, Matt Busby's scout happened on a cast match and saw him. Within days Connery was offered a trial at Old Trafford.

'Sean came knocking on my door at the guest house,' said Henderson, 'and he was very excited, because he had been playing football for fifteen years and knew he was good. He could hardly speak with the excitement, repeating again and again the importance of Manchester United, and the privilege of it. I listened, and I told him, "Don't take it. Remember what we discussed. If you can take Tolstoy – and *you can* – you'll make it big in the movies."'

Connery slept on it, then rejected Old Trafford in a phone call. When Jerry White heard the outcome, he was appalled. Backstage at the Opera House he confronted Henderson in a rage. 'Do you know what you've fucking done?' he ranted. 'You've built up this kid's hopes with baloney about movie success. United was offering him a *career* chance, the chance to earn bloody good money for a couple of years. In this business, he'll probably sink like a stone. He's a nobody, he might always be a nobody.'

Henderson showed no remorse: 'Forget White. In the space of a few weeks, Sean proved his worth to me. Lots of young actors are dead keen to become stars. Lots of young actors are also dead lazy. Sean had an insatiable desire to learn the business. Later, when people looked at the cool urbanity of Bond and the huge success, they said, Wow, that was easy for him. But, by God, I know it was labour and risk and sweat from the word go.'

On stage Henderson, along with other central characters in the cast like Millicent Martin and Michael Medwin, were intrigued by Connery's confidence. 'He had his qualms in daily life,' Michael Medwin said, 'but once on stage, he hadn't a nerve in his body'. In many unscheduled incidents along the two-year run, Connery distinguished himself with sheer neck, always demonstrating, said Henderson, 'a complete resistance to the word "failure"'. Michael Medwin recalled the simulated night-time bomb attack sequence, where black-clad bit-part actors ran on an unlit stage, invisible to the audience, flashing flare lamps that burnt briefly bright, like ground gunfire, while in the background sound effects duplicated an air raid. On one occasion Connery, draped in black, leapt out to the wrong cue, slap in the middle of a quiet dialogue scene. 'For a frantic second he hopped round, arms swirling with the flare torches, like some maniac on the loose. A gasp of shock came from the audience. In mid-stride Connery realised, in the sudden horrific silence, that his timing was wrong: he belonged backstage at the poker table, not here. He froze, dropped his torches by his side, grinned widely and ambled off. The audience breathed easy, and the show rolled on.'

About a year out on the tour, at the Brighton Hippodrome, Connery was at last elected on to the printed programme, taking over the part of Lieutenant Buzz Adams, originally performed on the West End stage by Larry Hagman, later JR of *Dallas*, the record-breaking television soap. A small-time Australian actor had inherited the part and, when he quit, Henderson led the group of principals in a deputation to demand Connery's promotion. Jerry White needed little persuasion. Connery became Lt Adams and assumed responsibility for his first true acting scene. 'It wasn't a very big slice,' Henderson said, 'but it was important. I was playing Captain Brackett and Adams had to come to my hut and tell me about the marine landing on the Japanese islands. It was quite an intense little scene, I suppose, and Sean delivered it beautifully. From the first night he was flawless, not a bit intimidated to be holding centre stage.'

Two women figured large in Connery's touring life: one he loved; the other adored him and, like Henderson, was convinced he was a budding international talent.

Carol Sopel, a raven-haired, petite actress, joined the company in the middle of the tour to take over the part of the Polynesian love interest whose famous 'Happy Talk' duet was, traditionally, the show-stopper. Carol replaced the popular Eurasian actress Tsin Yu, but, claimed Henderson, 'She transcended anything Tsin Yu gave us; she didn't act, she just presented herself as the serene ingénue and she was touched with near genius.' Henderson adored her. 'She was dedicated, but also she was great fun – everyone in the cast loved her. Her experience wasn't wide, but she was eager to cultivate the flair she had and, in that, she found her soulmate in Sean.'

Within just days of her joining, Connery developed a close friendship with Carol and, though Robert Henderson stressed he involved himself hardly at all in Connery's private life, he was close enough to observe that 'Sean fell deeply, deeply for her. They were the closest of friends and naturally the relationship intensified as the tour progressed.' Henderson saw that Connery confided his ambitions to Carol. 'It was everything a great love affair should be,' Henderson said, 'but that didn't alter Sean's disciplines. At night in his lodgings he still read into the small hours. During the days, he studied with the aid of a portable tape recorder, practising those

speeches from Ibsen and Shaw and working on his accent.'
Whenever the tour hit a major city, Connery took Carol to every
matinee in town – 'all the theatres and the local reps, in whatever
plays they were doing, avant-garde, anything'. Connery assimi-
lated material and ideas unusually fast, said Henderson, 'displaying the quality of a sponge – as though that cultural desert [of
Fountainbridge] had wrung him out and he needed to absorb
nourishment fast'.

Carol kept the pace and though Connery was – and is, according to Honor Blackman and most others – 'first and foremost a
man's man', for several months through the winter of 1954 the
couple were inseparable. Eventually Connery hinted at an upcoming engagement. 'He wanted to marry her,' said Henderson, 'that
much I know. Everyone knew, because they talked openly about it.
To many of us they were already the new married couple on the
team. It was just a question of where and when.'

Temperamentally and professionally Carol and Connery suited
each other, but the cloud that darkened their lives from the day
they met finally overtook them. Carol was Jewish, and her parents
strongly orthodox. Henderson said, 'They might have liked their
daughter's choice, but tradition would never allow them to permit
marriage. Carol plotted and begged but in the end she was forced
to give in. It was an overnight thing. Almost as suddenly as it
began, the love affair with Carol ended.' Connery was shattered,
his closer male friends on the cast truly surprised.

Carol's decision upset Connery greatly. When he lunched with
Henderson to explain the break-up, he wept. 'You can't imagine it,'
said Henderson, 'but it was just terribly sad to see this tough guy
we've all come to see as the ruthless James Bond so heartbroken.'

Consolation came from another girl Connery had met in a
London pub. Julie Hamilton, step-daughter of Labour Party-
leader-to-be Michael Foot, was a freelance photographer specialis-
ing in theatre tours, who mostly worked for the *Daily Mail*. After
visiting her friend, the actor Ronnie Fraser, at a show at the Lyric
in Hammersmith, Fraser made the introductions. Julie had at first
disliked Connery, seemingly finding him arrogant and average, but
weeks later, at Fraser's wedding in Hampstead, when Connery

showed up in a kilt, fell for him. 'She was a nice girl,' said Ian Bannen, who himself later became romantically involved with her, 'but she was not a great photographer. She photographed me at the Old Vic in *The Iceman Cometh* and for some damned reason the pictures were always out of focus. I liked her a lot, but I used to tease her that she was eyesight-impaired.'

According to Henderson, Julie's attraction to Connery was a combination of his ambition and 'the kind of who-cares confidence that made him comfortable in a kilt'. From Connery's perspective, she was young, well-educated and impressively versed in the history of theatre – all definite pluses. Henderson believed the relationship was fated from the start, that 'there was a compensatory measure at work and Sean was open to any fellow-traveller who was prepared to share his chosen road'. In character Julie was Carol's absolute opposite – she was witty, articulate and pushy – but Connery started to date her, and for a while they appeared every bit as close as he and Carol had been. 'But it was a totally different chemistry,' said Henderson. 'Julie wanted to help Sean's career. That was the foundation of their affair. Sean, for his part, wanted all the help he could get, but he hadn't really gotten over Carol and I saw no future for [Sean and Julie].'

As *South Pacific* neared the end of its two-year tour, Connery recognised the watershed he was approaching. He could look back on a bumpy period of his life which had marked him emotionally, given him real education, real fun and, above all, unscrambled his needs. The joys of the childhood freedom he cherished in Fife were distilled and crystallised in the acting life.

On the second tour visit to Edinburgh Effie greeted a rowdy bunch from the cast at 176: Tommy had brought them home to show them off, indifferent to whatever any thespian 'nob' thought of the rundown stair. According to Neil, Effie knew then with certainty that Tommy had chosen a career. Even Joe learnt to encourage what to him appeared a wayward and distinctly strange profession. Big Tam was truly, consistently happy: that was all that mattered.

*South Pacific* ended its run in Dublin at the Gaiety Theatre and Connery toasted his success in a Grafton Street pub. In all he had understudied five parts, succeeded well with Buzz Adams, and advanced further than any other Seabees in the cast. He had saved a few pounds, and had the loving support of Julie Hamilton. But the future, in work opportunity terms, was a colossal question mark. Henderson said goodbye to Connery to go on to *Damn Yankees* at the Coliseum. 'It looked like it was going to be a lean time for him, but he made it clear that he'd decided to stick it out, hell or high water. We promised to keep in touch, and I wished him luck.'

Back in London and out of work, Connery moved into a one-room basement flat at 12 Shalcomb Street, off the King's Road, which Henderson organised for him. He signed on at Westminster Labour Exchange, drawing £6 weekly benefit, and, on Julie's recommendation, started elocution lessons. Neil, who would share accommodation with his brother for a spell, reckons Connery's outgoings were about £10, so the economic pinch was felt immediately. Various steps were taken to address the crisis: his motorbike was traded for a lady's bicycle, costing £2; the usual nightly binge of cinema and pub was curtailed; daily food was rationed. The staple diet became a tomato-based Hungarian hotpot, usually meatless. Henderson visited and 'never forgot that pot bubbling on the stove from day till night ... it was a combination of porridge and stew and I never, ever touched it'.

Connery toured the big agents' offices, but achieved nothing. Every week he petitioned the theatres, and read all the trade papers. Throughout, he regularly phoned Henderson, who offered constant encouragement. 'He never let any of us [in Edinburgh] know anything was wrong,' Neil says. 'Even when he was ill and in bed for something like three weeks with a soaring temperature we knew nothing about it until months afterwards – and only then because one of his friends happened to mention it to us.'

At the lowest ebb, after nearly four months' idleness, Henderson came to the rescue. Assigned to direct Agatha Christie's *Witness for the Prosecution* at the Q Theatre near Richmond, Henderson phoned Connery and offered him a small non-speaking part as a court usher. Connery jumped at the £6-weekly fee, but kept drawing the dole.

Any doubts that Henderson may have harboured about Connery's readiness to play bigger roles were quickly put to rest. 'Rehearsals went well, but I was concentrated on the main actors and didn't pay attention to Sean. He was background, just your average usher, wearing this sweeping, full black cloak.' Then came the first night. 'It went as I wanted it to go, but suddenly someone called my attention to Sean. The main actors were compelling, but Sean's movement across the stage was so eye-catching – so grand – that it just wiped them out. He had this absolutely amazing way of walking, a great, elaborate stride that swished the cloak all over the place, and distracted half the audience. After a performance or two I had to take the cloak off him. It was just *too* impressive.'

The Q Theatre became a home-from-home for Connery at this critical time and he won further introductions from Henderson and parts in productions of *Point of Departure* and *A Witch in Time*. Beyond Henderson's circle, however, progress was stodgy, if not non-existent. Several West End productions turned him down and, at the Old Vic, Michael Bentall auditioned and rejected him on the basis of inadequate diction.

Ian Bannen first met Connery in the foyer of the Q Theatre at this time: 'I was appearing in an Anouilh play and Sean was wait-ing to see the director, hoping to land a part, the usual acorn trail. My first recall is of a towering, huge fellow with hair everywhere – all over his cheeks, huge eyebrows like a squirrel's tail, very hairy and sinister. He looked formidable, like some sort of gangster. I remember thinking I wouldn't have wanted to meet him down some alley – but we were fellow Scots and we made a connection.'

Lewis Gilbert, who was shortly to direct Connery's wife-to-be Diane Cilento in *The Admirable Crichton* (and would later reshape the Bond series with *You Only Live Twice*), also encountered Connery at the Q: 'I can't say there was anything striking about him, no sense that he would one day be a superstar. But he was good-looking, and he had a build that made you look twice.' Michael Caine, another struggling beginner, also met Connery on the audition circuit, but saw him differently: 'In my eyes, he had it from the word go. If Lewis was less than impressed, it's because he was already working with established great stars like Kenny Moore and Virginia McKenna. He was operating on a different plane from the rest of us in fringe theatre. It's significant that he took any note of Sean at all. But it figures. Sean, from Day One, had charisma.'

A sustained burst of job-hunting in the middle of 1956 finally broke the ice with decent stage parts and the first, lukewarm incursion into television. A recommendation from the Q Theatre forged an invitation to appear at Oxford as Pentheus opposite Yvonne Mitchell's Agave in *The Bacchae*, and, weeks later, with Jill Bennett in Eugene O'Neill's *Anna Christie*, a play which, in its revival on television the following year, would assume a special significance in Connery's life. Television was at last breached with roles in *The Condemned*, *Epitaph* and *Dixon of Dock Green* at the BBC.

No major breakthrough came during this jerky run: media reviews didn't mention him and the only press coverage worth bragging about was a bland local hero interview in a small Edinburgh paper. Connery didn't mind, said Robert Henderson, though Julie Hamilton probably did: 'She was impatient for him in a way that was kindly. But the joy for Sean then was just the regular work.' In fact, Connery was finding theatre life fulfilling and energy-creating. During the Oxford run of *The Bacchae*, he later told a journalist, 'I was driving back [from Oxford] to London late every night to rehearse *The Square Ring* for TV in the daytime, and then driving all through Saturday night to play football for the Showbusiness team on Sundays. I didn't feel I was being done out of my free time. I was enjoying myself. I believe a lot of people would enjoy themselves going hard at it if they had the kind of work they like and created the kind of surroundings they could respond to.'

By the end of 1956 Connery was in no doubt that he had found exactly the work he liked. But he was less sure of Julie who, said Henderson, had learned 'the knack of making a nuisance of herself' in Connery's company. The lean time at the beginning of the year taught Connery a lesson about showbiz that crowned the advice Henderson had given and created a very clear pattern for future survival: very little about showbusiness was 'a giggle'; one must study and graft, and one must *push*. Such effort required most, if not all, one's energy. There was time for social schemings

– indeed, social teamwork was part of making the grade – but a live-in girlfriend was a liability.

In the spring of 1957 Connery was doing well enough in theatre and bit-part television to quit the dole. He had also acquired an agent-with-attitude, Richard Hatton, who was then just starting to make a name for himself with the television companies. He had a motorbike again and a few pounds' savings, and in no time, as he knew it would, a plum role landed in his lap.

At the BBC in Wood Lane, Canadian producer Alvin Rakoff was in pre-production on Rod Serling's *Requiem for a Heavyweight*, a play about a dimwit boxer that had already been aired and applauded as a minor classic in the US. It was to be a live trans-mission – standard for the time – from Studio D of the new Television Centre, at 8.30 p.m. on 31 March. Rakoff had already considered some oddball names for the lead, among them the boxer Freddie Mills, before he settled on Jack Palance, who had played in the American version. Ten days before transmission, three before rehearsals, Palance's agent phoned to cry off, citing a delay caused by a Hollywood overrun. Rakoff rushed into confer-ence with his assistant Kay Fraser and Drama Chief Michael Barry. A shortlist of three major actors was drawn up, and Rakoff saw each that afternoon but by the night of Friday 22 March was still uncertain. On Saturday morning, en route to the BBC to prepare Monday's rehearsals, his girlfriend (soon to be wife), the actress Jacqueline Hill, suggested Connery.

Rakoff had already employed Connery for *The Condemned* the previous year. Then, Connery had first been assigned just one walk-on, playing a soldier, but he was 'so full of ideas and so keen at it,' Rakoff recalled, 'that I had to expand the work for him.' On location at Dover Castle, Rakoff cast him as the soldier who throws a hand grenade – and the bandit who receives it. Later, during studio taping in London, Connery was given yet another small role. In Rakoff's eyes Connery was distinctly a background player: 'And so I asked Jacqueline, who was set to play the love interest, why she would even consider him for this demanding lead role. And she just laughed her head off and said chirpily that every woman would want to just *look at* Sean.'

At the BBC canteen Rakoff tossed around the idea and received a surprisingly positive response. A lot of people remembered the Scotsman who had been eye-catching in the wings on *Dixon* and *The Condemned* and who had just won himself a big screen part, with Richard Hatton's help, in a minor movie called *No Road Back*.

Rakoff decided to interview Connery afresh.

# 6. HEAVYWEIGHT SUCCESS

In the summer of 1956 Connery had earned his first few days on a film set, auditioned and employed by second-feature writer-director Montgomery Tully to play near-silent stooge to Alfie Bass's dumb villain in *No Road Back*. Korda's old assistant Steven Pallos's Gibraltar Pictures understood exactly the market they were feeding: rattish gangland thrillers facelifted by the appearance of a 'name' American star – in this case Skip Homeier – were always popular B movies no matter how improbable the story or incompetent the cast. In this case Tully's task was made immeasurably easier by a reasonably original storyline (even a credible sub-plot love story) and the crack performances of Margaret Rawlings and the stage-trained Canadian Paul Carpenter.

Guaranteed oblivion by its rigorous adherence to current conventions in plot and style, *No Road Back* was released without promotion of any kind. Connery understood fully, as did everyone else involved. For Alfie Bass, the movie was just another exercise in conveyor belt thriller-making; but for Connnery it was a memorable first – the break into the rarefied acting life – the movies – where everything was larger than life. 'I doubt if Sean was paid a hundred quid,' said Bass, 'because a system was popular then whereby studio chiefs giving breaks to newcomers smartly drummed down fees. I'd suffered that myself a few years before when I was contracted to Sidney Box. It was very nice and above board, but by the time all sorts of considerations were out of the way, one was coming out with pennies. The interesting thing about Sean, though, was his intelligence. We had a lot in common. My background was in cabinet-making, too, so we could talk shop easily. At Pinewood, where the film was shot over six weeks, we shared a dressing-room. Sean liked to natter and it came over clear that nothing short of "making it" was on. He had great ambitions. And he had talent. He was competent, he had presence and he never forgot a line.' Emphasising the impact the eager newcomer had on the movie-weary veteran, Bass elaborated: 'How able was Connery then? Let me say this. I'm known as the shrewdest git in the business. And I would have happily become his agent.'

Connery was at ease on the movie set and, instantly, he saw it as some sort of terminus. The stage and television were bristling with challenge; but the movie world was the pinnacle. Stage stars belonged to the toffee-nosed of Edinburgh's West End; movie stars were for Fountainbridge, for everyone. Connery also liked to observe the fuss around Homeier and Carpenter, the limos at the studio, the fragrance of wealth wafting from others' dressing-rooms. At the same time, he wasn't so success-obsessed as to be impervious to the side-show offerings. Bass remembered, 'One thing everyone knew about Sean very soon: he wasn't queer. A couple of days after he started on the film he was befriending young starlets and production assistants like they were going out of fashion.' Inevitably, Connery was asking Bass to vacate the dressing-room at the convenient time. 'He wanted to entertain some birds,' said Bass. 'And a half-hour was all he ever needed.'

Toronto-born Alvin Rakoff, later one of television's pre-eminent directors of the 60s, had one major credit behind him with 1955's National TV award-winning *Waiting for Gillian* when he set out to tackle *Requiem for a Heavyweight* not long after *No Road Back*. A literate, experimental young director, he had a reputation for taking wild chances, an attitude that did not endear him to certain BBC executives, but one that produced the results. Rakoff had not seen Connery's debut in *No Road Back* when they met again at the BBC to discuss the possibilities of *Requiem*, and he remembered him mostly as a 'beefcake boyo'. Now, very quickly, he was struck by the actor's new confidence. After a reading, without reservation, he cast him as *Requiem's* lead, Mountain McClintock.

At rehearsals everyone felt a quality production was on the cards. Warren Mitchell and Fred Johnson as trainer and ring doctor were, said Rakoff, 'powerfully good' and Connery's relaxation, given his inexperience, was remarkable: 'He was not intimidated by the centrality of his role, or the huge amount of lines, nor did he seem in any way conscious of his mistakes. He blundered and was corrected: it was simply professional as that.' Michael Barry, the much-liked Drama Chief, sat in on one rehearsal and told Rakoff he was frankly disappointed, that Connery 'hadn't got it'. Rakoff was unmoved. 'As far as I was concerned, what he didn't have we could fix with camerawork. What he did have was animal power.'

On the night of transmission Rakoff sat in his control box, anticipating an important television experience. Then just minutes before the 8.30 p.m. green light, a group of grey-suited and grey-faced BBC executives stormed in, led by Michael Barry. 'They looked like Mafia wise guys,' Rakoff recounted, 'and I knew there was trouble afoot. I tried to ask Michael, but before we knew it, we were rolling, the show was on. It seemed edgy and uncertain because of the interruption, but on the floor everything cruised smoothly. Through the play I missed only one shot, and that was of Fred Johnson stitching some of Sean's facial cuts. I wanted a close-up, but Fred's hands were shaking so bad I didn't do it. The pressures of live TV took their toll on everyone.' During the inter-mission half-way through the ninety-minute play, Rakoff asked Barry what the fuss was about, to be told that the studio electri-cians were striking and had threatened to pull the plugs. 'The junior executives had agreed to stand by to push the plugs back in. Half the nation was watching us. The show had to go on.'

At home in Fountainbridge Joe, Effie, Neil and a neighbour from the stair, Mrs Pearson, watched on Joe's new 17-inch TV set. It was the first time any of the family had seen Tommy on screen. Neil, an impressionable 18-year-old, drank in every growling syllable of the drama and, he says, Effie was moved close to tears. When the play ended Joe was lost for words. 'The best he could manage was, "By heavens, that was smashing."'

Across the country viewers – and critics – concurred. JC Trewin in the *Listener* approached the play warily, but was won over by Connery. 'At first I thought I might take the count ignominiously in the first minute,' he wrote. But, within minutes, he was 'grateful for the oddly wistful performance of Sean Connery as the man who was once almost heavyweight champion of the world'. Trewin remained unmoved by the mechanics of the story: 'But its pro-ducer, Alvin Rakoff, let it have every chance, and the dramatist ought to go down on his knees to Sean Connery.'

In the *Evening Standard* the Boulting brothers, respected arbiters of movie-world taste, lavished praise on Rakoff and Connery. *The Times*, bizarrely, thought Connery 'physically miscast as the fighter', but praised 'a shambling and inarticulate charm that almost made the love affair [with Jacqueline Hill] credible'.

Before leaving Television Centre on that wet Sunday night, Connery later admitted, he knew he had pulled off a coup: he did not need Julie or any of his friends to tell him. Rakoff too was pleased – 'but also drained, as was everyone after such a fraught play'. Usually the post-transmission knees-up took place at the nearby Black Prince pub in Shepherd's Bush, but that night, because everyone was exhausted, a small party in one of the dressing-rooms sufficed. 'Then,' Rakoff said, 'we all went off into the night and caught our buses. It was the norm to take a long lie-in on the following morning, to recover. I remember I didn't come alive till midday, then I bussed back to the Beeb. I read the evening papers with the glowing tributes on the bus and later on Sean phoned me with a big thank-you.'

At his new one-room flat in Brondesbury Villas, Kilburn – recently arranged by Julie – Connery celebrated with his staple stew and a glass of beer. The pay cheque for the play was £25, but that was to represent the tip of the iceberg in terms of the material pay-off. The very day after transmission, according to Connery, the film companies started their pursuit of him. 'That wasn't unusual for that era,' said Rakoff. 'British films, though they didn't realise it then, were giving their dying gasps. Movie producers watched TV and stole whatever of quality they could from it. I knew what the direction of Sean's career after *Requiem* would be. I told Richard [Hatton] so. Rank was the first on the phone to Hatton, suggesting a long-term contract. Then a number of other production companies came on the line.' Knowing what he knew from Bass, Connery demurred with Rank, but was thrilled to hear that an international major, Twentieth Century Fox, was making overtures. Still, he hedged. Already, as a result of *No Road Back*, he had engagements on two other movies scheduled for shooting at Pinewood and Beaconsfield. Connery suddenly wanted breathing space, time to meditate and orientate himself. At Brondesbury Villas the people he shared the house with later recorded in a newspaper interview his cool and mature reaction to the exciting shock waves of *Requiem*. No one was surprised when he took time off to go home, with Julie, to Edinburgh.

At this key time in his career, when choosing the right avenue to take caused much suppressed concern, Julie's demands over-reached. In Fountainbridge he introduced her happily, but the confrontation that others like Henderson foresaw, developed quickly in what must have been, for Julie especially, an unusually strained environment. The incident that ended the love affair concerned what Neil called the Scottish 'masculine prerogative' – a jar in the local pub. The family was gathered round the fire in the but-and-ben, with Julie chatting to Effie, when Connery silently gestured to Neil his desire for a drink. Both brothers slipped quietly away, crossed to the Fountain Bar and ordered their pints. 'We had no sooner settled ourselves with a drink apiece,' Neil later told a newspaper, 'than Sean's girlfriend put in an appearance.' Julie was insulted at being left behind and let Connery know it. There was a row and 'that did it ... that was another of Sean's romances that died the death'.

In Henderson's view, Connery and Julie outgrew each other. Over the year and a half of their friendship, as they drew closer, so too they recognised the facets of their lives that did not match the other's needs. If there was any anger or sense of failure at the break-up, said Henderson, it was 'no more than tepid emotion'. They split, and Julie went back to her thriving London life and Connery to his chances.

Connery's second movie role, in Cy Endfield's *Hell Drivers*, at Pinewood, gave him no chance to shine, though the film was above average in every way. Written by John Kruse, who later went on to inject such vitality into the television *Saint* series, the part afforded him no more than a dozen lines, alongside Sid James, in a movie about murder and long-haul driving. Rank distributed *Hell Drivers* through the Gaumont cinemas, where it played to good business – best judged by the reruns – but failed to win the kind of recognition director Endfield had hoped for. Within the industry, the film was admired for its racy pace and good photography by Geoffrey Unsworth, a cinematographer bound for glory with classics such as *2001: A Space Odyssey*. Later Endfield, who would direct a number of slick box-office heavyweights, notably *Zulu* in 1963, considered *Hell Drivers* to have been a valuable market gauge that pointed him away from conveyor-belt thrillers.

Side by side with Endfield's film, Connery did a few hours on *Time Lock* for the Gerald Thomas–Peter Rogers director–producer team, then just months away from *Carry on Sergeant* and the beginning of the outstandingly popular comedy series which would, in its quiet way, be the only consistent rival to Bond during the 60s. Made at Beaconsfield, *Time Lock* was a long set piece about a 6-year-old boy accidentally trapped in a Canadian bank, in which Connery had second-to-last billing as a welder who tries to open the vault.

Before *Hell Drivers* or *Time Lock* had made their appearance in the late summer of 1957 Connery had hammered out a deal, under Hatton's guidance, with Twentieth Century Fox. The contract was long term but Connery had reason to be optimistic: Fox, above most, held a high profile in international production and had major projects on the go in Britain and the States throughout 1957. Connery had no reason to believe they would do anything other than push him hard for a return on their investment. And their investment was considerable. Under the terms, Ian Bannen reckoned, 'Sean was taking in £120 a week. In today's terms you're talking about a contract actor sitting back and taking in more than a thousand a week.' At Brondesbury Villas, Connery's initial reaction to the Fox signing was described as 'silent delight'. His landlady recalled, 'Any other actor would have been delirious at the sudden upsurge in his fortunes, but not Sean. He took the whole thing very calmly. He did not even celebrate.'

The silent delight hinged on sudden wealth: Connery did not shout about it, but his friends were aware of the deep satisfaction triggered by real financial security at last. Counter to that, however, was a troubling awareness, which unfolded quite quickly, that Fox, in spite of the outlay, was not about to fling its neophyte star into any star dressing-rooms. There followed, to Connery's astonishment, a few auditions, a meeting or two with important directors – and then silence. The closest stardom call was dead-end talk of casting opposite Ingrid Bergman in *The Inn of the Sixth Happiness*, a part eventually given to Curt Jurgens. Connery was disgruntled. He wanted to work, to test himself, to prove himself. It was then, he complained, he suffered his 'too' period: 'I hit the audition trail again and all of a sudden I was too big, or too square, whatever. I just couldn't fit the parts they wanted to fill.' Finally, one part was conceded. Director Terence Young, casting *Action of the Tiger* for MGM, offered a speaking role opposite Martine Carol. Fox signed the loan-out papers and Connery travelled to Southern Spain, keen to impress.

Young's plotline was, at least, geographically ambitious. Van Johnson played a philanthropic mercenary persuaded by Carol to help her sneak her political prisoner brother out of Communist Albania; Connery played a sailor encountered en route. The best parts of the movie were the tensions of its chase framework, and the conviction of the actors, Connery included. But, as so many reviewers were to note, the cinema had not quite got to grips with the Cold War and efforts to tell political parables – like *Action of the Tiger* – tended to founder in caricature.

To Terence Young's thinking, he had personally botched the movie: during his triumphs as template-director of James Bond he would look back on it as 'a pretty awful film' – though Connery continued to believe, or hope, he was on to something good. According to Alvin Rakoff, Connery held fast to the view that 'a movie like this, with stars like Van Johnson and Carol, *had* to be good ... But you have to make allowances, because he was quite green, and he had little or no understanding of the pitfalls, or compromised cuts and finance limitations ... of how the industry operates.'

As *Action of the Tiger* neared completion Connery approached Young on set, speculating on the likely success of the movie. 'Sean equated the foreign locations, big stars [Johnson was the highest profile and highest paid performer he had yet worked with] and the recognised director with success,' said Ian Bannen. 'He definitely considered this movie to be crucial.' Young was sympathetic towards the actor's naive expectations: 'Sean came to me and said in that very Scots accent of his, "Sir, am I going to be a success in this?"' Aware already that he had 'irredeemably mucked it up', Young was blunt: 'I told him, "No, but keep on swimming. Just keep at it and I'll make it up to you."'

# 7. ANOTHER PLACE CALLED HOLLYWOOD

The 'glamour' of success that interested Connery in a secondary way became a very palpable reality in the middle of 1957 when Lana Turner walked into his life. The Sweater Queen of MGM had just been fired after eighteen years with the studio and her career was nose-diving. Paramount, never one to miss a bargain, picked her up cheaply and found the ideal vehicle for her, a fire-and-ice love drama that embraced both her sophisticated acting style and her reputation as a man-eater. Turner's love life was, to say the least, chequered. Her five marriages were incident-filled, her romances – with Fernando Lamas, Sinatra, Howard Hughes, gangster Mickey Cohen – legendary. Tyrone Power, everyone knew, was her truest love but Lana's thirst for varied male company was unquenchable. In the spring of 1957, after the break-up of her marriage to 'Tarzan' Lex Barker, former Cohen bodyguard Johnny Stompanato entered her life.

Stompanato, according to writer-director Kenneth Anger, had been in big demand from certain prominent film ladies on account of his 'prominent endowment which had earned him the sobriquet "Oscar"'. Stompanato was a harsh and aggressive lover but Turner, it was widely reported, craved excitement and wasn't averse to being knocked around a bit. She had been thrown downstairs by one husband, struck in public by another, drenched in champagne at Ciro's by another. Stompanato's violence satisfied her needs and when they separated for her trip to Britain to make the Paramount movie *Another Time, Another Place*, her love letters home made explicit her yearnings for his rough handling.

Though Fox was profiting nicely with films like *The King and I* and the seemingly endless Monroe moneyspinners, no one had yet come up with a suitable niche for Connery. 'One of his main problems,' a Fox publicist later recalled, was 'that damned accent. Sometimes it seemed tolerable, but when he speeded up, like all Scotsmen, you couldn't interpret the babble.' Hatton kept the pressure up and finally Connery was auditioned for the Turner movie. Turner had co-star approval and she watched Connery's test, and liked him. In build and looks, many noted, Connery and Stompanato were not a million miles apart. Fox signed the loan-out and Connery had his first major movie part. In an incredible stroke of luck, his Fountainbridge friends thought, he was featuring opposite, and making love to, a Hollywood goddess.

Turner's initial personal response to Connery was favourable, though it was reported he had caused her some embarrassment by picking her up for an early social date on his Lambretta, 'clad in T-shirt and slacks while she was in formal fur and jewels'. It was, the tabloids reported, something of a fiasco, 'but they got into her car, or at least one she'd managed to commandeer, and things went along all right'. According to Alfie Bass, rumours circulated very quickly that romance was in the air. Unquestionably Connery did date Turner and told friends he liked her and that her professional advice was helpful. At that time there was no special woman in his life, but he certainly wasn't at a loose end and, according to Ian Bannen, most of his energies were absorbed by the small mews house in North London he had bought and was beginning to renovate, and by the nightmare atmosphere on the set at MGM's Borehamwood Studio. 'I got to know Sean and women,' said Alfie Bass, 'and he was nobody's fool. If he appreciated Turner's company it still didn't divert him from what that golden opportunity was all about.'

'The script wasn't entirely satisfactory,' Connery later said, 'and they were rewriting it as they were shooting. They started with the end first, and I was dead at the end ... so by the time they led up to me I was just a picture on the piano. The movie wasn't very good. It was beautifully lit by Jack Hildyard, but dreadfully directed by Lewis Allen.'

In fairness, Allen was working with a tricky story – a movie that divided neatly in two, the unbalanced halves seeming to belong to different genres. Connery had fourth billing, playing Mark Trevor, a BBC war correspondent who seduces American newspaper-woman Sara Scott (Turner) in London during the Blitz. Their brief affair is passionate, then Mark is killed in an air crash. Devastated by the news, Sara has a breakdown, then makes a pilgrimage to Mark's hometown in Cornwall, where she discovers his secret family life.

As shooting advanced and Connery's friendship with Turner grew, out of the blue Stompanato arrived in Britain. Turner arranged a house for him in West London but the friction between them was there for all to see. More than once Stompanato arrived unannounced at Borehamwood, frequently insisting on observing the love scenes with Connery, to the obvious annoyance of both Allen and Turner.

'It doesn't take imagination to understand Stompanato's rage,' Alfie Bass observed. 'He'd been in Hollywood and around film people long enough to know when make-believe is make-believe. But he knew Sean and Lana were getting too close for comfort.' Old friends of Connery's broadly hint that the friendship did eventually bloom into an impassioned affair. Big Tam, said one, had Hollywood incarnate in his arms and he did with it what he did most effortlessly – he made love. His intention wasn't the cold calculation of a nepotistic leg-up, rather the idea of proving something to himself; rough-hewn and all, as he may still appear, he was capable of comfortably navigating the star world.

In his book *Hollywood Babylon*, Kenneth Anger suggests that Stompanato 'outranked Connery in giving Turner the kind of treatment she wanted'. He pushed her hard, said Anger, warning her, 'When I say HOP, you'll hop! When I say JUMP, you'll jump! I'll mutilate you, I'll hurt you so you'll have to hide for ever.' Anger describes Stompanato's arrival on the set, brandishing a gun, ordering Connery to 'stay away from Lana'. 'Connery decked him,' said Anger, and the studio, with a little help from Scotland Yard, had Stompanato deported.

Though Connery was fond of Turner – 'a lovely lady', he remembered twenty years later – he was relieved when the film ended and she flew to Mexico for a reunion with her gangster boyfriend. The publicity he had gained while co-starring was advantageous, but he was personally depressed by the movie. His professional associates had told him this was the key film, the one that would get wide distribution in the US and could make his name overnight, but he knew before he saw the release print that everyone had, in the words of Alfie Bass, 'blown it'. 'Sean is not a patient man – least of all when it comes to incompetence or stupidity from so-called senior movie people,' said director Richard Lester – and in the case of *Another Time, Another Place* he was annoyed that rich potential had been crippled. The script, Turner, possibly Connery himself in his newness to star playing, were contributive factors, but Lewis Allen took the brunt of Connery's blame.

At Wavel Mews in north London where Connery had his new home – a spacious three-room flat above a large garage that he later converted into a sitting-room – he defused his disappointments by embarking once again on a strenuous get-fit programme. It served a dual purpose: it helped work off his frustrations and it reminded him of home, of adolescent pleasures from a life that now seemed rosier from afar. Ian Bannen was as close as anyone to Connery during this period and, while he too was into weight-training, he saw himself as 'a total amateur' compared with Connery. 'He had all the equipment, the weights and expanders and bars, and he was deadly earnest about it. I spent quite a bit of time at the house; very ordered and pleasant it was – that was Sean's way, he liked things tidy – but sometimes it felt like a gym!' Despite his sizeable weekly earnings from Fox and his admiration for the movie glamour-world, Connery still favoured a style of living that was not far from frugality. 'He went around on this rattlebag motorbike,' said Bannen, 'which remains in my memory only because he was always falling off. Didn't seem he could go down a bloody road without hitting a tree or something.' He ate simply too, confining his restaurant sprees – which in themselves were never extreme – to occasional weekend binges. Michael Caine, whom Connery had got friendly with during *Requiem*, was himself struggling at this time, with only tenth billing on a movie called *How to Murder a Rich Uncle* to boast about. 'It was hard and worrying obviously – as it was for me,' Caine said. 'But Sean never showed any doubts. He had a star temperament, he knew what he was about.'

During the tough era of *Another Time, Another Place* Connery did not despair because, in his own simple expanation, 'I was eating regularly.' Others from cosier backgrounds might have expressed alarm at the failure, but Connery, outwardly anyway, kept his cool. He had had two big non-starter flops so, to rekindle his sense of purpose, he turned back to television.

His best part came in August 1957 in the ATV Playhouse production of the Pulitzer Prize-winning *Anna Christie*, the dark O'Neill play that had fared so well at the Oxford Playhouse the year before. The role of the prostitute struggling for redemption, haunted by the sea, was given by producer Philip Saville to a movie actress, relatively new to TV but very able, the ash-blonde Diane Cilento. Connery portrayed her lover. A taxing and wordy play, *Anna Christie* required extensive rehearsal to establish the rapport between the main characters. Since Connery' had the upper hand of familiarity with the work, he suggested to Cilento they rehearse after hours, in their free time. Cilento was married to Italian writer Andre Volpe and had a baby daughter Giovanna, but the couple's living arrangements were casual; Ian Bannen contended they were on the point of separation even then. So Connery was invited to Cilento's flat, where work commenced.

Two more different people, socially and academically, it would be hard to find; and yet temperamentally Connery and Diane had a lot in common. Cilento was from the top of the social ladder, a 24-year-old multi-linguist, whose deep love was for literature. Her Italian-born father, Raphael Cilento, had settled in Queensland, Australia, in the 20s and had received a knighthood for his services to medicine. Phyllis, Lady Cilento, was also a physician, but her passion, and the gene she handed on to her daughter, was a devotion to the arts. Diane's early life in Queensland was one of luxury, but at 15 a gypsy spirit akin to Connery's led her to pursue drama studies in New York. Later, transferring to RADA in London, she rejected her parents' support allowance and earned her own way working in a wine shop and, for a spell, at a circus. Her first movie part was in 1952. Four years later she was high on the billing working with director Lewis Gilbert, and by the time she met Connery she was regularly tagged in the popular press as 'the high IQ sex kitten'.

Robert Henderson remembered her as a 'tough, independent little cookie'. Her crusty core, combined with fierce single-mindedness, appealed to Connery and he later admitted that, from the beginning, 'She swept me off my feet.'

Initially Cilento's reaction to Connery was discouraging. Quite apart from the shadows of her marital ties she found him a jagged personality, too free with a lashing critical tongue and, beyond the passionate range of the character he was rehearsing, a shade heartless. 'My first opinion of him,' she said, 'was that he had a terrific chip on his shoulder. He would come to my place and stretch out on the floor. I felt he was trying to see if he could make me angry, so I purposely didn't react. Finally I realised he had no ulterior motives, that he was just being himself.' An actor friend who knew both paints a different picture: 'Maybe he didn't admit it to himself – and he could be stubborn, so that wouldn't surprise me – but Sean was in awe of assured actors and actresses. Lana, Diane – he saw them as some sort of challenge to his ego as women. They were the best any man could get, so he wanted them for that reason. But, as well, there was this need to assert his talents against theirs. In those circumstances Diane considered him – probably rightly – to be overweening.'

But Cilento thawed, and a close friendship arose out of *Anna Christie*. Artistically the play was a success, not exactly in *Requiem's* league but certainly, to Connery's mind, the best thing he had done in half a year. He was pepped up, not only by the quality of the results but also by the nature of this new relationship. Cilento, he told Bannen, was like no one he had yet met in the business. In effect, he was saying she treated him – as she did – with the kind of respect he believed was an artist's due. Raw and all as most considered him, she, the experienced movie actress, had relied heavily on his support during the play. He was flattered, but enthralled too by her obvious competence, her self-possession, her iridescent intelligence. They dined together and enjoyed many social evenings, and she encouraged him to talk about his fears and ambitions within the business. 'Diane was his first real confidante in the industry,' Ian Bannen said. 'Up till then, with the exception of Hatton, he kept his troubles to himself.'

Cilento pushed Connery towards formal dramatic training. He enrolled alongside her in Yat Malgrem's Movement School – an extraordinarily pointless exercise, Robert Henderson believed, because, 'even from *South Pacific* days, Sean's grace in movement was amazingly good'. Yat Malgrem, a Swede, was not an actor but a former dancer in the Kurt Joos Ballet Company. 'He taught the study of action, attitudes and drives,' Connery said. 'It was based on the concepts of time and motion evolved by the Hungarian dancer Rudolf von Laban. I used to go there three times a week, doing theory. We learnt a cohesive terminology that applied to the whole group, so that there was no problem of communication as there so often is with expressions that mean one thing to one person and another to somebody else. It was a remarkable period for me. It proved that with the proper exercises you can reshape yourself physically, completely, so that you become a much better tuned instrument.' As late as 1989 Connery was still waxing eloquent to *GQ* magazine about the value of these movement studies.

Under Cilento's influence he read more widely, extending himself with Stanislavsky, Flaubert and the Shakespeare he hadn't covered during *South Pacific*. For a time, said Bannen, the tone of his conversations changed: he became 'heavyweight' and seemed to disdain the philistinism that attended commercial movie-making. There was nothing pretentious about this posturing. On the contrary, having suffered disillusionment in his first run of movies, he was sensibly reassessing the criteria and focusing his own temperamental suitability – and his intellectual edge – for a better class of production.

Early in 1958 he concentrated his energies on renovating his home and resumed the theatre trail, but the bitterness of cramped opportunity returned. Fox's cash was comforting, but there seemed something indecent about earning ten times what Joe was pulling back home for doing no more than sitting by a phone. 'There were days,' said Bannen, 'when you didn't want to meet him. You asked a simple question, and he spat fire in return.' But the patience paid off. In March a casting crew from Disney Studios in Hollywood, scouting Irish and British actors for *Darby O'Gill and the Little People*, called him to audition and offered a major role in the movie, to commence shooting in Burbank in May.

Connery was ecstatic. Stanislavsky wasn't forgotten, but temporarily he was shelved. Robert Henderson recalled: 'I was appearing at the Coliseum in *Damn Yankees* and I wanted to see the new production of *Madam Butterfly* at Covent Garden. I couldn't get along at night, so I was given permission to attend a dress rehearsal in the afternoon. I'd just arrived when a phone call came through to the box office and it was Sean saying, "Robert, I've got to see you right away. I've been offered the chance to go to Hollywood for a Disney and I want to know if I'm doing the right thing." I told him a Disney movie was good for anyone, and I suggested he come right over to the theatre if he wanted a chat so desperately. About a half-hour later he arrived and I came out to the lobby just as the marvellous first act climax was on. We had our talk and he decided himself happily to take up the Disney offer.' Even in his distraction, Henderson reflected, Connery displayed that 'specialness, the divine curiosity that distinguished him from the bunch'. Overhearing the strains of *Madam Butterfly* as they discussed the Hollywood option, Connery suddenly asked, 'What is that?' 'Well, that's the next step to becoming a good actor,' Henderson replied. 'That's grand opera, Sean. That's fine art. You're earning a little money now. So why don't you buy a ticket and go see some, learn about it?' Connery did, to Henderson's great satisfaction: 'Very shortly he was *telling me* about Maria Callas and the whole opera business. That encapsulated Sean's attitude. He didn't just want to make it big, he wanted *to learn*. He wanted to be big *and* good.'

While Connery was packing and preparing to hand over his house to Ian Bannen for the duration, *Another Time, Another Place* opened, as expected, to dire notices. British papers revelled in the fiercest criticism, tagging it melodramatic rubbish played 'without any style or enthusiasm' (*Monthly Film Bulletin*). By the time it opened in America Turner was in serious trouble. On 4 April Cheryl, her 14-year-old daughter with in-between husband Steve Crane, stabbed and killed Stompanato, having eavesdropped on a violent row in which, according to the police report, the gangster 'threatened to cut up Turner'.

Cheryl was charged and brought to trial, with Turner as a defence witness. As it turned out, a jury which retired for only

twenty minutes pardoned Cheryl by finding her guilty of justifi-
able homicide. But for the months the case held public interest,
Turner was scandalised and pilloried, her scarlet past raked over
and over. The moralists saw to it that none of this new-found
notoriety helped *Another Time, Another Place*. Countrywide, the
movie was either publicly savaged or abandoned by exhibitors.
Connery's first big chance to win Hollywood attention, which he
held little hope for anyway, was buried under an avalanche of dirty
linen. The *New York Times* tore the picture to shreds, declaring it 'a
long way from making any contact with any interests that might
serve to entertain. This one was made in England, evidently as part
of the current Go-Home-Yank plan.' A few reviewers did notice
Connery. One anonymous syndicated New York journalist noted,
'The BBC commentator is played by a newcomer called Sean
Connery who will not, I guess, grow old in the industry.'

For all the flak, Connery arrived in Hollywood in a mood of
optimism – not quite wide-eyed but, said Henderson, 'absolutely
zinging with drive'. Michael O'Herlihy, the Dublin-born technical
adviser and dialogue coach, greeted him and understood immediately his optimism with Disney. 'Walt was a benevolent despot,' said
O'Herlihy. 'He was a fine boss and many people, like myself, were
fortunate in getting our breaks from him. Once he took to you, you
were his for life. He took a fatherly interest in everything his
employees did. In my case, after *Darby* I did a spell with Warner
Brothers, then a long run on *77 Sunset Strip*, where I broke into
directing proper. A few years later, in 1966, Walt gave me my first
chance at a feature, *The Fighting Prince of Donegal*, and I was utterly
amazed that he'd seen *everything* I'd done in the intervening years.
He was a very caring, charming man, and I think he quite liked
Sean. That was the way his system worked. He had to be interested
in you to hire you, and then, when you came to work for him, he
met you and assessed you, and that decided your future. He met
up with Sean in Burbank, and the stamp of approval was granted.'

The rigid professionalism of the working atmosphere at
Burbank Studios appealed to Connery. *Darby O'Gill*, like many
Disney productions, was an ensemble show and the team spirit
shared by Albert Sharpe, Janet Munro, Kieron Moore, Estelle

Winwood and a group of Irish-Americans, comfortably recalled *Requiem* and his best theatre days. The entire movie was shot within the studios, with the verdant Irish backgrounds matted in. Disney visited the set every day and, said O'Herlihy, often chatted with Connery about his Scottish life and theatre experience, even gave him a tip or two. For a first exposure to the Hollywood system, Connery had fallen on his feet. 'I suppose he, like so many, had a vision of a licentious, crazy holiday camp governed by demigods,' said co-star Kieron Moore. 'But in fact Hollywood was – is – a duty-conscious business town. People went to bed early and rose early. There was work to be done and the standards were high. It was a town for professionals. Disney was the most professional, and Sean admired that.'

The problems of a pedantic, conventional director were leavened by Disney's charm, and the jollity of the Irish group sharing lodgings at the modest Disney-funded Burbank motel actor Jimmy O'Dea had christened 'Fatima Mansions', after a slum estate in central Dublin. According to O'Herlihy, the biggest bugbear of the movie was the director. 'What the hell was Walt thinking? Robert Stevenson was the most inappropriate choice for the movie. He was an Englishman with an all-American outlook, here stage-managing a bog-Irish leprechaun yarn. It was worse than that. He was working with actors as well as with special effects, but to judge by the script, you would never know it. Most of [the script] was story-board and he seemed more interested in his pictures than in anything else.' Kieron Moore was equally critical: 'Stevenson didn't talk to actors, that was his trouble. He just couldn't relate.'

But Connery bore up well. From his experience with Lewis Allen he had learned the trick of conserving energies while directors wrestled with themselves. 'Nothing much bothered him,' said Moore, 'not even Stevenson's infamous buckshot theory of shooting, where as many as twenty takes were called for one small scene, and then the best selected from the print-ups.' O'Herlihy remembered the grief: 'In the heat of the Californian sun, that was the real agony. It was extremely exhausting for everyone because it created constant make-up and continuity problems and some of the actors were floored by the time a scene was declared in the can.

As a result of this so-called trademark style, there was a lot of hatred aimed towards Robert Stevenson.'

In the evenings equilibrium was established in 'wakes' at Albert Sharpe's favourite Irish-styled pub, the Skid Lid. 'Sean was brave all day,' said O'Herlihy, 'then he sank a few at night – like myself. I won't say I ever saw him flattened on the floor, but he had a hell of a lot of fun in the Irish way, which was an eye-opener for a lot of the Hollywoodites.'

Wary of the real-life dramas surrounding Lana Turner, Connery made no effort to renew contact with her but the gossip circulated anyway. 'Sean didn't speak about Lana,' O'Herlihy said, 'and as far as I was concerned he was just another contented bachelor in the best town on earth for bachelors to live in.'

With a few white lies and his British motorcycle licence, Connery rented a flashy American Pontiac to explore his environment. He learned to drive around Burbank and took his casual dates for nerve-shredding spins in the Hollywood Hills. Once, on a wall on Sunset Boulevard, his date showed him bullet holes. The marks were the result of an attempt to assassinate Mickey Cohen. Knowing Cohen to be another former lover of Turner's, O'Herlihy said, Connery was shaken. 'But he didn't panic until somebody who knew Turner and knew the rules phoned him up and spelled it all out for him.' In his calm indifference to locale, the caller suggested, Connery was offering himself as a sacrificial target; Mickey Cohen, still faithful to Stompanato's memory, wanted to see blood spilled. Connery got the message. He later spoke openly to an American magazine about his reaction: 'Cohen was out for revenge. Apparently he didn't believe that Cheryl had killed Stompanato. He thought the killing had been engineered in some other way for some other purpose. A pal warned me: "You don't know how these boys work out here. They play for real. Anyone who had any association with Lana Turner and Stompanato in London would be wise to get out of the way." So I did.'

Towards the end of the fifteen weeks on Disney, Connery moved to a backroads hotel in the San Fernando Valley, several miles safe from Hollywood. 'Disney himself must have known about the rumours,' O'Herlihy said. 'I'm not saying Sean had any charges of misconduct to answer, but Walt Disney had an image to protect. Let's put it this way: Disney would no more have employed Lana or Mickey Cohen – right?' Whatever gossip persisted, Connery evidently managed to quash it and to maintain Disney's approval.

Special effects and process work, murderously laborious in the pre-digital age, remained. 'It was a helluva job to superimpose all those "little people" and fake that kind of magic,' said O'Herlihy. 'At one stage we overloaded every circuit and blew every dynamo in Burbank. I often looked at those actors and envied them, feeling sorry for myself because I was so involved in the technical end. But then I'd see Stevenson babbling around them and sequences going on for ever and I'd say, No, I'm better off with electrical wires.'

Still, Connery enjoyed himself. Privately he felt the story was good; his third billing part was the romantic lead; and he even had the chance to sing, serenading Munro with 'Pretty Irish Girl', a tune impressive enough to be released as a single in Britain some months before the July 1959 premiere.

'Sean arrived with his tail between his legs,' said Kieron Moore, 'because *Another Time, Another Place* was something of an embarrassment. But the Disney movie was a real shot at the title – the Disney cachet, the neon lights, full Technicolor, the works. He had a crack at it, and he pulled it off creditably.'

# 8. FALTERING FOX AND THE CLASSIC ANCHOR

As befitting the nature of the project and the conscience of a man who claimed to be a descendant of a General D'signy who fought on the right side at the Battle of the Boyne, Walt Disney premiered *Darby O'Gill* in Dublin in June 1959. The film was Connery's first hit and though he later dodged attempts to analyse his work on it he told the journalist, Freda Bruce Lockhart, 'I wish I'd had a share in the profits.' Probably because of the surfeit of family-orientated and fantasy films on the market at the time Disney, whose praises had been deafeningly sung through the early 50s, was now on the critics' hit list. Despite the huge business the movie did all over the world very few journals reviewed it favourably. For *The Times*, it was 'fatally lacking in lightness and charm' – an evaluation that suggested to a heartier reviewer that *The Times*'s man was facing the wrong way in the theatre. Connery's notices, along with those of the leprechaun king, Jimmy O'Dea, were good, though the dissenting voice of the *New York Times*' Disney-jaded AH Weiler, branded him 'merely tall, dark and handsome'.

But Disney's magic worked, as Robert Henderson anticipated, very quickly for Connery. Before he finished the movie Paramount sought to borrow him again, this time for a *Tarzan* feature. 'He was a rich man then,' Bannen said. 'The tables had turned since I'd met him in the foyer at the Q. Then, in my eyes, I was the one on the up. Now there I was, still treading the boards for sixpence, while Sean was hopping from one colour feature to the next in Hollywood. All of us looking for film work at the time – Mike Caine, Finney, Courtenay, all the young Brits – envied him madly.'

When Connery returned from *Tarzan* Bannen vacated the mews house and Connery poured the money he had earned into a massive renovation, converting the garage into a 35-foot-long sitting room. A resumption of the pre-Hollywood dynamics – Diane, the Yat Malgrem's studies, the workouts – kept his feet on the ground but it was clear that life had changed. Connery still appeared intellectually earnest, yet he was equally keen to ride this new populist wave. *Darby O'Gill* won him his first young fans; *Tarzan's Greatest Adventure*, solid formula fare directed by John Guillermin, consolidated that fan base. 'He had insight and perspective,' said Ian Bannen. 'Even at this early stage – and let's face it, he was still brand new – he could separate good from bad brilliantly. It might or might not have been *Tarzan*, but I remember him brooding over an early script, learning lines, then tossing it into an armchair. "What's it like?" I asked him, suspecting he was less than thrilled. "Lots of lines," he said. "Just lots of lines – but it will work."'

The appetite for serious work was still intact and in October he appeared on the Edinburgh stage with the esteemed Sybil Thorndike in Chekhov's *The Seagull*, casting so far removed from Disney and *Tarzan* that Bannen, himself renowned for versatility, was in awe. Immediately following came the ATV production of Arthur Miller's *The Crucible*, alongside Susannah York. The actor Robert Hardy, who met him at that time, said: 'Sean told me he enjoyed that classics-quality work more than anything. I'm sure it had nothing to do with his relative lack of success in the cinema till then. I think the appeal was in the austerity [of the productions], which forced him to deliver his best.'

In 1960 he returned to the Oxford Playhouse stage where his new champion, the gifted producer Frank Hauser, carved better and better roles for him in *The Bacchae*, then a reprise of *Anna Christie*, starring with Gordon Pitt and Jill Bennett. Director Lewis Gilbert remembered: 'He wasn't always good [on stage], but he always found some *business* within a role, he was *always* interesting – and that is something you cannot say of many actors in any sphere.' Joan Littlewood, architect of iconoclasm in her Theatre Workshop, where she nurtured the likes of Michael Caine and Richard Harris, also saw Connery at Oxford and was impressed by his leap in skills. Then planning for her *Macbeth* tour of Russia and Eastern Europe, she offered him a lead role with her troupe. To her great surprise, he turned her down. 'He spoke to me about Littlewood, giving no reasons for turning her down,' Robert Henderson said. 'It was a wonderful offer, but our way of communication had matured. He wasn't much asking my advice then. He was telling me what he felt was right and what he had decided was to commit himself fully to movies.'

There was also the issue of Cilento's health to deal with. In 1959, shortly after he returned from Hollywood, she was diagnosed with tuberculosis and hospitalised. The illness occurred at a time of great stress in her unravelling relationship with Volpe and the growth of her own theatrical career. According to Bannen she came close to death – a shock, Cilento later admitted, that forced 'a two-year rethink about my life', leading to a deeper relationship with, and eventual marriage to, Connery. During the crisis of illness Connery put his career on hold. As Bannen recalled it, 'He was either by her bedside or by the phone.' In the middle of the panic, the Hollywood producer Samuel Bronston, famous for epics like *The King of Kings*, offered Connery the co-lead, starring opposite Sophia Loren, in the eleventh-century Spanish epic, *El Cid*. Connery instructed Hatton to turn it down. 'It was the worst timing,' Bannen said. 'Most of us would have slaughtered our mothers for something as big as that. But Diane was slowly getting well again and Sean wanted to be with her. She had a chance to do a Pirandello play – *Naked* – for Minos Volanakis at Oxford. Sean could do it with her, and that's what he chose to do. It was Diane or *El Cid*, and he chose Diane.'

Across Britain in the winter of 1959–60, as Connery worked the boards in Oxford, both *Darby O'Gill* and *Tarzan's Greatest Adventure* were playing in provincial towns and big cities. For the first time he was experiencing wide recognition in the streets, but there were wars yet to be fought to secure his success. After the rejection of *El Cid*, Fox reportedly was less than happy and was considering terminating his contract. *Picturegoer* magazine speculated that the end was in sight with Fox, and friends were quoted defensively insisting that Connery's patience had run out, that Fox had done little to push him. This, in large measure, was true. Connery had pulled off Hollywood and was consistently proving his talents in a vast range of disparate parts in theatre and television, yet Fox only sporadically tossed him scripts and mumbled about longshot projects. The power of momentum, however, kept him moving. In 1960 he was loaned out again, this time to Anglo-Amalgamated, but he conceded this time with some enthusiasm because the script on offer, by Leigh Vance, was among the best he had read. Brian Doyle, publicist for the new film, which was called *The Frightened City*, remembers Connery's distinct satisfaction with the ambitions of the film. 'Sean let it be known that he was pleased with the movie – and he did that by being extraordinarily professional and good-natured. We had a wonderful cast, Herbert Lom, John Gregson, Kenneth Griffith, but Sean went a long way towards creating the perfect work ensemble atmosphere. On most movies, you get good chemistry and bad chemistry. On *The Frightened City* working relationships were all good, and a lot of it was down to Sean's affability and joke-telling. People liked being round him. When the working day began, you were glad to be there. And when it ended, you were in no rush to go home. That's about the best compliment you can pay to an actor. Our goal was something better than the standard English thriller. Sean went along with that as his starting reference and his finishing point. At the end of the day, it might have been his presence more than anything that made that movie notable.'

*The Frightened City*, directed by John Lemont, was the peak of Connery's pre-Bond cinema effort though, strangely, it failed to gain anything like the recognition that was its due. Connery was 30 when it was made, amply experienced and splendidly aggrieved by Fox's mishandling: the resentment of Fox's lassitude brought a tight-lipped ferocity to his part as a protection enforcer that made the story strikingly credible once he sidled on to screen. His character, Doyle observed, was a complex one, 'a tragic figure psychologically worthy of Shakespeare', couched in a plot that had the intelligence of fine allegory. Everything Connery had filched, stumbled upon and been taught in six years of acting was piled in ideally concentrated measure into *The Frightened City*. The much-commented-upon 'rawness' that was the inevitable legacy of Fountainbridge, the dance-movement studies (particularly noticeable in his elegant hand gestures), his laconic speech deliveries learnt from long-time film performers like Diane, all blended to create a memorable character who, as Henderson prescribed, looked one thing – indomitably tough; but was another – humane.

On the circuits *The Frightened City* did very average business and though the popular dailies called it 'the toughest crime exposé ever made', just such a clichéd commendation assured box-office stagnation. Dosed to drunkenness with the annals of Scotland Yard at work in the East End, moviegoers were refreshing themselves with the sour medicine of working-class life-as-it-is in kitchen-sink dramas like *Saturday Night and Sunday Morning* and *A Taste of Honey*. The genre stamp, in effect, killed *The Frightened City*.

After the failure, Connery's relations with Fox were suddenly strained beyond endurance. Film historian David Shipman states that 'the facts about the termination of the long-term contract are muddy'; but what is clear is the unfortunate timing of the collapse of the partnership. In 1961, as kinship and trust disintegrated, Connery finally won an undisputed co-lead in Cyril Frankel's *On the Fiddle* (entitled *Operation Snafu* in the US), released just a month after *The Frightened City*. Here was the acid test – a lump-ish British comedy, based on a thin story by RF Delderfield, in which Connery played a gormless gag feeder to Alfred Lynch's smart-arse. A lesser actor would have sunk or, worse, been sub-sumed in the mire of music-hall sidemanship. But Connery soared like an eagle, elevating pap to promise and imbuing the whole with warmth. The input of gifted technical contributors like the editor Peter Hunt (who would, in years to come, help mould the James Bond franchise) further enhanced the movie. The movie flopped financially, but the benevolent elements did enough to win wide industry attention.

Among the people who sat up and paid attention was Dennis Selinger, an influential agent on the rise, who had reason to remember Connery unfavourably. In the *South Pacific* days, Selinger's girlfriend was Carol Sopel – until Connery won her affections. Seeing *On the Fiddle*, said Selinger, all was forgiven: 'It was really quite a coup, I felt, because the movie itself was unspec-tacular, but Sean was quite fun, against all the odds. Now, superfi-cially, that might not seem like much of a compliment, but "quite fun" can make the difference between a bad-performing film and a disaster. It suddenly struck me that he had that clichéd commod-ity, "star quality". Everyone in this business is on the lookout for it, because somewhere, sometime, it will be their only fallback, the thing that saves their necks.' Guy Hamilton, later to direct Bond, observed the flaws in *On the Fiddle* but, like Selinger, admired the actor's survival skill: 'His power as an actor was clearly built on strength, not on the kind of dumbness [in *On the Fiddle*]. You can shade down [Connnery's] strength or build it up, but it struck me then that you are wasting a great gift like Sean's by casting him as the also-ran. Simply, he was a born star. He was a star before Twentieth Century Fox even knew what they had on their hands. It was his loss *and* their loss that they didn't recognise what they had.'

In some ways Connery benefited from the widely contradictory notices for *On the Fiddle*. After its release in October of 1961 magazines were filled with debates about his future. 'It is a real mystery to me why no film company has built Sean into a great international star,' wrote Freda Bruce Lockhart in *Woman*. '[In a recent TV play] Sean reminded me of Clark Gable. He has the same rare mixture of handsome virility, sweetness and warmth. His attractive speech has the vigour which many find lacking in the pinched vowels of London-trained actors. Above all, Sean has size. I don't just mean height. I mean, too, the breadth and all-embracing effect of his personality.' Connery agreed: 'They'll offer me anything on TV, as opposed to stage or films.'

Lockhart concluded her feature with word of his newest TV venture. BBC producer Rudolph Cartier had chosen him to play Vronsky opposite Claire Bloom in *Anna Karenina*, a prestige Tolstoy adaptation scheduled for November. Before that there would be some more theatre work, in a new West End version of Jean Anouilh's *Judith*, at Her Majesty's. 'I hope Cartier's production brings him luck,' Lockhart enthused, 'for it is my conviction that he is one of the biggest hopes among promising present-day actors.'

But Fox remained indifferent. According to Brian Doyle, Connery was 'too problematic and demanding' for their liking. The pubs and billiard halls of Shaftesbury Avenue were choked nightly with aspirant new talents who would be more compliant and less tetchily ambitious. Sean Connery had proved himself, but who wanted a Scottish Clark Gable in kitchen-sink drama? And as for

Hollywood? Well, Disney hadn't asked Connery back and Mickey Cohen was still alive. Sean Connery had been on Fox's books a long time and not done much. He might never make Hollywood again.

Michael Hayes, who had directed Connery in a version of Shakespeare's *Henry IV* the previous spring was disdainful of the notion of a major studio dropping him. 'It was ludicrous to consider dropping Sean. When I directed him, eighteen months before James Bond, it was clear he was a star. You know that by performance skills, but you also learn to detect some *je ne sais quoi* – a confidence in behaviour, perhaps. He wasn't loud or smug but compared to the other fine people we used on *Age of Kings* – Esmond Knight, Julian Glover, Patrick Garland – he was gold-plated. With the exception of Esmond, who had vast experience, we were all new young bucks trying to make our way. But Sean was different. He had a car – in fact, he had several over the short period I was friends with him. I remember once he bought a little Fiat, around the time of *Henry IV*. I asked him, just in passing, what had become of his old model, which had been very respectable. "The ashtrays were full," he replied. Sounds like a cliché "star-defining story", but it's true. And the funny thing was, there was next to no arrogance in him. There was just a very centred, total confidence about his understanding of his medium, and his ability to deliver. Backed up by a sound intellect, those qualities are rare in good actors. Fox was insane to ignore him in the way they did.'

Hayes's live broadcast Shakespeare production – one of fifteen mounted under the banner title *An Age of Kings* – was a significant landmark for Connery, who played Hotspur alongside Robert Hardy's Prince Hal. Reviews then were unanimously good and *The Times* called the series 'an astonishing achievement'. But most important, in Connery's eyes, was the respect afforded by his experienced co-workers like Hardy, who judged Connery 'exceptional' tackling Shakespeare: 'To anyone who'd watched him on television or in those early films, it was evident in the Shakespeare that he had achieved a new intellectual control. He had grown. It sounds bizarre to say it, but the truth is, many actors don't grow. They sail into the profession on their confidence and strength of character and give the same performance after ten years as they did on day one'. Hardy's roots were in Shakespeare, stretching back to the Histories in Stratford in 1951, and he had understudied Richard Burton's Prince Hal. For him, in terms of a universal acting standard, Shakespearean drama separates the men from the boys; in this regard, to his thinking, Connery had mastered technique. 'Hotspur's speech is not versified in the way others' are, so Sean had an advantage there, but he carried it off with such dash. His relaxation – that's what I remember; that's the gift he brought to us from films. That, and a technical proficiency which allowed him to bawl.'

Among those round to comfort and encourage Connery during this time of conflicting signals was Julie Hamilton. Ian Bannen recollected meeting her at a Wavel Mews party after *Henry IV*. 'Diane was in his life, for sure, but there was no lady in residence, to my recall. Julie hung on in there – hardly his exclusive paramour – but there was still some up-and-downing going on, that's for sure. I know their close relationship had ended, but there were reverberations going on right into the early 60s, perhaps even later.'

Diane Cilento had, however, undeniably replaced her in Connery's affections. Recovered from her illness, with her marriage firmly behind her, Cilento was work-active again and devoting all her extra-curricular time to Connery. 'Of course I knew about Diane,' said Michael Hayes, 'but I didn't know her. Sean brought only one face to the studios: that of the consummate pro. One was left in no doubt about his priorities.'

*Anna Karenina*, the major production that Lockhart had expressed such high hopes for, further established Connery's confidence and reputation at the BBC. Recorded over three weekend nights in June 1961, this famous Marcelle Maurette play, adapted by Donald Bull, tested Connery every bit as much as the Shakespeare, pitching him against Claire Bloom, recently triumphant in *Look Back in Anger*. Ian Bannen said that Connery was 'anxious at the prospect of the play' and a BBC producer, serving then as a floor technician, remembered Connery's 'obvious nerves, facing [director] Cartier and extremely experienced people like Bloom and Jack Watling ... There were many retakes, but you got the feeling of general competence and a desire to make it perfect from him.'

While awaiting transmission of *Anna Karenina* on 3 November Connery returned to the stage for a short run in the West End biblical play *Judith*. 'He was the one who, in the Bible, slays Judith,' said Robert Henderson. 'He hadn't got much to say, but here again was an instance of his ability to command an audience by his appearance. His body was in peak condition, and he riveted everyone because he was almost naked, wearing only a loincloth. Never before, in my view, had the legitimate stage seen such remarkably graceful masculine physical beauty. It didn't help the production, but it was mildly sensational, it was remarked upon.'

*Judith* was panned by critics and its run cut short, but Connery's opportunity to flex his pecs in high drama proved important. Among the audience at Her Majesty's was his old ally Terence Young, already in discussion with two struggling producers about a strategy to launch Ian Fleming's James Bond in movies. The names currently mooted were Rex Harrison, David Niven and Cary Grant, none of whom particularly interested Young. Watching Connery, and remembering his promise after the failure of *Action of the Tiger*, Young later said he made a mental note to review his career to date, and perhaps audition him.

In the middle of this television and theatre run, Fox at last mustered a prestige project for Connery: *The Longest Day*. Based on Cornelius Ryan's epic account of Operation Overlord, the Allied invasion of Europe in June 1944, four directors vied to leave their imprint on this mega-documentary that featured no less than forty-three headline stars. Ken Annakin directed the Juno Beach British sequences in which Connery played Private Flanagan, 'the seasoned veteran,' said the handouts, 'whose Irish temperament saw him through the landings' – a fleeting role necessitating only a couple of days' location work for the actor.

On its release in 1962, both the movie and Connery's short performance won plaudits, but the strain of mounting this gargantuan production – two years in the making, nine months and seventeen days in principal photography, thirty-one locations, one hundred main actors – showed in every foot of every reel. Bosley Crowther of the *New York Times* summed up its key failing: 'No character stands out particularly and no event stands out as more significant or heroic than anything else.'

To friends like Bannen, Connery was dismissive of the film even as he made it. It belonged, he felt, to John Wayne and Robert Mitchum, the Hollywood heavyweights. He did his best, but there really wasn't much meat on the role. 'It was no compliment to his talent,' said Bannen. 'And no gesture of appeasement from Fox. He knew the Fox contract was as good as dead, and he wanted it that way.'

All the hopes pinned on *Anna Karenina*, on the other hand, were fulfilled. Audience response was excellent and most of the dailies greeted it warmly. The *Listener* thought it deserved, if not prizes, then at least 'a distant salute'. *The Times* was unequivocal in its estimation of a hands-down success. While the players were 'variable', the 'most successful was Mr Sean Connery, a headlong, passionate Vronsky'.

On Terence Young's advice, Harry Saltzman and Albert R Broccoli, the producers discussing James Bond with him, watched *Anna Karenina*'s transmission. Both were intrigued, Young later said, by 'the old-trouper tricks this new boy employed to knock Claire Bloom right off the screen'. Connery suddenly joined Rex Harrison and Niven at the top of their casting poll.

# 9. ENTER THE WALKING APHRODISIAC

The first attempts to put James Bond into movies failed. Under the intended sponsorship of millionaire businessman Ivar Bryce and his one-cylinder Xanadu production company (their sole venture had been Kevin McClory's financial failure *The Boy and the Bridge*), Ian Fleming, McClory and top British screenwriter Jack Whittingham developed a plot – which later became *Thunderball*, book and film – but abandoned it when Bryce and Fleming got cold feet. It had been Fleming's hope that established producer-directors like Anthony Asquith or Alfred Hitchcock would take up the rights of the *Thunderball* treatment, but when Hitchcock flatly rejected it Fleming withdrew. Jack Whittingham's fee for the first script was £5,000 and the project was shelved indefinitely. Fleming wrote to Bryce: 'Show biz is a ghastly biz and the last thing I want is for you to lose your pinstripe trousers in its grisly maw ... nor, of course, do I want the first James Bond film to be botched.' A literary perfectionist with a penchant for collecting rare classics but reading trash, Fleming had more in common with Sean Connery, the man who was to breathe life into his dream-hero, than many recognised. Compared with Connery's upbring-ing, Fleming's childhood was crème de la crème – country seats, town houses, Eton, Sandhurst – but both men shared an ambition which, to some, was angry in its intensity. Both enjoyed risk-taking, both had nomadic spirits, both acquired sophisticated tastes. 'Don't be misled by Sean's lorry-driver press,' the actress Honor Blackman said, evaluating Connery's aptness for the role. 'He may have had humble beginnings but the man I got to know [on *Goldfinger*] simply gushed high-living refinement.'

Within a few months of Fleming's postponement of screen Bond, the Canadian producer Harry Saltzman, acting on the advice of his and Fleming's lawyer, Brian Lewis, optioned the existing Bond novels. Saltzman's option covered seven books in print. One Bond title, *Casino Royale*, was unavailable, having been sold to

Gregory Ratoff for $6,000 in 1955. Another title, *Moonraker*, had been purchased by Rank, but Fleming's movie agents, MCA, retrieved the rights in 1960. Saltzman's track record was superb. He had been the driving force behind Woodfall, the production company partnership with John Osborne and director Tony Richardson responsible for the success of Britain's contribution to new wave cine-realism in *Saturday Night and Sunday Morning* and *The Entertainer*. He was also, Honor Blackman recalled, 'a hard man, a dedicated deal-maker'.

With Bond, however, his deal-making prowess initially faltered. Having paid Fleming $55,000 for a six-month option, 28 days before the time expired he was all at sea, no nearer a financing deal than he had been at the start. At the eleventh hour his writer friend Wolf Mankowitz introduced him to Broccoli, a 50-year-old New Yorker who was himself a longtime Bond admirer, and whose contacts in financing circles were impressive. Broccoli's experience was every bit as colourful as Saltzman's, though he was frustrated by the relative lack of success of his major productions. A good scholar and avid reader, he had a degree in agriculture and a spell as assistant to Howard Hawks behind him when, after the war, he transferred operations from Hollywood to London and started a series of adventure films in partnership with Irving Allen, earning the distinction of producing the first true Anglo-American features. Saltzman's proposal for a partnership arrangement to launch Bond was based on his belief that, after kitchen-sink, people wanted 'something different, strong plots with excitement, fast cars, bizarre situations, drink and women' – an antidote to a post-war, post-50s malaise. Broccoli needed no persuasion. In 1959 he himself had tentatively tried to acquire the Bond rights: and he still wanted in. A fifty-fifty deal was struck, though Saltzman would have preferred terms more favourable to himself. All that then remained was choosing the book to film, drafting the screenplay and casting the essentials – Bond and his bedmate.

Richard Maibaum, who had written Broccoli's *The Red Beret*, went to work, initially on *Thunderball*, while Broccoli commenced talks with the major studios throughout April 1961. Columbia Pictures considered the Bond proposal, but rejected it as being unoriginal. In the middle of this money chase, the producers were obliged to switch to pitching *Dr. No*, having been cautioned that Kevin McClory's High Court action against Fleming's rights in *Thunderball* could muddy the waters.

Peddling *Dr. No* then, on 20 June 1961 in a short boardroom meeting at United Artists' offices in New York, a deal was finally agreed. David Picker, later UA's London chief, was the Bond fan in the studio camp who swayed the company president Arthur Krim. Broccoli and Saltzman asked for a million dollars to make *Dr. No*; they were given, and accepted, $800,000.

Back in London, in high excitement, the producers reconsidered their crew and cast objectives. Their first-choice directors Guy Green and Bryan Forbes had refused the project, as had Guy Hamilton. But both liked Terence Young, who came on high recommendation from Broccoli, whose *The Red Beret* he had directed to budget eight years before. United Artists agreed to accept Young provided *Dr. No's* budget was guaranteed with a completion bond funded by the producers.

Casting for *Dr. No* was a fits-and-starts operation. When Cary Grant refused the project (because he didn't want a multi-movie contract) and both Rex Harrison and David Niven passed, Patrick McGoohan, Roger Moore and Richard Johnson came up for consideration. Fleming, who was quite happy with the professionalism and generosity of Broccoli and Saltzman, still promoted the idea of an established name lead. He mentioned Michael Redgrave and Trevor Howard but, after the fiasco of *Thunderball*, was content to stay away from 'all this side of the business and all those lunches and dinners at the Mirabelle and the Ambassadeurs which seem to be the offices for all this huckstering'. By the time the search for Bond was at full cry, according to Connery, Fleming was keen on the idea of an unknown, someone who would not overshadow James Bond.

Saltzman and Broccoli had first met Connery at a party, and liked his looks. Broccoli enjoyed his accent in particular and had further food for thought when, in Hollywood, he viewed *Darby O'Gill and the Little People* and observed his wife's enthusiastic response: like Jacqueline Hill on *Requiem*, Dana Broccoli found

Connery's macho presence hugely attractive. At the same time, in London, film editor Peter Hunt was recommending *On the Fiddle* to Harry Saltzman.

According to Broccoli, Terence Young was not consulted in the final casting of Bond. It was Saltzman who phoned Richard Hatton, requesting a meeting with the actor. Connery approached the producers' South Audley Street office, he later said, 'casually, expecting nothing at all'. He drove his green Fiat 127, wore a brown shirt, brown suede shoes and no tie – garb befitting the Buxton on a Friday night, Ian Bannen observed. In their first-floor office suite Broccoli and Saltzman greeted him coolly and Saltzman, ever the inquisitor, fired the opening questions. Connery answered pat, in the thick burr Broccoli found fascinating. Yes, he had read a Fleming novel – *Live and Let Die*, some years back. Yes, he thought the idea of a Bond movie series exciting. No, he didn't regard himself exclusively as a classics actor, or a stage performer or whatever; he had yet to find his niche. The polite conversational tone altered only when Broccoli questioned Connery's dress style. Feeling he was being patronised, Connery told the producers, 'Look, you either take me as I am or not at all.' Saltzman had reservations – according to Lewis Gilbert 'Harry always liked his subordinates to know their place' – but Broccoli found Connery's authority a plus. 'He pounded the desk and told us what he wanted,' Broccoli said. 'We agreed, he walked out of the office and we watched him bounce across the street like he was Superman. We knew we had got our James Bond.'

Others had yet to be persuaded. Though Saltzman and Broccoli had emphatically decided their choice, they knew they still had to satisfy UA. With audition footage in mind – though Connery was unaware of this – test scenes were filmed at Pinewood and sent to Krim in New York. The response, now legendary in the annals of show biz gaffes, was a cable from UA with the unadorned moan SEE IF YOU CAN DO BETTER.

Broccoli and Saltzman ignored the cable. In November they had signed Connery for a multi-picture deal that would engage him till 1967, allowing one non-Bond picture a year. His up-front fee for

*Dr. No* was meagre – just £5,000 – but this was a relative fortune to Robert Hardy, Ian Bannen and his theatre friends.

Connery had not undertaken *Dr. No* and the long-term deal lightly. When the offer was made he took time to consider it, consulting Hatton and Cilento. After Disney, he had been offered long-term Hollywood television contracts, for *Maverick* and *Wyatt Earp*. Those proposed deals were financially modest, but either would have guaranteed him the permanent access to Hollywood he sought. He'd turned them down, firstly because he thought he would be short-selling himself to American television and secondly, he told Bannen, because he wanted to be near Diane. Now, with Bond, Diane took a hand, giving forceful advice. Fleming's books were immensely popular, with yearly sales nearing the million mark. It was significant too that they attracted praise from all sections of the community, and had been likened to Buchan, Sapper – the best of twentieth-century popular fiction. The poet William Plomer had been instrumental in securing Jonathan Cape as Bond's publisher and Raymond Chandler and Somerset Maugham were devotees ...

Cilento urged him to take Bond. 'If it were not for me,' she told an American magazine in 1964, 'Sean might never have become James Bond.'

Reflecting on his casting interview with Saltzman and Broccoli, Connery later admitted he had 'put on a bit of an act'. Intuition carried the game. He hadn't, he claimed, scientifically worked out the pros and cons, but, even before he consulted with Diane, he'd sensed the importance of James Bond just as, seven years before, he sensed *South Pacific* was right for him.

With shooting scheduled for January 1962, just weeks after *Judith*, Terence Young and his assistant Johanna Harwood entered a preproduction dash that gave every indication of disaster looming. There were five different scripts, all scrappy, and Broccoli, who had been largely absorbed with casting, was at war with Saltzman, in charge of the writing. Young recalls that, in the end, Broccoli's nerve went. Flinging the mountain of wildly derivative scripts aside he shouted to Saltzman: 'Look, we've paid all this fucking money for this James Bond book and we're not using a word of it.

Now, Terence is a writer, he's the quickest writer I know. He's got ten days to put it back. He can take all the scripts we have … and whatever he writes we're going to be stuck with and, Harry, if it's bad it's your fault.'

Young and Harwood took a room at the Dorchester Hotel and began rewriting, going day and night. Meanwhile, Saltzman had equal reason to lose patience with Broccoli. 'Cubby was the tit 'n' bum man,' Guy Hamilton said. 'He had fixed ideas about the type of girl he wanted in Bond's bed. And one thing he wanted was good tits.' Julie Christie, among a score of others, failed the tit test. Broccoli had seen her on television and summoned her. No one doubted her talent, least of all the discerning Cubby, but, close up, her breasts just didn't reckon. Finally, in a stack of newcomer photographs, Broccoli came across Swiss-born Ursula Andress. In the cheesecake publicity shot she was wearing a wet T-shirt that moulded her hard-nippled breasts. Glancing over her curriculum vitae, Broccoli was encouraged: she was the right age (25) and height (5′ 9″), had made films in Rome – which stood for little in talent terms – but had been briefly on contract to Paramount. Without meeting her, Broccoli wired a Hollywood friend for testimonials and received exactly the affirmative response he wanted. Interviewed later, Saltzman unwittingly mocked the casting process that had cost so much concern and cash: 'We chose Ursula because she was beautiful and because she was cheap. We didn't have the money to spend on anyone else.' Andress received £300 per week for the scheduled six weeks. (The film overran: in the late 80s she claimed she had still not been paid her dues for the extra work.)

Among Connery's friends at the West End actors' clubs word was out that the role of Fleming's hero superspy was his. 'I was amazed,' Michael Caine stated frankly. 'I was sure they'd give it to Rex [Harrison], because he was the living image of upper-crust good-living.' Robert Hardy thought it 'oddball casting, but a tremendous compliment to Sean. Everyone expected something contrived and Englishy.' Around the Buxton in particular surprise – and sour grapes – were hugely evident. The *Saturday Evening Post* quoted an anonymous movie director who knew Connery saying,

'He was on the garbage heap of acting until Bond.' Connery himself experienced what might best be termed polar affections once news circulated. 'Actually it was a bit of a joke around town,' he conceded. 'There were those in the Buxton club who thought Bond a backward step, B movie stuff, and those who imagined Sean Connery clad in anything other than Levis and beatniky suede shoes a travesty.'

Young hurried Connery into a crash course in social graces that made the cynics snigger. 'Terence *was* James Bond,' said Zena Marshall, who starred as the murderous sex tigress Miss Taro in the film. 'When he cast me, all he said, the way he behaved, told me he was projecting himself as Bond. He had incredible style and complementary gentleness and strength.' For sure, Young's background was closer to Fleming's superspy than Connery's. The son of Shanghai's Commissioner of Police, he was educated at Harrow and Cambridge and served in the war with the Guards Armoured Division. His tastes were for the good things of life. 'Terence loved to be surrounded by pretty furnishings, champagne, attractive people,' said Molly Peters, whom he cast in *Thunderball* three years later. Young had also worked, for a short time, as an assistant to Hitchcock, as, significantly, did screenwriter Richard Maibaum. (Though Young and Harwood rewrote much of *Dr. No* with Berkely Mather, Richard Maibaum received the main screen credit. He went on to write most of the Bond films.) Elements of Hitchcock infested all the early Bond movies, by way of tribute rather than accident. 'I sent Sean to my shirt maker,' said Young. 'I sent him to my tailor. I used to make him go out in these clothes, because Sean's idea of a good evening out would be to go off in a lumber jacket.'

Feeling much out of his depth by the workings of this curious film world, this same domain that had defeated him two years before, Fleming's reaction to progress was confused. At first he wasn't happy with Connery, though he kept up a brave face when he cabled Bryce about Saltzman's conviction in the 'absolute corker, a 30-year-old Shakespearian actor, ex-navy boxing champion, etc, etc.' With Young, whom he knew through mutual acquaintanceship with Noël Coward, he was more cruelly honest.

At a UA London function he squared up to the realities of an untested director guiding a half-known ex-labourer star into James Bond's elegant world. 'So they've decided on you to fuck up my work,' he charged Young. Young was unperturbed. 'Let me put it this way, Ian. I don't think anything you've written is immortal as yet, whereas the last picture I made won a Grand Prix at Venice. Now let's start even.'

*Dr. No* 'started even' with location shooting in Jamaica on Tuesday 16 January 1962, and Andress joined the team ten days later to film her Crab Key sequences on the north shore. Her husband John Derek (later self-styled 'creator' of third-wife star Bo) accompanied her. She fitted in well, though Young found her strangely built: 'She had the shoulders, stomach and legs of a boy, but with this great face and breasts. Shooting her to advantage was not as easy as it might have been, though by Connery's side her bulky proportions looked about right.' Connery liked the Dereks, and laughed a lot with Ursula. She had a waspish, rebellious side to her that brightened the mood of relentless time-is-running-short tension and though her squeaky accent caused trouble from the start, her discipline impressed him. Later he called her his favourite Bond co-star – and indeed she proved an invaluable asset to the perennial rethreading of the Bond mythology: for a million Bond fans Andress, white-bikinied with hip knife on a Caribbean beach, became the symbol of luxurious, sexy, inviting adventure.

Pleased with Connery's work in Jamaica, Young brought the team back to Stage D at Pinewood in the middle of February, where Ken Adam, a long-time associate of Broccoli's, had been labouring on some imaginative set designs with a budget of only £4,000. Here the interiors would be shot, and the famous introductory scene, where a suntanned Connery announces himself as James Bond to Eunice Gayson's Sylvia Trench across a gaming table, went in the can on the second day. A few days later the seduction of busty, dangerous Miss Taro was filmed. Zena Marshall recalled: 'I spent the entire day in bed with Sean, so you could say it was fun – but it was hard work too. Ian Fleming came on the set and had several words with me. He seemed to think my role important, this enemy agent making love with

Bond, each tacitly knowing the other is out to kill them. There were a few retakes, because Terence wanted us to relax into the mood of love-making, and we did some publicity shots twice for the different markets. In Ireland, for example, they couldn't see my tits, so more covered-up shots were taken. It was all like a military exercise, very thorough and well thought out. Sean was a kind of contrast in the sophistication of everything. He was very rough and raw, but his charm was exceptional.'

Day by day Young preached etiquette. Once he checked Connery for eating with his mouth open (during dinner with Doctor No), on another occasion Connery's accent thickened to a burr in the excitement of a scene. One or two errors of class slipped through: Bondphiles blast the sartorial blunder of Connery at Strangway's house, buttoning down the last of his suit coat buttons, spoiling the cut of a finely figured outfit, a transgression Hardy Amies – or Young himself – would never have been guilty of.

The film story of *Dr. No*, Fleming was relieved to see, differed only in small detail from his novel. Young considered the yarn ordinary, Connery thought it good. John Russell Taylor, the film historian, isolated the formula shrewdly: Bond spends one half of the movie getting into the villain's clutches – and laying the girls on the way – and one half fighting his way free. In *Dr. No* the journey into trouble begins when a British agent in Jamaica is murdered while investigating the 'toppling' of American rockets from nearby Cape Canaveral. MI6 agent Bond is ordered into the inquiry and follows the trail to the Caribbean Island of Crab Key, where he thwarts Doctor No's attempt to hijack the American space programme. Along the way his accomplice through incarceration, torture and escape is the naive island girl, Honey, played by Andress.

The completion of the film in March marked an occasion for muted celebration. Small problems had still to be addressed: Andress, it was decided, would have to be dubbed throughout. Monty Norman's music score was deemed non-cinematic and a thematic reworking by John Barry was commissioned. Connery was good, but . . .

UA officials flew from New York to watch the first cut in a private Mayfair cinema in Connery's absence. Saltzman liked the picture well enough, 'but then I liked *Look Back in Anger*, and that died the death of a dog'. The distribution executives watched ninety minutes of Connery then, in unison, grimaced. He was 'all right', average detective hunk, self-conscious in the close-ups. One top-ranking executive reportedly said, 'I can't show a picture with a limey truck driver playing the lead.' Someone else took consolation from the fact that Broccoli and Saltzman had only overspent by $110,000.

Thus decreed, UA would splash nothing on promoting *Dr. No* in America. One executive allegedly concluded that it would earn a few bucks, but held out little hope for a follow-up.

Connery, on the other hand, remained optimistic. He told Michael Caine the film 'felt bloody good' and, no matter what UA thought, he was prepared to 'sit tight and wait'. The actress Sue Lloyd had become close to Connery, having met him at the Buxton, and shared a few loving evenings with him at her flat – 'never his: I never saw the inside of his place, and only had the vaguest notion he lived somewhere in the NW region.' She too found him 'quietly optimistic'. A few weeks later she met Andress at Shepperton Studios where both were vying for an upcoming part in a small movie. 'Ursula had no idea what the repercussions of *Dr. No* would be. We were chatting and she said, "I've just been in Jamaica enjoying the sun, doing this thriller with Sean" – and it might have been any thriller, with any actor. It meant nothing to her beyond another job. She held no hopes for it.'

But James Bond remained at least a literary institution and Connery was intent on doing his share of pre-promotion. Long before the movie opened he was on the media mill, stressing his pedigree (the whistle-stop *Macbeth* he had done for Canadian TV the previous autumn, figured large), and promulgating an entire philosophy for James Bond. He told the *Daily Express*: 'I see Bond as a complete sensualist – his senses are highly tuned and he's awake to everything. He likes his wine, his food and his women. He's quite amoral. I particularly like him because he thrives on conflict – a quality lacking in present-day society.' With wary respect for the producers he added, 'I've been asked if I'm worried about getting tagged as Bond. Well, Bond is a "bracket" for me. It's a one-million-dollar production and the people who set up and cast the film have a healthy respect for a pound and dollar tag.'

While, professionally, Connery sat tight during the summer of 1962, in his private life great changes were underway. The desultory love affairs that filled the vacuum of an actor's 'resting' days – brief flings with model Joyce Webster, Sue Lloyd, Shelley Winters and others – were suddenly overtaken by a new and vigorous relationship with Cilento. 'As far as I was concerned,' Ian Bannen said, 'Andre Volpe no longer existed.' Diane's marriage had been over for quite a time, but now divorce proceedings were going and she and Sean had settled down together. They spent several nights a week with each other and we waited for the knot to be tied. We waited for a move from Sean, anyway. Diane was another kettle of fish. You see, under all the baloney of Scottish chauvinism, Sean was a one-woman man. Diane, on the other hand, had a career to be catching up with.'

At home in Fountainbridge, Effie and Joe were told of Sean's new love in a phone call. Later, briefly, Sean brought Diane home and the family reunion was serene. Effie, Joe and Neil read between the lines and guessed the seriousness of the affair. Effie smiled when, in the autumn, she read a national newspaper interview where Sean extolled the bachelor life: 'No one to tell you what to do. I can leave my socks on the floor, play poker all night, come and go as I please. I couldn't ask any woman to put up with that.' By the time the interview was published Diane Cilento was several months pregnant, expecting Connery's child, and he was about to apply himself to the difficult task of persuading her to marry him.

As Connery contemplated marriage, *Dr. No* opened in Britain, to be followed weeks later by an inglorious opening in the American Midwest where, if destined, it could die a quiet death. But by the time of the American opening the movie was a massive European success. It premiered at the London Pavilion on 6 October 1962, with Paul Getty in attendance, and production costs were covered within weeks. Unstinting reviews sang paeans of hope for a British cinema with American production values – at last! – and reversed anything ever breathed in blasphemy about Connery's talent. Thrilled by the MGM-at-its-peak-style decor, the Fritz Lang echoes, the uniformly excellent acting, *Films and Filming* could only gasp, 'There hasn't been a film like *Dr. No* since – when? There's never been a British film like *Dr. No* since – what?' 'Carefully, expertly made,' agreed *The Times*.

Connery's personal reviews were his best yet. Critic Peter Green in *John O' London's* believed there was 'no doubt that Sean Connery with his Irish [sic] good looks, splendidly hairy chest, and tough but elegant charm, embodies this modern male compensation factor [James Bond] better than most actors could'.

At the premiere, where Zena Marshall took Connery's arm and Saltzman for once sat back to allow his movie to speak for itself, audience response was electrifying. Marshall, viewing the whole assemblage for the first time, could not but be impressed: 'The theatre was deadly silent at the beginning, but as it went on they were shouting for Bond. Sean's performance was so smooth he riveted the eye. I remember Anita Ekberg was there, sitting just along our row from Sean. Throughout the movie she couldn't keep her eyes off him – not on screen, in person. Later at the reception at the Ambassadeurs it was the same. Whatever effect he'd had on women up till then was doubled. James Bond made him a walking aphrodisiac.'

The explosion of media attention that accompanied the New York opening at the Astor, the Murray Hill and other theatres in the Premier Showcase group in May firmly and irrevocably stamped 'stardom' on Connery. Bosley Crowther in the *New York Times* commended the film as 'lively and amusing' though 'not to be taken seriously as realistic fiction or even art, any more than the works of Mr Fleming are to be taken as long-hair literature'. *Variety* predicted, 'As a screen hero James Bond is clearly here to stay. He will win no Oscars, but a lot of enthusiastic followers.' Tongue firmly in cheek, *Time* welcomed 'the varlet pimpernel' on screen at last: 'He looks pretty good. As portrayed by Scotland's Sean Connery, he moves with a tensile grace that excitingly suggests the violence bottled in Bond.'

As the New York critics applauded, *From Russia with Love* was already filming at Pinewood, backed by $2 million from a humbled UA. On the home front Connery was decorating his new property, a three-storey mansion overlooking Acton Park, and settling into married life with Cilento and a ready-made family – step-daughter Gigi and five-month-old son Jason.

Fame had taken its time. But in some regards matters were moving too fast.

# 10. HITCH, EFFORTLESSLY

'I don't think I'm meant to be married,' Diane Cilento told an interviewer in March 1961, propounding tersely the reasons for the failure of her union with Volpe. Two years later, six months after marrying Connery, she was reminded of that conclusion. Asked to comment she replied tartly, 'I got married.'

The beginnings of the new marriage were not auspicious, though the affection and regard Connery and Cilento held for each other is beyond question. By Cilento's own admission, Connery had to talk her into tying the knot. Beneath the dedication to his craft and his pugnacity of purpose, Connery in his 30s was surprised to find 'the old John Knoxian influence' working away – a realisation that struck him whenever, after long absences, he came back to Fountainbridge. On discovering Cilento was pregnant in the summer of 1962, shortly after just such a refresher trip to Edinburgh, he promptly set a course for marriage. Time and circumstance were right for him: with his Bond contract he was assured good money for a few years; his existing savings were considerable; he was past thirty, and tired of philandering; most important, Diane was a supreme career navigator, blessed with intuition that divided good from bad irrefutably. He proposed, but she refused. 'I didn't want to get married,' she said later. 'Having made a bodge of it already I didn't rate marriage. I thought it was too stifling.' Discussions about alternative lifestyles stretched into September, but Connery was adamant in his reluctance to settle for separate lives, with the new child farmed on loan every other week. 'Sean was never enamoured of the idea of children,' Ian Bannen said, 'but he was anxious about the baby once he knew the die had been cast. And he loved Diane, remember. He told people she reminded him of his mother – bright, strong, firm.'

In the heady afterglow of the *Dr. No* premiere, over dinner, Connery finally persuaded Cilento to agree to his proposal. He had already made a major gesture of resolve: for £9,000 he had purchased a twelve-room house in Centre Avenue, Acton, formerly the home of twenty-five nuns of the Order of Adoratrices. He had drafted in an interior designer and decorators, and he was building a nursery. Cilento was flattered, but she laid down conditions. She told the *Sunday People* later: '[Sean] was so sure we could make a go of it … I wanted us both to retain a fair amount of freedom. I don't like ownership in marriage. I don't like too many promises either. There is no way of being sure you can keep them.'

Days after Cilento accepted Connery's proposal the wedding ceremony took place in Gibraltar. Gibraltar was best for many reasons: in Britain the couple would have had to wait three weeks after the posting of banns, and the bush telegraph that operates through registrars' offices would have meant unwanted press coverage. As it was, jaundiced circles were still abuzz with the scandal of the scarlet lady, just one month divorced, seven months' pregnant and hopping in and out of love with Connery. 'She jilted him a few times,' one actor acquaintance claimed. 'He was never too sure of her.'

At first in Gibraltar Connery thought he'd got the ultimate jilt. Cilento was in Spain, staying with friends, and arrangements had been made by telephone for her to meet up with him at the appointed registry. Connery, travelling on his British passport, had no trouble entering the colony but Cilento, with her Australian documents, was delayed at the frontier. The ceremony was postponed for a few hours, new witnesses had to be roped in – two taxi drivers, for convenience – but, at last, the vows were exchanged. Connery's mood was foul, though Cilento thought the whole affair 'like a funny TV show. He was all feet, all thumbs, frustrated.'

Nerves were not given long to settle. A walking trip up the Rock was attempted, with the romantic intention of watching evening fall over Africa. But the couple stayed up too long, and got lost in the military camp on their way down. Locked in, with night descending fast, it took them an hour to find a sentry with a sympathetic ear. According to Cilento, they repaired to their honeymoon base, the Rock Hotel, exhausted, facing a night of anticlimax after the dramas of the day. Subsequently they spent their honeymoon days at a beach front villa rented from the Marques de las Torres ten miles away on the Costa del Sol.

Six weeks later, in London on 11 January, Jason was born, by which time the family – with Gigi Volpe looking ever more on Connery as Dad – had moved into Acacia House. Connery personally supervised the several thousands pounds' worth of reconstruction, frequently haggling with the builders and challenging costings. 'I'd been on building sites,' he said. 'I knew how corners could be cut, what was feasible and what wasn't.'

Space and colour were the main considerations. For the 37-foot living-room Connery insisted on 'bright red carpet, white paint, lots of very bright cushions ... colour is necessary'. A year later he was 'watching Jason reaching for the lights and the brightest colours, laughing. He will grow up to memories and experiences that will be inescapable.' The simple sentiment revealed the urge to displace Fountainbridge once and for all. 'Sean was never ashamed of Edinburgh,' said Ian Bannen, 'but he acquired a liking for good material things. I suppose he even tried to impose it [on Fountainbridge]. For instance, I remember he took me home there and he'd bought this very modern gigantic fridge for his parents. It was a huge thing, crammed into this tiny room where everyone had to squeeze round it. It was quite ridiculous.' With the upfront money from *From Russia with Love* he was now trying to lure Effie and Joe away from the stair. He offered them a flat in London, but Effie insisted that she needed to be near Helen and Neil, her parents, then living in Corstorphine and very dependent on family support. The fact that McEwan's Brewery was beginning to annex nearby properties did not deter either Effie or Joe. 'Fountainbridge is so handy,' Joe told the *Sunday Express*, fending off his son's offer. 'London is such an enormous place, and there's always too much bustling and hustling.'

As *Dr. No* swept through Britain, playing virtually non-stop in cinemas during 1963, inevitably Fountainbridgers had the chance to measure Connery's climb. Tom O'Sullivan saw it and felt, 'This was different from some Ealing comedy, this felt like Hollywood. [From then on], all of us sat up and paid attention.' John Brady saw it and told Neil, 'That's it, Tommy has done it, he's made for life.'

United Artists agreed, investing more executive interest, as well as cash, in *From Russia with Love*. Terence Young had earlier tested their patience and resolve, spending the months after the completion of *Dr. No* laboriously casting the new movie. For the key villains he finally chose Robert Shaw (ordering him to put on weight and muscle), and the torch singer Lotte Lenya. Seeking a heroine to outstrip – in every sense – Ursula Andress, he commuted for weeks between European capitals, interviewing more than two hundred girls for the role of Tatiana, the turncoat Russian. Among those in the running were Austria's Elga Anderssen (dropped by UA decree when she spurned an executive's advances), Roman Lucia Modogno, English roses Margaret Lee and Sally Douglas, Pole Magda Konopka, Yugoslav Sylvia Koscina and a Miss Universe 1960 runner-up, Italian Daniela Bianchi. In March Bianchi was told she had the job and on 1 April filming began, once again at Pinewood's Stage D, utilising most of the proven technical talents from *Dr. No*.

Over sixteen weeks Young took his crew from Pinewood to Turkey, Madrid and Scotland, shooting more extravagantly than he had on the first Bond, and running weeks over in Turkey where there were union troubles and serious cast illnesses. Connery was exhausted, but he perked up when director Basil Dearden offered him the lead in his upcoming *Woman of Straw*, co-starring with Ralph Richardson, an actor Connery had admired since his days at the Blue Halls. Connery accepted the Dearden project without seeing the script, and revived for Bond.

As a consolidating choice, the one to secure the Bond series, *From Russia with Love* was evidence of Broccoli and Saltzman's brilliant market sense. Undeniably Fleming's most literary and strangely structured book, Fleming himself had reservations about its worth. Before the book was in proof in 1956 he wrote to the publishers Jonathan Cape about his fear of staleness and the contrivances used 'to fill the vacuum created by my waning enthusiasm for this cardboard booby'. As it turned out the public, and no less a luminary than President John Kennedy, loved the novel and turned it into a perennial best-seller. Richard Maibaum, the screenwriter, wisely chose to retain as much as possible of Fleming in his script, a punch-heavy story of a plot by an international crime organisation, SPECTRE, to kill Bond, steal a decoding machine and confound both British and Soviet spy agencies.

Superb photography by Ted Moore, adventurous editing by Peter Hunt, Bianchi oozing sensuality with every timid arch of a brow and the coincidence of the mysterious assassination of President Kennedy six weeks after the London opening all joined to elevate *From Russia* into the realm of stellar mega-hits. Effie and Joe came to London to join Diane and Connery for the premiere and were floored by the degree of unanticipated success. Effie maintained that deadpan aloofness that had kept her through the bleak days of the Depression, but Joe was at a loss. The crowds, the glaring manifestations of a wealth he could only have dreamed of in drunkenness, the autograph hunters screaming for Tommy – it was all too much to digest. At the reception after the screening he told a film journalist he believed his son 'might get quite popular' in the immediate future. Already at work on *Woman of Straw*, Connery seemed almost unaware that film history was in the making: *Dr. No* could easily have been a fluke, but with the triumphant premiere of *From Russia with Love*, a heavily backed series was guaranteed. Pressed to give an account of his personal recipe for Bond's success, Connery yielded to the hyperbole he would soon grow to detest. He spoke of the lack of humour in Fleming's novels (a gross unfairness in the eyes of Fleming and those familiar with the sardonic undertone of the books), and of his and Terence Young's tricks to lighten the material with one-line gags and some self-mockery. Hyperbole was the order of the day. Fleming, who had privately expressed doubts about 'the labourer playing Bond', was now reported as saying Connery was 'much as he had imagined Bond'. Were he writing the books all over again, he said, Connery would be his clothes-horse.

In Young's trademark style, champagne had, literally, flowed day and night during the making of *From Russia with Love*. Now it seemed more than justified. Following the October premiere floodgates opened. It seemed as if the worldwide media gave 007 an ovation. As a feat of technical virtuosity – the American production values again – the movie defied any negative criticism. But there was much more than just appreciation for American-style British thriller-making. Wry political elements in the plot teased the highbrow critics prone to analysing cinema as a mirror of life. There were, of course, dissenters. Philip Oakes in the *Sunday Telegraph* catalogued the 'voyeurism, sadism and lesbianism for kicks. Guns go off; girls get undressed; people have sex; people die. Happening succeeds happening, but nothing and no one is of real significance.' What Oakes was circumspectly describing was the social fall-out of a new, youth-driven liberal era, an era dominated by the hedonistic overtones of the Beatles and now rubber-stamped by Bond.

In due course, America fell. After the assassination of President Kennedy on 22 November, the Cold War intensified and the cartoon relevance of Bond versus the Beast was sealed. *Playboy* magazine, sub-literary voice box of all America – young liberal and, in its own way, conservative – adopted Bond as its standard-bearer instantly, and in so doing assured colossal popularity through all strata of society during the confused 60s. (*Playboy* earned the distinction of serialising Fleming's last few novels prior to book publication. It also specialised in features on Bond movie girls, running nude or topless shots of Ursula Andress, Martine Beswick, Margaret Nolan, Molly Peters, Mie Hama and Lana Wood. Incisive articles and interviews with Fleming, Connery, Richard Maibaum and Roald Dahl, who wrote the script of *You Only Live Twice*, also frustrated lesser journals keen to cash in on the Bond boom.)

Connery's notices for *From Russia* jousted for pride of place with those of the lovable Pedro Armendáriz as Kerim Bey, villain Robert Shaw and Daniela Bianchi. Bianchi particularly did well and many enjoyed her endearingly waiflike performance, which, in spite of her newness, was consistent (though she was dubbed by Shakespearean actress Barbara Jefford). In America, where the film opened in April 1964, the acid pen of hard-to-please critic Manny Farber decided the winner, though backhanding equal honours to the runner-up. In an article in *Cavalier* magazine he waxed eloquent on 'Robert Shaw's scene stealing ... which is done alongside Sean Connery, who is a master in his own right in the art of sifting into a scene, covertly inflicting a soft dramatic quality inside the external toughness.' Bosley Crowther, meanwhile, in the *New York Times* was hollering, 'Don't miss it! Just go and see it and have yourself a good time.'

'About half-way through *Woman of Straw*,' a film colleague relates, 'Sean's attitude to acting and stardom changed – overnight. Diane was behind him, so was Harry Saltzman maybe – though he lived to regret it – but suddenly Sean was it.' Strengthened by financial security and the gradual realisation of his greatest ambitions, Connery did appear to alter tack during the winter of 1963–64. One *Express* article of the period quoted a press agent ranting: 'Sean Connery? You want my honest opinion? Sean Connery is a great, big, conceited, untalented, wooden-headed ninny.' Whispering tales were already circulating about his greed and big-headedness ('You couldn't drag him to a party unless there was something in it for him'). At Pinewood Studios, filming with the short-tempered Gina Lollobrigida, Connery was, allegedly, asserting his equal-star-billing status. The on-set mood was reputedly horrendous and technicians reported daily conferences, where director Dearden cast oil on troubled waters. Connery was constantly suggesting script rewrites, though Stanley Mann, later his close friend, had co-drafted the original. Many suggest Cilento had much to do with proposed alterations. 'Her stock was high,' Ian Bannen said. 'She'd just finished Tony Richardson's *Tom Jones* and gotten herself an Academy Award nomination. She was still full of energy, and full of ideas for making Sean an "artist".' On location in Majorca cast relationships deteriorated alarmingly. Connery was allegedly 'sick and tired' of Lollobrigida's lapses. (Connery later denied any rift: he liked working with La Lolla, he said.) One scene called for him to roughen her up with a shake and a face slap. Furious after an earlier argument, Connery hit Lollobrigida too hard, sending her reeling. He later apologised, claiming accidental force, but expanded in an interview, 'Acting is a job, like carpentry or building roads. There are a hundred people involved in putting you up there on screen. The trouble with a lot of stars is that they develop heads as big as their close-ups.' His own head, he made clear, was unchanged by his good fortune. 'If I wore hats,' he snapped, 'I think you'd find I still take the same size.'

Close friends like Bannen and Michael Caine supported Connery's declaration. His home life was simple. He kept one secretary whose function was to answer fan mail. He drove a Volkswagen (later a second-hand Jaguar) while Cilento had a small Austin Healey. His only notable indulgence was good restaurants. The only appreciable change concerned his attitude to the work on offer. 'It must have been after the first or second Bond that he decided to quit the stage,' said Ian Bannen. 'He suddenly said he never wanted to do it again, that all the shouting hurt his throat. Simply, he wanted to do first-class films, and only films.'

Michael Caine said, 'He'd brought to Bond the gift every star actor has: he'd made Bond his own, doesn't matter what Ian Fleming originally visualised. Sean *was* Bond. But he knew his talents were bigger than that. Of course there was lots more he wanted to do while the going was good. He was smart about his breakthrough.'

In December 1963, just after *Woman of Straw* concluded, and distressingly early in the day for Harry Saltzman, Connery was telling *Photoplay* the extent of his unease at the prospect of type-casting. 'I remember once going to see a casting director for a role in a picture,' Connery said. 'When she asked me, "And what type of actor are you, Mr Connery?" I just got up and walked out. An actor hates to be typecast. I don't want to be Bond all the time. It rattles me when people call me Bond off the set. That's why I'm making pictures like *Woman of Straw*, in the hope that audiences will accept me in other parts.'

*Woman of Straw*, as it turned out, did little to enhance Connery's reputation beyond Bond, though its critical assessment was unfairly based on comparison with the lavish production values of the Broccoli–Saltzman pictures. The film was criticised, not unfairly, for its pseudo-Hitchcock approach, and had a stagey feel (the alternative stage version by Catherine Arley and Ian Cullen was generally better received). In the story, nurse Maria, played by Lollobrigida, is persuaded by Connery's Anthony Richmond to con an unsympathetic invalid uncle (Richardson) into marriage in order to divest him of his fortune. The plot twists dated from the Golden Age of detective fiction but rich dialogue kept the movie buoyed. The *Monthly Film Bulletin* approved of Connery, but wished for greater inventiveness with the material, invoking the names of Orson Welles, Losey and Hitchcock. The *New York Times* was resolutely savage: 'Try as the script and camera may to convince us that Miss Lollobrigida is the most irresistible of females, she stubbornly remains her placid, matronly self – hardly the type to draw a passing snort from an old lion like Sir Ralph. No wonder Mr Connery double-crosses her in the end.' William Peper in the *New York World Telegram and Sun* complained that Connery was 'much more fun as James Bond'.

Connery's immediate response to the cool reception for his first major role since Bond was submerged in the pre-production of the third Bond, *Goldfinger*, and of another special feature in the works, called *Marnie*. 'I wasn't all that thrilled with *Woman of Straw*,' he said afterwards, 'although the problems were of my own making. I'd been working nonstop since goodness knows how long and [was] trying to suggest rewrites while making another film (*From Russia with Love*). It was an experience, but I won't make that mistake again.'

Many of Connery's peers felt that both he and the media were unreasonably dismissive of *Woman of Straw*, which stands staunch in retrospect, removed from Bond comparisons. As in *The Frightened City*, the angst that Connery displayed supercharges the film and La Lolla remains unforgettable in black underwear. There was also the matter of financial returns. According to *Variety*, within twelve months *From Russia with Love*, which cost $2 million, had earned its money back (ultimately its US gross would total $10 million). *Woman of Straw*, running alongside it, grossed almost $1 million in the same period, proving something of its worth, notwithstanding the Bond association.

Recognising his golden moment, Connery urged Hatton to find the gilded projects and directors and sure enough, in this first flush of unequivocal stardom, Hatton produced the best: Hitchcock. Almost precisely two years after hoofing out of his little Fiat and signing on for *Dr. No* at £5,000, Hatton was writing a thank-you to Universal for $400,000, the agreed fee for the lead role in a pet project of Hitchcock's, *Marnie*. *Marnie* began life as a novel by *Poldark* author Winston Graham. It was acquired by Hitchcock in 1961 as the ideal property to reintroduce Grace Kelly, Princess of Monaco, into movies, and had Universal's backing from the start. Joseph Stefano, who had so brilliantly adapted Robert Bloch's *Psycho*, wrote the *Marnie* treatment and Grace Kelly accepted Hitch's offer. But at the last minute, the citizens of Monaco blocked Kelly by popular protest. Hitch shelved *Marnie* and made *The Birds*, testing the lead-playing potential of a new discovery, 26-year-old New Yorker 'Tippi' Hedren (Hitch always insisted on the quotes round the name Tippi). *The Birds* did well enough to encourage Hitch to try Hedren in a stronger character role and, to the surprise of the industry, in 1963 he reactivated *Marnie*, engaging a woman writer, Jay Presson Allen, to pump up the female role.

Connery had come to Hitch's attention in *Dr. No*, which he watched with interest, having rejected Bond two years before. But it was Cubby Broccoli who claimed credit for securing Connery's casting in *Marnie*. At Connery's request, said Broccoli, he rang Hitchcock and expressed the actor's wish to work with the master. Hitch complied, and even agreed to Hatton's inflated asking price. Less digestible was Connery's second demand: before committing, he must read and approve the screenplay. Hitchcock thought twice, concerned at the possibility of being hampered by the condition he despised above all, the star ego. But, as Michael Caine pointed out, 'The one thing Sean lacked was star ego: in that sense he was always an actor's actor and a director's actor.' Hitch quickly established this, and conceded the script.

In London the pop press made much of Connery's alleged macho posturing. The story was published that Hitchcock's London agent had told Connery, 'Even Cary Grant doesn't ask to read a Hitchcock script.' To which Connery was supposed to have replied, 'Well, I'm not Cary Grant.' This Bondian devil-may-care was milked by the press, much to the satisfaction of Saltzman and Broccoli. Even *Time* magazine took up the *Marnie* propaganda baton, eulogising a new breed of movie man 'whose individualism is just right for Bond, who makes steely love, is a wine snob, and likes to rub people out without leaving blood on the carpet'.

Privately Connery dismissed the fuss over his request to see the script. For a start he was exhausted, having worked without a day's break for more than a year, first promoting *Dr. No* throughout Europe on an all-cities tour, then dashing through *From Russia with Love* and *Woman of Straw*. Asking to read a script was a safety check, to ensure that *Marnie* was no quasi-Bond rip-off foisted on Hitchcock by Universal, who were in serious need of some good box-office. Protesting about the to-do over what one newspaper described as his 'failure to conform to the established patterns of the film business', Connery explained, 'Look, for the first time in my life I can ask to read a script, and if you had been in some of the tripe I have, you'd know why.' In the end, he got the script, liked it and saw immediately that UA's intentions were true. *Marnie* was the strongest script he'd been offered since *Dr. No* and – best lure of all – Hitchcock was giving him Hollywood again.

At Christmas 1963 Connery flew to Los Angeles alone and was picked up by two Universal VIPs at the airport. He refused the chauffeured limousine placed at his disposal and asked for a small runaround 'like my Volks back home'. Taken to the Chateau Marmont on Sunset, according to the *People* newspaper, he expressed displeasure. 'A nice place,' he said, 'but what's wrong with the motel I stayed at in Burbank six years ago? That was easy to get in and out of and very inexpensive.' And so he was taken to Jimmy O'Dea's beloved Fatima Mansions, the low-rent motel originally laid on by Disney. 'It was the same little game about restaurants,' said the *People*. Asked how he felt about Chasen's or LaScala, 'Connery bluntly stated his preference for American hamburgers. His idea of entertainments also caused surprise. No, he didn't want to take in elite strip shows or star parties or touring musicals. He wanted to swim a bit, knock a golf ball round [he had just been introduced to golf by Terence Young], maybe collect a suntan more in fitting with the swanky American businessman-sophisticate he was to play.'

If Hitchcock or Universal harboured fears about a star temperament, those fears were silenced within days of Connery's arrival. Ian Bannen said, 'It was a *huge* chance, and he went there wanting to avoid distractions and work hard. It was Hitchcock, for Christ's sake!'

From their first meeting Connery and Hitchcock got on well. Hitchcock was a little unsure of Connery's blatant lack of social grace in some areas, but he enjoyed Connery's appetite for rehearsals and his speed with lines. Connery, for his part, liked the respect afforded to him, not just by the master himself, but by the serious film press. There was still nonsense talk of Bond, but there was also intelligent discourse. Later he guessed the reasons for his smooth professional acceptance: 'Most of the younger British actors today, like Finney and O'Toole and me, are more organic, down-to-earth actors than the previous generations. In America there is much more feel for realism than in Europe, where there is still a conception of an actor as being somewhat divorced from real life, and in Britain, where acting is still often associated more with being statuesque and striking poses and declaiming with lyrical voices.'

But Bond was taking America by storm while Connery was making his declaration of independence and, because a minimum of three Saltzman–Broccoli pictures lay ahead of him, he was forced to make some concessions to the pop press. Between takes at Universal Studios and on location in Maryland he was photographed with busty aspiring actress-models, and an informal chat with Hitchcock about the relative merits of British and foreign women received massive cover. His hands clasped around his paunch, Hitchcock restated his devotion to the English ice maiden: 'They are three-dimensional women. The other type of beauty, the Italian, big voluptuous figures, may look 3-D but, believe me, they're just cut-out dolls.' Connery responded wryly: 'You've just described my type.'

*Marnie* progressed in fits and starts. A rift between Hedren and Hitchcock, who had a complex emotional interdependency, slowed proceedings for a couple of days, but Connery remained cautiously detached, befriending Hedren, befriending Hitch. Hitchcock had been through the mill so many times he could, in the words of screenwriter Anthony Shaffer, 'direct with his eyes shut and his cigar stone cold'. The plot had been doctored to accommodate a young lead. In the book the Connery character was an elderly man. Connery plays Mark Rutland, a rich company executive, who discovers that a junior in his employ, Marnie (Hedren) is a kleptomaniac. When he discovers her criminality he covers for her and cajoles her into marriage, believing loving attention will change her.

Hitchcock outlined for François Truffaut the attraction of the storyline. He wanted to make the movie, he said, because of 'the fetish idea. A man wants to go to bed with a thief because she is a thief, just like other men have a yen for Chinese or coloured women.' Mark was, to Hitchcock, mildly neurotic too – though none of this was relayed on set or in script to Connery. 'I had a great time with Hitchcock,' Connery later said. 'He tells you on the set what moves he wants. The only major direction he gave to me was when I was listening to what somebody else was saying in a scene, and he pointed out that I was listening with my mouth open – as I often do – and he thought it would look better shut.' But of the neurotic slant to Mark: 'He never got into anything like that. He used to tell me funny stories before a take quite often, but he never dwelt upon the psychology of the character. His humour is pretty schoolboyish.' At one stage Hitchcock told Connery, 'If I'm paying you as much as I am and you don't know what you're doing, then I deserve what I get in the way of performance.'

For the latter part of the movie Cilento flew out to Hollywood with the children, and the family rented a lavish $1,000-a-month Bel Air bungalow complete with swimming pool where, the press lustily reported, Cilento bathed naked daily. From there, on his free days, Connery made telephone arrangements with director John Ford's agents to read and consider a starring role in Ford's upcoming biography of playwright Sean O'Casey, scheduled to start in Dublin towards the end of the year when, it was hoped, *Goldfinger* would be out of the way.

Hitchcock disappointed himself with his final cut of *Marnie*. In his published conversations with Truffaut he said he felt the neurotic conundrums had not been delineated sharply enough and, though Connery had handled tough emotional variations well, aspects of the character which seemed to work on set did not carry over on to celluloid. Truffaut suggested that the role may have been miscast: Laurence Olivier might have reached the subtler heights.

Hitchcock was inclined to agree: 'I wasn't convinced that Sean Connery was a Philadelphia gentleman. You know, if you want to reduce *Marnie* to its lowest common denominator, it is the story of the prince and the beggar girl. In the story of this kind you need a real gentleman, a more elegant man than we had.'

The comment was not intended to insult Connery personally. Hitchcock admired Connery more than many of his leading men, rating him somewhere between Cary Grant and Jimmy Stewart – his favourites – and Rod Taylor and Paul Newman, his newer collaborators. The technicians on *Marnie* shared the maestro's admiration. When the movie wrapped they presented Connery with a memento of respect in the form of a gold watch valued at $1,000. Connery found the sentiment 'rather touching', though he was less than touched by the postscript. On re-entering Britain in March, en route to start *Goldfinger*, Customs demanded a £25 duty on the luxury goods import.

*Marnie* opened in the summer of 1964 to mixed reviews and reasonable business, helped, like *Woman of Straw*, by the oblique Bond link. For Eugene Archer in the *New York Times* it was 'a clear miss, the master's most disappointing film in years'. Connery worked, he judged, 'commendably and well, but his inexperience shows'. *The Times* of London was kinder, its critic believing the film 'manages remarkably well . . . it is easy to see why the plot outline should have taken Mr Hitchcock's fancy: it is essentially *Spellbound* turned inside-out . . . moreover, the film has plenty of material for the nuttier French Hitchcock enthusiasts: a dash of amour fou in the hero's obsessive devotion to a beloved he knows to be from the outset almost impossible; lots and lots about the crucial word which can set free (shades of *Under Capricorn*), and the exchange of culpability.' Almost all reviewers – and early audiences – condemned the unusually bad process work, back-projection and obviously painted backdrops, while backhanding praise to Connery. In later years the very factors that damned *Marnie* secured its place among the cult elite. It was, the revisionists decided, a picture that resided outside time, a compendium of all Hitchcock films, an 'illuminating portrayal', wrote Donald Spoto, 'of the delicate balance between sickness and health in everyone'.

Connery, however, was suffering the grey realities of the present. He had revelled in the balm of the Californian winter and hated returning to the damp drudgery of another Bond at Pinewood. Hollywood was twice as attractive the second time round, because now there was the deep cushion of cash and recognition, and Lana Turner was small fry in the deep and misty past. But, for now, contractually bound to Bond, Hollywood remained as remote as ever.

The frustrations piled up. Despite high hopes, Cilento did not win the Academy Award in her nominated category of Best Supporting Actress, losing out to Margaret Rutherford for *The VIPs*. Shortly after, Ford's offer of *Young Cassidy* disintegrated because of scheduling clashes and Connery was left instead to trudge through a slush pile of clichéd sub-Bond pastiches on Richard Hatton's desk.

Back at Acton the fans huddled round the high stone walls of Acacia House, as they had done intermittently for months, anxious to catch a glimpse of the neo-establishment superstud hero who was cheekily outpacing the Beatles in the rapid-growth-phenomenon stakes. They saw instead a balding, angry man in a heavy overcoat, glowering, ready to do battle with Harry Saltzman and Cubby Broccoli.

# 11. AGONY AND ECSTASY

'James Bond came of age with *Goldfinger*,' said new Bond director Guy Hamilton, 'but in so doing he stirred up a hornets' nest.' Greed, ruthless ambition, pomposity and a pervasive fear of failure almost strangled the Bond series at this bountiful time. The spring of 1964 was not a peaceful spring for anyone associated with Bond or the Broccoli–Saltzman company, Eon. Terence Young, who had been preparing the new script with Richard Maibaum, fell out with the producers because he demanded a cut of *Goldfinger*'s profits, and was replaced by ace action director Guy Hamilton whose credits included *The Colditz Story*. A new screenwriter, the esteemed Paul Dehn, was summoned, and Hamilton began daily work at Dehn's Chelsea flat, rebuilding Maibaum's unfinished script. Saltzman, always the gadget man, was at war with Broccoli, ever the tit-and-action man, though both felt, in line with Hamilton's thinking, that the best and worst of the first two movies must be sifted and analysed in order to consolidate. Hamilton was keen from the start not to fall into the trap of 'doing the obvious in merely following what had gone before'.

Amidst this tumult, this measured strategy to make hay while the sun shone, Connery sauntered in with his gripe. 'Sean had risen to stardom very fast by most standards,' Hamilton said. 'Only five or six years before I'd had a nodding acquaintance with him at Gerry's Drinking Club, opposite the stage door of Her Majesty's. I didn't think he had too much going for him, but by *Dr. No* he was proving his salt. He matured rapidly as an artist, and the difference in performance between *Dr. No* and *Russia* is vast. And so with the Bond success he was picking up offers here, there and everywhere. But the big problem, the cause of his disillusion before *Goldfinger*, was that the offers he could consider were restricted by the contractual commitments of doing Bond. Those Bond pictures took a hell of a time to do, and Cubby and Harry weren't naturally prepared to allow Sean to go after other jobs as they arose. *Woman of*

*Straw* gave Sean no particular satisfaction because it wasn't the kind of film he wanted to be doing. He was concerned about his craft. He came back from Hollywood wondering what and who he was. He wanted to test himself and see if he was more than just any Mickey Mouse playing James Bond.'

Connery also wanted greater compensation for cramped opportunity. He had grown to dislike Saltzman intensely – 'mistrust him', in the words of Lewis Gilbert – and was suspicious of placatory suggestions made by Eon. Finally, reluctantly, he accepted $50,000 plus a percentage for *Goldfinger*, stemming his annoyance by putting out word, via Hatton and other close friends, that he was seeking radical, type-smashing parts. The 'integrity' some associates snigger at seemed quite real. Despite the eagerness for change and challenge, Connery rejected the first draft script of *Young Cassidy* submitted by Ford, thereby causing the scheduling delays that lost him the movie to Rod Taylor.

'After this one [*Goldfinger*],' Connery told Honor Blackman over dinner, 'it's got to be classy parts or nothing.'

Physically, making Bond was tougher than ever, though Hamilton was a more ordered director than Young, the kind who plans every move, allows little improvisation and believes 'sorting out the locations is the hardest part'. Shooting began in March at Pinewood in an atmosphere co-lead Honor Blackman describes as 'furiously professional'. A director of proven commercial instincts, Hamilton more than anybody was responsible for the key success of *Goldfinger*, the movie that rechannelled Bond from the edge of amorality to untouchable U-certificates. 'The difficulty was often the divergence of opinion between Saltzman and Broccoli,' Hamilton said. 'It became a case of why-is-your-idea-better-than-mine? One had to sit around for hours awaiting decisions. But once that obstacle was overcome, it was fine. I had my say in casting. I believed Bond must play opposite someone strong, someone to draw out his strengths. That's why I wanted Gert Frobe, the German actor who was very accomplished – and Honor. With Honor, who is a powerful actress, there was a certain "Oh my God, she's that *Avengers*' girl and how do we overcome that?"' There was also a feeling that she looked older than some of the young Bond girls they'd used. 'But I told them, "Don't worry, she's a fine actress, that's what is important. And we can shoot her with filters to make her look whatever way you want her to look."'

Honor Blackman herself knew that she had been assigned because of her wide experience – plus the personal fan-following she had won with her kinky, leather-costumed Cathy Gale in TV's *The Avengers*. 'I'm sure the appeal of macho Bond versus kinky me was at the back of Harry and Cubby's minds,' said Blackman. 'It obviously worked on screen, this strong female persona – it substituted for the lesbian aspect of the heroine Pussy [which was in the book]. It was decided this [lesbianism] would be understated in the movie.'

Pussy Galore was Bond's first unfriendly lover, a lesbian gang leader who assists megalomanic Auric Goldfinger (Frobe) in his outrageous attempt to contaminate the gold supplies at Fort Knox, Kentucky. Against the odds (indeed, against character credibility), Bond seduces Pussy and wins the day. 'It was simple fare,' said Hamilton. 'But we had the advantages of great dialogue from Dehn and a really original prototype sub-villian [Oddjob, played by Harold Sakata].' Those, and the gadget-laden Aston Martin DB5 introduced by Saltzman, took the movie to realms hitherto unreached in the series.

'I was naturally helped by what had gone before,' said Hamilton. 'But I wasn't, for instance, prepared to shoot miles of film and leave half of it on the floor, as had been the case with Terence. In *Goldfinger* Bond was sweetened, I suppose, by the perfection of formula. In *Goldfinger* there were only about twenty shots that never appeared on screen. Myself, Sean, Honor – we all knew *precisely* what we were aiming for from day to day.'

To Honor Blackman, Connery cut an impressive figure in two ways: 'Firstly, he was downright perfectionist, as I am. I liked that. He would never expect one to buy a bad take. If he fluffed, he was the first to call a halt. But he wasn't a directorial voice. Guy had full command – so much so that he didn't balk at putting me in my place! There were elements of the lesbian character I would have liked to try out, but Guy said no. An in-joke or two was fine – like me calling my co-pilot girl Harry or Joe – but that was all Guy would allow.' Blackman also admired Connery's scepticism of 'the publicity machine', a wariness made acute by what she saw as his essential shyness. 'He was a very reserved man,' she said, 'confident but private. As the film went on, obviously we got to know each other better. Privately. I found him attractive, sexy ...' She laughs mysteriously. 'I think he's got a pair of the best eyes that have ever been seen on screen, apart from anything else he might have that's good – and let's say there's plenty of that.'

Shyness alone was not the root of Connery's troubles with publicity. Hamilton is quick to emphasise that, regardless of threatened rifts with the producers, Connery was keen to outdo *From Russia with Love*. He was willing to do whatever had to be done, but his patience was frequently tried by the constant interruptions at Pinewood, where publicists brought casual journalists on to the set. In one incident, during a key scene, a French woman writer was landed abruptly on Connery. The familiar questions began. 'First she asked what the film was called,' said Connery. 'I told her. Then what part I was playing. I told her that too ...' The backbreaking straw came when the journalist took note of Gert Frobe's name and said, 'I've never heard of *her*.' Connery exploded. 'I just blew up and walked off the set,' he recalled. 'So, as a consequence, I suppose I'm considered rude by that person. Well, I consider her disrespectful and incompetent, and both are definite sins. If someone treats me rudely or dishonestly, I repay them an eye for an eye.'

As she had done with *From Russia with Love* and the later films, Cilento coached her husband through *Goldfinger*, helping him learn his lines in his study at Acton by sitting in as Pussy and Jill (Shirley Eaton in the film). She confessed she enjoyed the Bond girl parts, but thought them fundamentally too facile; she herself would never wish to star in a Bond movie. As it was, her own recently rocky career was stabilising. With Jason growing spirited and independent she had room to breathe again – and chase good parts. *Rattle of a Simple Man*, a minor movie that attracted good notices, was her first worthwhile job since *Tom Jones*, and now Carol Reed was offering a prestigious role in *The Agony and the Ecstasy*. Cilento was delighted with the script on offer and keen to have her husband star opposite her, but the movie was already fully cast, and he was stuck on Bond anyway. An alternative, for the future, was sought.

With perfect timing Terence Young came back into the picture. He was preparing his own movie version of the Defoe classic *Moll Flanders*, and was agreeable to the notion of pairing husband and wife in the leads. No sooner had Connery's appetite been whetted than the idea was dashed. Reed's film was scheduled to start in Italy in June, but no definite finish date could be given. Young had to start shooting in the autumn. For a few days it was heart-rending stalemate; then Young moved on with other actors and the Connerys lost their chance. Cilento flew to Rome with her mother and children, *Goldfinger* duly wrapped in July and an atmosphere of gloom descended on the Eon camp. 'We knew Sean was pissed off with Bond,' a publicist said. 'We knew the series was threatening what he regarded as his actor status. I think he wanted out there and then but, like Harry and Cubby, he was mesmerised by the potential.'

United Artists rolled out the red carpet for *Goldfinger*, promoting it massively and staging major premieres in London and New York in September and December respectively. Connery, meanwhile, began his first holiday in nearly two years, flying to Rome to join Cilento with a script in his briefcase that he had turned down when *Moll Flanders* was in discussion, but which now filled the gap. The script was an adaptation by Ray Rigby of his successful stage play, *The Hill*, about a North African detention camp for would-be deserters in the Second World War. It had been given to Connery by Pinewood-based producer Kenneth Hyman, and was immediately attractive for the subtlety of its plotline and depth of its characters – factors manifestly absent in Bond. Sidney Lumet, the celebrated American director of provocative films like *The Pawnbroker*, was to take the reins – another definite plus. In Rome Connery made his positive decision to sign for *The Hill*, and overnight the post-Hollywood, post-Bond depression lifted. There was other good news. Telephone negotiations began with producer Doc Merman to co-star husband and wife in a movie version of the novel *Call Me When the Cross Turns Over*, hopefully to be shot in Sydney early in 1965.

The paparazzi and scandal-thirsty Italian journalists inevitably fastened on to Cilento, Connery, Cinecitta Studios and the shortest distance between those points while 'James Bond' was in residence in their capital city, but excitement was hard to find. Cilento was a conscientious and discreet actress, liked by co-stars Charlton Heston and Rex Harrison and rigid in her disciplines. Connery, for his part, lived quietly in the pretty pink villa in the hills, reading, idling, going shoeless day and night, growing a moustache for *The Hill*, tending Jason, chit-chatting with the cook and Cilento's mother. A French journalist who spent a lunchtime chez Connery reported them 'ideally suited and as content as any young family could hope to be'. Connery found preparation for *The Hill* more satisfying than any movie experience in his life. He ascribed his profound pleasure to 'the time to prepare, to get all the ins and outs of what I was going to do worked out with the director and producer in advance, to find out if we were all on the same track'. There were minor rewrites, but Rigby's script was so good and Lumet's vision for it so assured that Connery felt that insistence on small alterations would be churlish.

Just before he left for the Spanish location, the word came that Ian Fleming had died in Canterbury Hospital after a heart attack. Connery had liked Fleming – 'a dreadful snob, but a marvellous companion, we shared many fascinating conversations and his knowledge was vast'. Connery was playing golf with Rex Harrison at Rome's Olgiata championship course when he heard the news. In smiling tribute, the two stars played an extra eighteen holes, Connery teeing off with a Penfold Hearts, the brand of golf ball Fleming dictated for James Bond in his match against Goldfinger. 'It seemed appropriate,' Connery said. 'I think Ian would have liked that.'

Fleming missed the triumph of the *Goldfinger* opening by just five weeks. For the first time mob-style crowds crammed Leicester Square for the Odeon premiere, attended by Honor Blackman 'wearing a solid gold finger cast, quite stupid actually, and flanked by colossal security men'. Autograph hunters were everywhere. Fans ripped down the poster hoardings and screamed for Connery as they screamed for the Beatles. BBC television news covered the premiere. Bond had come of age, all right – bigger in stature than anyone at Eon could ever have hoped for. The financial rewards, too, were astounding. The *Evening News* reported that 'nothing like *Goldfinger* has happened in films since they discovered the word "stupendous"'. For the last week in September the Leicester Square Odeon took £17,327 and the Hammersmith Odeon, which averaged £2,000 on its biggest Hollywood attractions, totted £10,000. In New York a few weeks later, the phenomenon was repeated and embellished. *Goldfinger* had cost $2 million. *Variety* reported it had become the fastest money-maker in history, grossing $10,374,807 in just fourteen weeks in the US and Canada. United Artists took the unprecedented step of announcing its expectations: by the time the movie ended its first-run engagements in America, a gross of $20 million was projected.

On the critical front, response was neatly divided between the perspicacious and the snobbishly begrudging. *Punch*, untypically, was effusive in its praise: 'The whole thing is glossy, entertaining, often funny nonsense.' In the *Spectator* Isabel Quigly was worried about the movie being 'the most overtly fascist of this unsanitary series', but had to admit the audience approved, clapped, laughed, cheered its head off – and 'not just a hooligan patch of it'. *Saturday Review* admired Hamilton ('who has paced the action even faster'), Fleming, and Connery ('who has the role down pat by now'). Penelope Houston devoted a huge chunk of *Sight and Sound* to in-depth analysis, concluding that *Goldfinger* was 'rather a symbolic film' which, as Penelope Gilliatt had suggested of the Bond boom, encapsulated 'the brassy, swinging, ungallant taste of the sixties'. The *Daily Worker*'s moan that the movie was 'one vast, gigantic confidence trick to blind the audience to what is going on underneath' was given short shrift. Leonard Mosley, always to the point, gasped, 'Even for eggheads, I swear this film is worth a visit. Honor bright. My word is my Bond.' And Alexander Walker thought it, and Honor Blackman especially, 'the best thing since spliced film'. In America, *Newsweek* took the heavyweight approach, noting dark Freudian undertones and concluding that Connery-Bond was 'the only guy in the world who has satisfactorily resolved his Oedipus complex. It is an odd entertainment when the hero's strength is as the strength of ten because his gender is pure.'

Connery – the purity of whose gender had never been in doubt – was unmoved by all the tub-thumping. He was glad to retreat to Almeria in southern Spain, away from prying flashbulbs and rubbish questioners, to join Lumet and his cast for what was to be his most physically gruelling film to date. Leaving the family again so soon might have presented problems, but Cilento was still contentedly dug into *The Agony and the Ecstasy* and Lady Cilento was there to be surrogate parent for Jason and Gigi.

Producer Ken Hyman had expressly made clear the likely strenuous demands of *The Hill*. With his construction crew, headed by art director Bert Smith and manager Dick Frith, he had been in and out of Almeria for three months preparing the ground. The exigencies of film-making made it more feasible to base the production in Spain rather than North Africa, where writer Rigby – on whose personal experience *The Hill* was based – had been a prisoner of war during the Second World War. But Almeria was no easy alternative. The entire action of the movie took place within a wired stockade under the blazing sun, but the ideal site was hard to find. Smith and Frith finally found a sandy wasteland at Gabo de Gata where, over ten weeks, an area of 400 metres by 150 was cleared (one sand dune, 90 metres square and 5 metres high, was painstakingly manually shifted), and the punishment hill of the title was built, using 3,500 metres of imported tubular steel, and more than 60 tons of timber and stone. From midsummer the sun was fierce – temperatures never fell below 115 degrees – and conditions worsened, as if on cue, when the cast arrived.

'We were in a bloody roasting desert,' said Ian Bannen, who was starring on screen for the first time with his old pal. 'The water and food were ghastly. I'd known tough locations before, but it'd be hard to find words to describe that one. A beast, that's all I can say. Real tough.'

Two thousand gallons of distilled water were shipped in to keep crew and cast alive, but that didn't stave off dysentery. In the beginning, after the rest in Rome and buoyed with the energy of breaking from type, Connery bore up while others fell to sickness. The actors' working day was long – ten hours or more, six days a week – and fitness was the prime requisite. 'If Sean was uptight about Bond, Sidney [Lumet] kept him smiling,' Bannen said. 'I think *Time* magazine summed it up when it said Sidney makes love to his cast and crew; he's a great sweetener. Sean was fine at the start – despite the fact the location was as smelly as Aberdeen on a hot day. Fishy – that's what it was like – fish smelling. Awful. But Sidney knew his first priority was keeping Sean content, so he tried hard to save him from ennui and illness and all the rest.'

Eventually Connery did fall ill, flattened by a combination of the heat, ferocious physical exercise and 'Spanish tummy', but he was on his feet in a day or two with not much shooting time lost. 'It was the one picture I was on where there was no yellow, pink and blue [script amendments pages],' said Bannen, 'and that pleased Sean more than anything. "At last," he said to me, "a fucking producer and director who know what they want on the screen."'

Connery rated Lumet – and the picture – very highly. Despite the stresses of Almeria, he loved every minute of the seven-week shoot (five weeks in Spain, two for interiors in MGM Studios at Borehamwood). Later he saw it as 'an example of a film which wasn't a success by the public's standard but eventually became, in terms of acceptance, a classic. The idea always was to make an ensemble movie, and we made it. The writer, the director, the cast and myself all agreed we'd succeeded in making the movie we wanted to make.'

*The Hill*, Bannen contended, was 'strictly a man's film'. The cast was all male, the story uncompromisingly brutal: in a British military stockade errant prisoners are repeatedly forced to climb an almost sheer man-made hill, weighed down with full kits, tongue-lashed by sadists like Staff Sergeant Williams (Ian Hendry). Joe Roberts (Connery), court-martialled for striking an officer, is one such victim prisoner, pushed beyond endurance, but fighting 'the system' to the end. Bannen, who played the righteous Sergeant Harris, judged the film a winner as soon as he saw the rushes at Borehamwood. 'But you can never tell from the bits and pieces. As it happened, it didn't take in the money and we were all, I'll confess, disappointed. Sean more than most, I'd say. There were things that maybe were misjudged. The black and white photography was aesthetically fine but the American drive-ins don't like it. On the other hand, the movie was a big hit across Europe. I saw it, as a paying customer, in France and Italy – which is the best way to evaluate. I was doing a Tony Richardson film, cruising the Mediterranean on a schooner, going from port to port. I saw *The Hill* in Greece and [the audience response] was incredible. I've never witnessed cheering and applause like it in a cinema before. In Europe, of course, it was subtitled, which made it easy to understand. But I feel it should have been dubbed in America, to get rid of some of the extreme regional accents – like mine and Sean's – and cut back some of the merciless background "left-right, left-right". I always felt that if that were done, it could have been massive.'

The release of *The Hill* early in 1965, overlapping early production of the new Bond, *Thunderball*, gave Connery his best personal reviews since his television work. The *Sunday Express* celebrated 'a masterpiece [with] Sean Connery reminding us what a really splendid actor he is'. The *Sun* called Connery 'startlingly good', and the *Daily Express* applauded a 'devastating film [where] Sean Connery gives one of the most disturbingly effective performances of the year. A more powerful film has not come out of a British studio for many a year.'

To Connery's intense annoyance, once back in London, publicity surrounding *The Hill* focused more on the fact that he had cast aside the toupee he had worn since *Marnie* and allowed the bushy eyebrows that had been cropped for *From Russia with Love* to flourish again. The fan magazines splashed 'Bond in *The Hill*' over double page spreads that bullheadedly resisted distinction of character, and the tabloids headlined the Spanish location shots as 'James Bond at Play', interpreting the drawn features and scraggy moustache of *The Hill* as evidence of a jaded Connery at war with Eon. The game seemed endless. When Connery won a few thousand on roulette at an Italian casino, the papers hollered, 'Bond Breaks Casino Bank'. At the launching of Israel's branch of Variety Club International, where Connery agreed to present the major cash donation, the *Daily Mail* ran the headline: 'Bond hands over £103,000 for Israel'.

Trouble, friends knew, was coming. 'Sean makes a point of controlling his temper,' Cilento said. 'Only twice since we've been married have I seen his wrath.' At the time the media gossip that the marriage itself was likely to be the first casualty of the pressures had begun. Cilento stayed silent but then suddenly, in the run-up to *Thunderball* in the spring of 1965, everybody was talking about an imminent separation. 'I don't know how it started,' said a friend from *The Hill*, 'but I will say Sean was a fairly faithful type. Diane, though, was a tough egg. When it began to look like their differences were going to open up into a real split, I guessed Diane was the one who wanted to end it.' It was obvious Diane was jealous of the Bond success while Sean was probably jealous of the highbrow society Diane attracted. There was more to it than that, though. From the beginning Diane had felt she wanted freedom in marriage but Bond certainly gave her none. In effect she was Mrs Bond.

*Thunderball* compounded the marital difficulties of Connery and Cilento in more ways than one. Firstly, its scheduling knocked out Doc Merman's plans for a partnership movie and effectively ended the dream of a co-starring venture. Worst of all, it focused an intense media spotlight on a couple in trouble, striving desperately to sort out their personal lives. Legal hitches temporarily delayed *Thunderball* but by February the new screenplay was ready, all production grievances settled, and finances once again agreed with Connery. His fee for *The Hill*, a relatively small-budget feature, had been an astronomical £150,000. For *Thunderball* it was reputedly upped by £50,000, with a percentage thrown in.

Filming started in France in late February, by which time Connery had already met his female co-lead, another pneumatic sex-siren called Claudine Auger, at a London press party. Auger was neither the producers' nor director Terence Young's first choice. Saltzman had wanted Raquel Welch, having seen her over-spilling a bikini top in the October 1964 edition of *Life* magazine, and tentative arrangements had been made with her. But in a last-minute phone call, head of Fox Richard Zanuck, a friend of Broccoli's, asked for her release to star in his forthcoming *Fantastic Voyage*. Broccoli complied and from Christmas 1964 through to

February a long line of glamorous unknowns was tested – by Eon's estimate, as many as 600. From them, after close misses by Yvonne Monlaur and black actress Gloria Paul (who would star with Roger Moore in *Live and Let Die*), the former Miss France, Auger, was chosen for the lead role of Domino.

Married to the French director Pierre Gaspart-Huit who was 25 years her senior, Auger said she 'always felt I would become Domino. I had read the book about seven times and knew her inside out. I am very much a Domino sort of girl myself, a fun-loving extrovert. Whatever I am doing I enjoy doing it: loving, driving, riding, all of it.'

Auger and Connery were photographed together at cocktail functions where she gushed fawningly about Connery's style and talent. Back at Pinewood in March rumours of romance started and on the second Friday of the month Connery quit Acton to move into a London apartment alone. The *Daily Express* conveyed a close friend's non-surprise: 'It is a great shame. They've tried to patch up their troubles, but it hasn't worked out.' The same article also reported that Twentieth Century Fox had just disclosed the indefinite postponement of any possible Cilento–Connery co-starring movie. 'It isn't true to say Sean's artistictally edgy mood after *The Hill*, or passing fancies on *Thunderball* or whatever else, were responsible for the separation,' Ian Bannen insisted. 'Anyone who understood their marital arrangement knew the process by which they broke up then. They were just two extremely independent types who had two very different-shaped careers. And ultimately Sean put his career before his home, and Diane did the same.'

A week after the trial separation Connery was back at their Acton home, sleeping overnight. The press pounced. Since his arrival from Spain he had been shadowed everywhere by reporters looking for a slice of Bondian wit or wisdom. Cilento brushed away the hysteria. Were husband and wife to be permanently reconciled? Was there another woman in Connery's life? Did he intend to stay at Acton now? 'You must simply draw your own conclusions from what you know,' Cilento hedged. 'All I can say is that Sean spent last night at the house and will spend tonight here too.' A reconciliation? 'If that is your interpretation, yes. I leave it to you.'

But it was not a reconciliation. Connery moved out again and, as the antidote to encroaching depression, flung himself inventively into *Thunderball*. 'He was lovely to work with,' said Molly Peters, whom Young had plucked from the crowd scenes of his earlier movie *Moll Flanders*, to star as Patricia, the sexy health clinic masseuse who 'works over' James Bond. 'He was very brotherly and protective towards me, because it was my first big part and I was desperately nervous – not only of the lines, but because there were these very sexy bed and shower scenes I had to do, one [the shower room] where I was nude with him. He encouraged me, and never showed any impatience – unless it was with outsiders who intruded, or with publicity people.'

Unlike Hamilton on *Goldfinger*, Young changed the script every day. Molly Peters's dialogue was altered and, in very un-Hamilton fashion, eight takes of the nude shower scene were run. 'But Terence made it easy, he kept the atmosphere humorous and he obviously got on so well with Sean that we were, in spite of all that was going on beyond Pinewood's lot, like a little happy family,' said Peters. 'For the shower scene the make-up people wanted to use sticking plaster on my pubic area and nipples, which I thought more obscene, if anything. In the end, they just covered my front, and my bottom was bare for the scene where Connery presses me against the glass and you see the outline. I remember, after all the takes, Sean joked it up. We went into the steam for take number eight or so and when it was over Sean came out on all fours, gaga, with a bowler hat on. He could laugh. And he could make one feel important, which was nice for a newcomer. Once, after a spot of trouble in my private life, I broke into tears on the set just before a take. Sean came up and put his arm round me and said, "Who has upset you? Tell me: who here upset you?" He was vexed for me, and I'd no doubt he would have sorted out whoever it was if I'd said a name.'

Molly Peters, among others, observed Connery's attraction to 'glamorous women who came to the set, especially one fabulous Hungarian', but kept apart from his social life. Another Bond girl from the movie said: 'Sean's attention was absorbed by Claudine. He went for continental types, and she suited him ideally.'

Late in March crew and cast flew to the Bahamas to resume filming and Cilento stayed behind with Jason and Gigi. *Playboy* reported that the tiny archipelago was 'in a state of siege, occupied by an invading army of newspaper reporters, magazine writers and photographers from every major publication in America, England, Europe, Canada, Australia and Japan; TV crews from ABC, NBC and the BBC, silk-suited press agents and swimsuit starlets'. Auger kept Connery company discreetly, though they were pictured together daily, embracing, languishing in the warm Gulf waters, ambling under the casaurinas along Love Beach. Perhaps the mandatory overt romance of Bond-and-bird was the most fortu-itous natural cover. Then again perhaps it was, as a film colleague said, a nuisance. 'Claudine was a good friend to Sean and they liked each other's company. But Sean wanted Diane to come out to Nassau.' After long telephone negotiations, Cilento cancelled when Acacia House was burgled and items of her favourite jewellery taken. Days later, however, she did catch a plane, accompanied by Gigi and Jason, and was collected at Nassau airport by Connery.

Badgered with questions about reconciliation at the airport, Connery played dumb. Asked whether he was pleased to see Cilento he answered angrily, 'Yes, of course.' Then the reunited group skipped into the unit Cadillac and motored to a bungalow specially rented for them at Love Beach. *Thunderball* kept rolling through Easter and Connery made love, for the cameras, to sexy, sad-eyed Auger. The word 'reconciliation' fell from the reporters' barrage. The couple was together again, the radical marriage resumed. Cilento told journalist David Lewin: 'I am through the other side now of being called Mrs Bond and although it still happens it cannot upset me any longer. Sean and I have our own lives to lead in our own way.' Ominously she warned, 'This industry can take hold of you and wrap you up like a piece of meat. Neither of us will allow ourselves to become that involved. We are not going to let ourselves be merchandised.'

Connery, unfortunately, was already bought, packaged and sold. Succeeding with Bond he had, for the moment, lost himself.

# 12. YOU ONLY LIVE ... TWICE?

A kind of insanity overtook Sean Connery's life from 1965 to 1967, the period during which the foundation of his fame and fortune was laid. In 1965, thanks to *Goldfinger*, he was number one box-office attraction in America, an unparalleled achievement in recent times for a British-based actor. In 1966 he still topped the polls, and his fame had spread to Asia. In Japan he was idolised, ranking high above the Beatles in cult status. In Germany, Scandinavia, Italy, Spain and France his celebrity had injected new vitality into cinema-going. The French, he later observed, were the first to comprehend the culture-changing values of the Bond films: 'In some ways the French are insular because of their chauvinism towards film, but they have always been very respectful of effort in new directions.'

'I suppose many actors envied him for the breadth of his popularity,' his friend Robert Hardy said. 'But the burdens of that kind of fame were just too extraordinary. You look at that period in his career and you simply shake your head in awe and respect. Others would have gone over the edge. He held himself together with dignity and integrity.'

Connery's fee per film soared to $500,000 during these heady mid-60s, but the strain of overwork showed in some of his performances. *Thunderball* was one. This new Bond had him tracking down a stolen Vulcan aircraft, equipped with atomic bombs, to its sunken hideout in the Bahamas. Largo (Adolfo Celi) was the SPECTRE villain and Domino (Auger) his unhappy mistress. As in *Dr. No*, *From Russia with Love* and *Goldfinger*, Bond beats the villain with the loving assistance of the girl while wallowing in the ambient holiday brochure locations.

It was, again, a subtle brew of sex and non-stop action, but this time the reviews were clearly divided. Bosley Crowther of the *New York Times* had turned sour: 'Mr Connery is at his peak of coolness and nonchalance ... That's the best I can say for [this] Bond film.'

In London, in the *Sunday Times*, Dilys Powell, ever eager to dispense with hype, wondered whether the mechanical ingenuity of the series wasn't undermining human interests. In the *Telegraph* Robert Robinson wrote: 'Bond is the magus to whom all things are possible, a sickly condition with a very poor prognosis, for once it is diagnosed by an audience it robs a character of individuality, and, at last, of interest. Where there are no limits, there is no story, and novelty is offered as a substitute.'

Connery, according to Ian Bannen, ignored the reviews and concentrated on distancing himself from Bond and Eon with all speed. With Cilento invited to Hollywood to make *Hombre* opposite Paul Newman, Connery plugged for any American deal that would put him close to her. Richard Hatton quickly tied down Warners' *A Fine Madness*, to be shot on location in New York by Irvin Kershner. By a happy coincidence Newman's wife, Joanne Woodward, had already signed for *A Fine Madness*, so the groundwork for after hours happy families was already set. Connery flew to New York with Cilento and though *Hombre's* principal location shooting was in Phoenix, Arizona, the couple agreed to commute as often as possible, the children staying with Cilento. 'Sean was just too jaded by Bond,' Ian Bannen believed, 'to feel any jubilation at coming back to America for such a big picture.' Michael Hayes, the *Age of Kings'* director, considered it 'quite astonishing that, amid all that Bond uproar and the obvious exhaustion, he would take on a subtle comedy like *A Fine Madness*. It was obviously a tough script – but Sean worked his magic and pulled it off. I admired him more than anything for that display. Tired as he was he could dash around as Bond, then trim himself to the finesse of *A Fine Madness*. It spoke volumes for his self-discipline.'

Of the four or five movies that followed *Thunderball* in rapid succession, *A Fine Madness* is Connery's best, undoubtedly because the character he portrays, Samson Shillitoe, the rebel poet, is an exaggeration of Big Tam the Fountainbridge rebel. Samson is portrayed as a wild beast, haunted by the epic poem he can't quite write and hounded by a wife he loves yet wants to leave. Sacked from his job for rudeness, he is chased all over New York for back alimony and falls into the hands of a sophisticated Manhattan psychiatrist, played by Patrick O'Neal, and his wife, played by Jean Seberg, who try to tame him, but are ultimately won over to his ways.

*Hombre* and *A Fine Madness* achieved more or less all their goals and the parallel success helped Cilento and Connery restrike the link of mutual confidence and commitment. Both movies were critically well received and Connery utilised his time in New York and the comfort of his 10 per cent in *A Fine Madness* to steel himself for what was now announced to be his last Bond, the Japanese-set *You Only Live Twice*, scheduled to start shooting in May 1966. (*On Her Majesty's Secret Service*, with Guy Hamilton directing, was originally announced as Connery's fifth Bond, with Brigitte Bardot as the heroine Tracey. Weather and set-building problems caused the cancellation.) A year earlier, reflecting on his gutsy role in *The Hill*, Connery had said, 'Some people thought I couldn't make a go of a movie without romantic interest.' That he obviously had was proved not only by the favourable notices, but by the earnest new attention paid to him by lofty 'names' in New York. While he was there, Sean made a go of fitting into the Greenwich Village, into the arty swing of New York which was so very different from the claustrophobic atmosphere of the Pinewood scene. He saw plays on Broadway and off Broadway and he made friends in LA with people like stage director Sir Tyrone Guthrie, who took him seriously and really treated him as an artist.

After the productive months in America Connery settled back with Cilento, Gigi and Jason in Acton in higher spirits. Revelling in the New York reviews for *Madness*, he was bursting with fresh, Bond-busting ideas. With a side jab at Eon he told the *Express*: 'One should be paid what one is worth. Money gives you freedom and power. I want to use that power I now have as a producer. In Hollywood I asked Sir Tyrone Guthrie why he had never made a film. "Because no one asked me," he said. Well, I want to ask him. In the same way that Burton asked Zeffirelli to direct *The Taming of the Shrew* when Zeffirelli had never made a film before.' With the fresh perspective of New York, Connery emphasised, he intended to put a stop to 'a lot of fat slob producers living off the backs of lean actors'. Despite previous declarations to the contrary, he wanted to go back to his purist roots and direct a play on

Broadway next year. 'Of course a lot of people say that's madness. When thirty-eight new productions out of forty-four have flopped in the past season this is hardly the time for an untried English director to be welcomed. But I'm going to do it because I like the play and I want to do it.' The determination was admirable but ill-founded and the play, London-based Ted Allan Herman's *The Secret of the World*, announced to star his old friend Shelley Winters, never materialised.

Before embarking on the last exhausting Bond, Connery and Cilento took advantage of the lull to put their house in order. They analysed and confronted the conflicting aspects of their lives together and decided they could not be an effective family unit while both pursued movie careers. Consequently Cilento decided to put her career on hold and concentrate on novel-writing. (Her book, *The Manipulator*, published in 1967, with the dedication 'For Sean' and a jacket designed by Connery, was a moderate success; as was *Hybrid*, its follow-up.) The continuing violation of privacy at Acton, especially after a spate of burglaries – five in all during *Thunderball* – was deemed no longer acceptable. Acacia House went on the market in April 1966, advertised openly under a rambling newspaper notice headed: 'Sean Connery, the motion picture actor, offers for sale the self-styled queen of the suburbs'. The asking price was £17,950, freehold. Connery explained his reason for wanting out with typical frankness: 'People knew the house – after all, there aren't many actors in Acton – and would come and sit and stare at Diane and me in the main room. If it had gone on I'd have been found guilty of assault.' As alternatives, property in Spain – a few vineyard acres with a nondescript farmhouse – was secured and, to the couple's initial great pleasure, a large Victorian house on Putney Heath, slap in the middle of actor-land. While Cilento remodelled her life as a home-maker, Connery dutifully taxied to Pinewood for script talks on *You Only Live Twice*. 'After this,' he told Bannen, 'I will only do the things that passionately interest me for the rest of my life.'

Lewis Gilbert, fresh from *Alfie* with Michael Caine (a movie destined to give Bond a run for his money at the box office through 1966), approached his first commission on a Bond with reservations. 'In the beginning I turned it down,' he said, 'because four films had already been done and the natural reaction was to say, Well, what can *I* contribute? – it's all been done. Then Cubby rang me again and said, You can't turn this down because you have the biggest audience in the world sitting out there waiting for you. And that was interesting. I mean, you can make the greatest movie ever and it will still not find an audience, but with Bond you are guaranteed. Then of course there was the budget. This picture would cost seven or eight million dollars, and, like a general in the field with his tanks and resources, that kind of back-up for a director is pretty alluring. So I decided I'd do this Bond, and try and contribute my own little something to making the saga different.'

With their fingers on the market pulse Broccoli and Saltzman saw the need to freshen Bond too, but their individual ambitions were dogged by personal unease. 'There was a dreadful divide,' Guy Hamilton said. 'Harry had wandered off into projects he whimsically wanted to do, like those Len Deighton spy films [Michael Caine as unglamorous agent Harry Palmer] and Cubby grew tired of Harry's irregular participation in Bond. Harry wasn't as fast on the uptake, ideas-wise, as Cubby – that was part of the trouble too.' Lewis Gilbert confesses he acted as 'a sort of go-between, keeping the peace' but stresses: 'Once the picture got going Cubby and Harry were terrific. With their vast experience, I knew I had people to turn to when I was in trouble and, good God, at times on Bond you needed support.' During pre-production, said Gilbert, Broccoli and Saltzman came close to dissolving their partnership. They finally parted in 1974, with Saltzman selling out to Broccoli and returning to theatrical management. Gilbert remembered, 'They really couldn't stand the sight of each other . . . and things got worse when Sean's dislike for Harry flared. It got so bad Sean wouldn't come on set in Japan when Harry was around. The scenario was, A: he didn't want to be in Japan doing Bond at all. And B: the last person he wanted looking over his creative shoulder was this hard-shelled slave-driver.'

Roald Dahl, the celebrated children's author who had never written a film, was engaged as an extraordinarily offbeat choice to screenwrite the Japanese film. Perhaps, Gilbert suggests, Noël

Coward's observation about Dahl's 'fabulous imagination' with its 'underlying streak of cruelty and macabre unpleasantness and a curiously adolescent emphasis on sex' endeared him to the producers.

Dahl later humorously recounted for *Playboy* his first contact with Broccoli. Never having heard of either of the producers and having seen only *Goldfinger*, he believed the man trying to reach him on the telephone to discuss a possible commission was one Archie Lockley. Patricia Neal, his actress wife who had answered the phone, insisted, 'No, this one is Broccoli, head of the Mafia. You'd better watch out.' Dahl wrote his script in a few weeks, ready for shooting at Pinewood in May. There were plot difficulties in translating this most arcane of Fleming stories, so Dahl and writer Harold Jack Bloom, Gilbert's regular script-fixer, flew out to Japan for revisions in July.

'There were so many problems,' Lewis Gilbert said. 'Apart from Sean's unease, we had a huge row over casting. Up till the very last minute there was no arch villain. Harry swore he'd found a superb Czechoslovakian actor, but the man did a few days in Pinewood and we had to let him go. We roped in Donald Pleasence to plug the gap. Then there was the hassle with the girls. The Bond movies are prepared on the highest diplomatic level – that's to say, Cubby was getting permission to shoot at key sites in Japan by approaching embassies and government ministers and all the rest. So, naturally the Japanese were insistent that certain requirements be met. First we tried to get our Japanese girls in Europe, then Hawaii. But they were too brash and Americanised and all wrong. Then the Japanese people said, in effect, use our own people or forget it. So we had to take Mie Hama and Akiko Wakabayashi, neither of whom could speak English. They went on crash courses, but the problem arose when Akiko picked up her English faster than Mie. Mie was lovely, but she just couldn't get her English down. So we decided to drop her, and I took Tetsuro Tamba [Japanese Secret Service chief in the film] aside and told him our situation and asked him to explain nicely to Mie. He was helpful, he took her out to dinner and told her. The next morning he came to Cubby's office and we were having a meeting and we said, "Well, does she know she's not in the movie?" "Yes," Tamba said, "I told her." "And how did she take it?" Tamba was very philosophical. He said, "She said OK, if she is off the movie she will commit suicide. She cannot go home to Japan and face the loss of honour after all the advance publicity. James Bond is the king of Japan, and she's got the big role opposite him." Harry and Cubby looked at Tamba with mouths open. Then we all said, "Well, on second thoughts she's not so bad. She can keep working at it and we'll fit her in somehow."'

Hama's part, originally to be the larger role of Aki, Bond's agent ally, was swapped with Wakabayashi's Kissy, the pearl-diving island girl Bond later falls for – a part that was less demanding in terms of dialogue.

Connery and Cilento tried desperately to make the three months of location shooting a holiday, attempting to stay close and distance themselves from the usual media mania. While a chartered jet flew the cast and crew one way round the world, the reconciled couple chose the alternative route, going via Manila. It proved a drastic mistake. In the sweltering jam-packed city they were mobbed, pestered in their hotel, ultimately trapped. On arrival in Japan, conditions deteriorated. The lobby of the Tokyo Hilton was crowded day and night by frantic, unsupervised camera-hung newsmen, keen as wild animals. The film trail led south, to Kagoshima – and the swelling, voracious press followed along. Alan Whicker accompanied the crew, travelling with his own, more subtly intrusive BBC camera team, and he had the good grace to sip his Kirin beer, play the distant spectator and admit appalled amazement. Connery, he noted, had 'abandoned his fierce professional concentration and seemed indifferent to the film's progress'. Cilento in an exhausted moment told Whicker: 'Sean's tried beyond normal limits, because everywhere you go there's always someone coming out from behind a tree. Photographers even follow him into the lavatory.'

After *Thunderball* Connery told columnist Sheila Graham only $2,800,000 plus a high percentage would buy him for another Bond; but when *You Only Live Twice* was over he said: 'I don't want to know. It's finished. Bond's been good to me, but I've done my bit. I'm out.'

'I can understand how he felt,' Lewis Gilbert said. 'If he seemed to be "cruising" in certain parts of our movie it was only because he knew the character was immovably second in line to the gadgets, and that bored him, I suppose. For myself, I tried to give Bond a human dimension. By introducing the emotion when the girl Aki is murdered, for example. But Sean had such a strain to put up with, with the fans. Once, when we tried to do a simple shot of him walking down the Ginza we decided the safest way was to hide our camera, let him slip out of a car and amble past – let him vanish in the street strollers. We tried!' Gilbert laughs loud. 'But Sean got out of a car ... and was just pounced upon by a million fans. It was a feeding frenzy, a nightmare!'

*You Only Live Twice*, a kind of advanced *Dr. No* in storyline, did not sweep the box office as its immediate predecessors had done. The reviews, by now, were reflex gestures, regurgitated superlatives primed to fill out entertainment pages in journals good and bad. Politically and socially, Bond was now neutral – a labourer with bourgeois style in a high-living, to all purposes apolitical universe. In *You Only Live Twice* Russia and America were testy brothers naturally vexed by the in-flight thefts of their respective manned space shots. The ubiquitous SPECTRE, led by Blofeld (Pleasence), was the real culprit, stealing the spaceships in hopes of inflaming East–West tensions to the point of annihilative war. Bond unravels all this with functional action and short-circuits a very unlikely Third World War. Not that Connery cared. Robert Robinson's prognosis on *Thunderball* seemed borne out definitively in the end result.

Ian Bannen observed that whatever slender grip the James Bond of *Dr. No* had on dramatic realism was lost for ever with *You Only Live Twice*. James Bond, not Sean Connery, had become the movie star and that, to Connery, rendered the option of vacating the role now imperative. 'It could have been different though,' Connery said later. 'Had the producers not been so greedy, today United Artists could belong to Connery, Broccoli and Saltzman.' It didn't happen like that, so Connery worked out his contract, pocketed his quixotic dreams and set off in 1967 in search of new worlds.

*       *       *

Out of Bondage, he had time to contemplate the compromises and the unreached goals. In Bannen's recall, 'He seemed to take a long, sharp intake of breath and reassess everything.' His love for golf – which now had him playing off a handicap of thirteen – was a focus, however whimsical, of what might have been. 'I considered turning pro,' he later said. 'But I'm not sure it would have made me any happier. I'm an actor, and I love my job most.' Always a scribbler, he concentrated for a while on drafting movie storylines and teasing out the screenplay-of-his-dreams: 'My own *Macbeth*, to be made in Scotland with Scottish actors, which I can direct myself.'

But none of these musings came to much. 'Writing, football and golf anchored him,' said John Boorman, who got to know him well in the late 60s. 'In the hiatus period he liked to write poetry, which he didn't show around. There was always the feeling that he withdrew to regroup, to reorganise his thoughts – but there was always the certainty that he would come back before the cameras, because that was the air he breathed.'

The opportunities afforded by uncontracted idleness provided Connery with what was to become an alternative ongoing intellectual stimulus – an outlet for investment, financial and cultural, in Scotland's future. The door was opened by the revolutionary Scottish industrialist Sir Iain Stewart, nationally known in the late 60s for his brave campaigns to reduce unemployment and rejuvenate Clydeside, specifically in his Fairfields Shipyard plan. Connery met Stewart, a Glaswegian, at a golfing society dinner in London and liked him. In casual chat, the industrialist detailed his five-year plan for Fairfields, a courageous labour-management experiment that had started with the support of George Brown at the DEA, Jim Callaghan at the Treasury and Ray Gunter at the Ministry of Labour. The plan, in essence, slackened potentially stifling union regulations and allowed a workers' voice in management. The real viability of the plan was never tested because in 1968 Stewart made the mistake of allowing Fairfields to enter the disastrous Upper Clyde Shipbuilders merger, a scheme that ended in bankruptcy within fifteen months. But, at the time, Connery was attracted to Stewart's radical experimentation and, a socialist at heart, offered to make a documentary film about the problems of Clydeside.

*The Bowler and the Bunnet* (a bunnet is the Lowlands Scots equivalent of the flat cap) was written and directed by Connery over a few weeks late in 1967 and shown on Scottish Television. Efforts to sell it to regional independent television, even the BBC, failed, but the documentary was regarded as good of its kind and served to highlight the positive progress Stewart was making at Fairfields. Connery was especially proud of his little film because it spoke up for Scotland and articulated, for the first time, his own nationalist spirit. 'Stewart was doing something at Fairfields that hadn't been done so successfully anywhere in the country, including England. He was bridging that terrible gulf between the bosses and the workers and he was breaking down the petty suspicions between unions. He even had carpenters doing painters' work when necessary and he had union men sitting in the boardroom. It was all working famously and production was going up. That was the social value. What the film did for me in personal terms was make me realise that part of me belonged to that kind of background. I couldn't turn my back on it.'

The failure of Fairfields in the UCS merger was an industrial and social tragedy, but it started Connery on a course of edifying social activism that has become a lifelong commitment. The friendship with the sagacious Stewart inspired a concept that was grander than union-management control. The Scottish International Educational Trust, founded in 1970 to provide bursaries for bright but underprivileged Scots and to supply cash for educational projects like the establishment of a drama chair at Strathclyde University, started life as a modest charity golf tournament set up by Connery along the lines of the tried-and-tested Bing Crosby Pro-Am, a perennially successful charity fund-raiser. In 1968 during early preparation for the tournament Connery announced that 'part of the money raised is going to be used researching the reasons why Scots leave Scotland. I've already talked to St Andrews University about an ongoing research programme.' Behind this, for those who knew him, was a personal liberation: the clarification of his nationalism and a dawning of his own political potential. 'I was reminded of the return of the prodigal son,' said Edinburgh friend Andrew Fyall. 'Sean had never actually got Scotland out of his blood, to give him credit, but he never gave any big indication till then of national pride. The full picture of his vision for Scotland wasn't immediately clear. It came in stages. But the Trust, and his work with Stewart, was the start of a political chain reaction.'

Following a firm restatement of his allegiance to 'Scottish interests first' on television in *The Eamonn Andrews Show*, Connery was formally approached by the National Party to stand as their candidate at the upcoming general election, representing an unspecified constituency. He turned the offer down because 'I would not be so presumptuous as to sit for any political candidacy without sufficient work, background and knowledge. I suppose it would be easy enough to let lieutenants spoonfeed me, but I'm not familiar enough with the details across the country. I'd get found out.'

Bit by bit, in the slowest increments, movies were drawing him back. But the movies on offer, initially, were, inevitably, quasi-Bonds. Charles Feldman's offer to bring him back to the big screen as a comedy Bond in the spoof *Casino Royale* was dismissed with contempt, as was a clutch of ridiculous 'cardboard booby' spy stories. When at last an offer took his fancy it surprised no one, least of all his brother Neil, that the subject was a Western, scheduled for shooting early in 1968 in Mexico, called *Shalako*.

Edward Dmytryk, the director, chose Connery as 'the ideal for Louis L'Amour's frontier scout hero', and producers Euan Lloyd and Dimitri de Grunwald endorsed this view with a $1,200,000 pay cheque (to be cashed in over a phased nine-month period) plus a generous 30 per cent of net profits. Connery was childishly enthusiastic about the project, though he cooled a little when told Brigitte Bardot would be his co-star. Bardot's star-studded ego was well known to be bigger than her going price ($350,000 for *Shalako*, plus a cut in profits) and, true to form, she insisted on a sounding-out meeting with Connery before she signed papers. In his intimate biography of Bardot, Willi Frischauer suggests Connery's first response was wary, but on meeting Bardot face to face at Deauville the good vibrations calmed things down. Gunter

Sachs, Brigitte's current husband, according to Frischauer, 'feared the worst', and left the party. But within a few days Connery was safely back in Putney and Bardot reconciled in Sachs's arms.

Honor Blackman, a co-star, describes *Shalako* as not a happy film. The threat of a labour strike in Mexico forced Lloyd to relocate to dusty old Almeria and events shuddered to an unpromising start when Bardot delayed filming by arriving days late in a showy Rolls-Royce and with an entourage of photographers and hangers-on, to take up queenly residence at the Hotel Aguadulce. 'It was a jolt to begin with,' said Blackman. 'But once Sean was over the bad start he just kept his head down and kept out of it. He took a rented villa nearby, where he stayed with his family and made a point of concentrating on doing as good a job as possible under distracting circumstances.' The circumstances were not conducive to the kind of ensemble work Connery loved. In her personal plot to remain the constant teenager, Bardot brought to Almeria exactly the kind of press-heavy circus that Connery had hoped to leave behind with Bond. Bardot's open rows with former lover, the actor Stephen Boyd, made matters worse. Worse again were her threats to quit the location before half her footage was in the can.

'Eddie Dmytryk's patience was truly remarkable,' said Blackman. 'Then, given Brigitte's temperament, I guess we all deserved credit.'

Ten years before, the story of a true-as-an-arrow Western hero despatched by the army to guide a party of wealthy aristocrats out of dangerous Indian country would have made Connery barter his soul. Now he almost regretted signing on. Satisfied enough with his own performance, he was relieved when the picture wrapped up only slightly over schedule. Returning to London, he awarded himself the gift of a new (well, second-hand) Jensen for endurance and self-control beyond the call of duty.

All the publicity promises – 'the most sensuous film BB has ever made', 'Connery and BB's electrifying twosome' – were not upheld in *Shalako*'s final screen cut. The movie was not a conventional studio production, rather Lloyd had pre-financed it by procuring advance distribution guarantees from 30 separate countries – which was just as well. Reviews clashed fiercely, divided between those who thought this first ambitious British Western an out-and-

*Right* In his early teens Connery joined the Sea Cadets, based at his old alma mater, Bruntsfield School. For a yearly fee of 25 shillings he learned the basics of seamanship. The Cadets also spent a week at Rosyth aboard HMS *Nelson* where Connery slept on deck under the stars and dreamed of a life in the Royal Navy.

*Below* Fet-Lor Amateurs was Connery's first football team (*third from the right, middle row*). While playing with them he was spotted by Bonnyrigg Rose, the top junior side in Scotland, and enlisted as an outside right for a series of trials. He was offered permanent placement as a semi-professional at ten shillings a week, but turned it down to pursue his bodybuilding.

*Above* Connery was 28 when he made his first Hollywood 'breakthrough' starring in Disney's *Darby O'Gill and the Little People* with Janet Munro. Having started his career singing in the chorus of *South Pacific*, he welcomed the chance to sing 'Pretty Irish Girl', which was released as a single but made no impact on the record charts.

*Left* Connery arrives in Nassau to film *Thunderball* in the spring of 1965, accompanied by Terence Young (*far left*) and co-producer Kevin McClory (*second from left*). With his marriage to Diane Cilento showing pressure cracks and the tedium of Bondmania, Connery's rows with Harry Saltzman and Cubby Broccoli (*right*) signalled the imminent split with Bond and a change of career direction.

*Above* In January 1962 the legend begins: Connery and Ursula Andress start filming *Dr. No*. The Crab Key swamp sequence was filmed near Ian Fleming's home on Jamaica's North Shore. Fleming visited the location, taking time out from writing *On Her Majesty's Secret Service*.

*Above* After the success of *Dr. No*, director Terence Young tested scores of European actresses for the role of Tatiana in *From Russia With Love*. Daniela Bianchi, a Miss Universe runner-up, won the role and turned in a memorably sensitive performance that consolidated the importance of the female counterpart in the movie series.

*Below* Connery's relationship with *Thunderball*'s Claudine Auger – on screen and off – was among the best in the Bond series. Auger, a former Miss France, said she 'identified' with Domino, the passionate, generous adventurer of the story.

*Below* Cashing in on Bondmania, Italian director Alberto Demartino cast Neil, Connery's younger brother, in a half-serious spy thriller called *Operation Kid Brother*, populated by Bond stars like Adolfo Celi and (seen here with Neil) *From Russia With Love*'s Daniela Bianchi. The movie was released in 1968, followed by Neil's second – and last – movie, Gerry Levy's camp horror flick, *The Body Stealers*, in 1969.

*Left* Bernard Lee, cast as 'M' by director Terence Young, became one of the cornerstone talents of the early Bond movies. He and Connery enjoyed a harmonious friendship.

*Right* Connery at work in Ireland with producer Kevin McClory (*right*) and novelist Len Deighton (*centre*) on the script for the 'alternative Bond' that would evolve over ten years of legal wrangling into 1983's misjudged *Never Say Never Again*.

*Left* By 1965 and the release of *Thunderball*, the fourth 007 movie, Connery's global success was paralleled only by the Beatles – at the age of 35, his name was a byword for blue chip entertainment.

*Left* Diane Cilento was an established stage and movie actress when she met Connery. It was she he consulted before accepting the role of James Bond, and they married on 29 November 1962, six weeks after the premiere of *Dr. No.*

*Right* On 6 May 1975, two years after divorcing Diane, Connery married Micheline Boglio Roquebrune in Gibraltar. He had just completed shooting *The Wind and the Lion* and was in the process of settling in permanent residence near Marbella, in Spain.

*Left* Connery with son Jason, who would follow him on to the stage, into films and, with some trepidation, play Ian Fleming in a television biopic.

Alfred Hitchcock liked Connery but told director Francois Truffaut he 'wasn't convinced' the actor fitted the role in *Marnie*.

With John Huston amid the Atlas Mountains in North Africa for *The Man Who Would be King*. The movie is widely rated as among Connery's best of the 70s.

*The Offence*, a dark thriller made at the height of the Bond boom, seemed strategically designed to smash typecasting. Here Connery teamed up with one of his favourite directors, Sidney Lumet – they would go on to make two more quality movies together.

Michael Crichton directed Connery in *The First Great Train Robbery* a decade before turning his attention to novel writing and hitting the jackpot with *Jurassic Park*.

*Above* Brian De Palma's *The Untouchables*, broadly developed by David Mamet from the 50s television series, finally won Connery an Academy Award in 1987.

*Below* After a throat polyps scare, ridiculously overplayed in the tabloid press, Connery returned to form, if not full vocal confidence, in *The Hunt for Red October*, based on Tom Clancy's naval bestseller.

*Above* A triumph to match the contemporary success of late-era conveyor belt Bond – *Entrapment*: sex, danger, wit and war in the company of Catherine Zeta-Jones.

*Below* Gus Van Sant's *Finding Forrester* was a profound personal triumph that coincided with millennial changes for Connery: a change of home base from Spain to the Bahamas, a knighthood and a gloves-off commitment to the Scottish nationalist cause.

*Left* From an Edinburgh tenement to the Hollywood Walk of Fame: a journey of seventy years and countless schemes and dreams.

*Below* Connery leaves Holyrood Palace, having received his knighthood from the Queen in July 2000. His response was humility and pride – for Scotland.

out dud, and those who admired the circuslike motley of black former football star Woody Strode as an Indian chief, purring over Honor Blackman as the faithless aristocratic wife and Eric Sykes, playing a French chef. No one said much about Bardot, though she herself conceded, '*Shalako* is Sean Connery's film. He carried the whole weight of it on his shoulders.' Marjorie Bilbow in *Screen International* declined this humble baton: 'Connery seems so determined to erase all memories of James Bond that he allows the foreground figure of Shalako to fade into middle distance.'

Few kids at the Blue Halls would have been impressed.

# 13. A 60s' HANGOVER

With Bond buried and the wound-licking spree of idleness with *Shalako*, the long-dreamt-of Western, past, Connery slumped to a career stance that appeared something between defeatism and apprehensive torpor. 'He was, momentarily, completely unsure of himself,' said Robert Hardy. 'Everything he did, he questioned. I remember a friend visited him in Putney, where he'd had this German hot-and-cold shower installed in the basement, and it had cost a few hundred quid. He agonised over it. A few hundred quid was a big deal! In Scotland his dad could've lived for a year on a few hundred quid. Sean wasn't happy, and didn't know how to *get* happy. He tried to give up cigarettes and cut down on his drinking. He tried many things. One got the feeling that here was a man who wanted to retrace his steps, go back to the past – all this was evident in his fixation with doing good for Edinburgh's poor, all that – but he'd lost his way.'

Dennis Selinger, Connery's new agent-manager, replacing Richard Hatton who had retired to go into production, was concerned too. He believed Connery needed to capitalise on the lingering Bond boom, but to work fast to establish himself as a separate, adaptable entity. At round-table meetings in Selinger's office in central London the agent outlined his proposals: Connery must recognise that his non-Bond films had largely flopped and, out of Bondage, he could lose ground fast. He must not sit and wait for offers, he must go out and grab whatever was available, meet directors and moguls, *work*. 'I'd proved this with Mike Caine,' Selinger said. 'If one wants to make international impact the surest system is to make as many films as possible. I told Sean, if one can do four or five movies a year, one is bound to hit and that one can up your price and keep you on top. Sean wasn't too convinced. "But *The Hill* won't come along every week," I advised him. "You must get out and push it."'

Very reluctantly Connery went back to work, taking on two

offers that were to prove disappointing culs-de-sac – *The Molly Maguires*, directed by Martin Ritt for Paramount, and the Italian–Russian co-production *The Red Tent*. To date, *The Molly Maguires* has lost about $10 million (negative cost, inflation adjusted) and *The Red Tent* about £9 million. Both rate among the fifty biggest box-office losers of all time.

Connery had been keen on *The Molly Maguires*, a project first suggested to him while Ritt was directing *Hombre* and Connery was visiting Diane. Blacklisted from TV, where he started his career during the McCarthyist drive of the early fifties, Ritt was enamoured of the idea of a movie about the abused, impoverished Irish miners in the Pennsylvania coal pits of the 1870s banding together (as the secret Molly Maguires) and taking murderous action against their employers. The story of *The Molly Maguires*, as written by Ritt's lifelong friend Walter Bernstein, revolved round the infiltration of the Irish group by a management agent, McParlan, played by Richard Harris, who eventually befriends the miners' leader Kehoe, played by Connery, and switches sides. Though based on fact, the plot was fictional and metaphorical and somehow, in its grey-faced telling, sank in arty analogy. The critics mostly disliked the film and found little to rejoice about in Connery's unsympathetic character. Many disdained specious crusading, though Connery himself defended the movie's *raison*, seeing it as an extension of his work-for-the-people on *The Bowler and the Bunnet*.

While the movie was being made in Pennsylvania and at Paramount Studios in Hollywood, *On Her Majesty's Secret Service*, the sixth Bond, progressed at Pinewood, with Australian newcomer George Lazenby portraying the hero. Connery declined to comment on Bond developments but, when questioned, saw no loss of face in his own second-billing on *The Molly Maguires*. Queried about his declining popularity, he said, 'They're paying me a million dollars for this picture. For that kind of money they can put a mule ahead of me.'

In Pennsylvania he was moody, said Richard Harris, but generally good company. Though he was ready to talk to the press, publicists were instructed that questions about a return to Bond were taboo. The weather was good, too good, during most of the shoot and he suffered dehydration – as he had done during the making of *You Only Live Twice* in Japan. The suffering eased some need for purgation within him and he bragged about doctors having to give him tea with whole lemons squeezed into it and salt crackers to stabilise his metabolism.

Ritt recognised the failure of his film just about as fast as Connery – though he certainly suffered worse for it. Later he admitted it 'went on its ass, didn't do any business at all, and though I wasn't completely without employment [after it], employment wasn't as accessible to me as it had been. *The Molly Maguires* was quite an expensive film, a costly exercise in every definition.'

Apart from three short weeks in Russia on *The Red Tent* early in 1969, employment was no richer for Connery, though this was largely by his own choosing. What followed was a period of film inactivity, which lasted almost two years. Ian Bannen said: 'Part of it was identity crisis, yes. Another part as the general late 60s hangover syndrome. All the icons were down. The Beatles were hobbling back from the Rishikesh, popping LSD, doing the drab, indulgent *Let It Be*. And James Bond was flagging out too. Sean had been on this speeding merry-go-round for six years and when he jumped off everything was swirly. He was trying to get on his feet, trying on various masks, one might say. For a while we saw him as the convert to art house films – that was the general impression after *The Hill* and *The Molly Maguires* – but he's a pragmatist, so that didn't last long.'

In the hiatus, whenever there was a hiatus for the mature Connery, business raised its head. Though part of his continuing association with Iain Stewart's pioneering interests arose from what Bannen called 'a hippie-trendy sense of social duty', many non-charitable, less altruistic investments were explored as well. The Fairfields friendship led to the establishment of a merchant bank, Dunbar & Co, with impressive panelled offices in Pall Mall, as well as a multitude of large-share investments in another bank and other companies in the US. He professed himself a socialist, but saw no conflict in his appetite for good investments and sound returns. 'Golf, food and drink: that's what I enjoy,' he told the *Express*. 'And the only point in having money is to indulge the [things you like].' Inevitably the dichotomy invited cynicism. *France Soir*, the French newspaper, was indelicate enough to suggest Connery had gone to seed and been forced out of Bond by the producers because his waistline had thickened from too much high living. Connery sued. In the High Court David Hirst, QC, for Connery told the judge, 'It was asserted quite erroneously that the producers of the James Bond films had dispensed with his services because he was no longer fit enough to play the role of James Bond.' Connery had, said Hirst, checked his waistline with a measuring tape, recorded an acceptable inch of flab and phoned his lawyers. On 17 February 1969 *France Soir* retracted its statement, apologised for the libel and settled with Connery for an undisclosed sum. Connery was as effusively delighted as he had been when Warners was forced to hand over $50,000 when *A Fine Madness* ran over schedule.

Having holidayed in Australia at Cilento's home and again living hermit-like, looking after the hundred muscat grapevines he had just planted on his Spanish farm, Connery moved on to Leningrad and Moscow for *The Red Tent*. He liked Moscow, despite the fact that his hotel room was routinely bugged, but found Leningrad drab. At a top-class Leningrad restaurant he deplored the ineptitude of out-of-step dancers performing to a balalaika band. 'They were hopeless. They wouldn't have lasted ten minutes at the Dennistown Palais.' Russia was all right, but not the kind of place he'd ever want to call home.

Deciding where exactly home should be, Bannen observed, had become a contentious issue. Suggestions that he was about to flee Britain and opt for tax exile in Bermuda were dismissed, as were reports that he banked all his loot in Switzerland and had some personal grand plan for a Swiss escape. 'Scotland would be as far as I'd consider moving,' he insisted in a television interview, but among friends he aired his angry views on British taxes and weather. 'Because he loved to play golf whenever he could, he sought out the sunshine,' Michael Caine said. 'But that wasn't the reason he started to consider emigration. The main reason was injustice. In Britain, because of the punitive taxes, he believed he was discouraged from working and the alternative of squandering time and talent by just sitting on his backside was morally offensive to him.' Ten years later Connery admitted that other upsetting factors were involved. Just when he'd thought he could take it easy, his finances were found to be 'really in a mess. The accountants were unscrambling what they could. But the practical answer for me was to get out.'

Before all the upheavals of the early 70s, *The Red Tent* unfurled. In concept an ambitious, metaphysical film, it failed through heavy-handed direction and dull acting performances. Peter Finch dominated the film as General Nobile, leader of the ill-fated transarctic dirigible expedition, who is visited forty years after the event by the ghosts of his comrades. The events of the debacle, and the rescue attempt led by Roald Amundsen, played by Connery, provided a jarring, never-fully-realised melodramatic narrative. Connery's fee for the film was not large, and though he received second billing it seemed hardly deserved. Roger Greenspun in the *New York Times* wrote, 'To have taken a situation with such potential and to have made it as dull as director Mikhail Kalatozov [did] must have taken great ingenuity.'

In November Connery's friend the journalist Roderick Mann was dreamily recording in his column: 'What a splendid year it has been for Mr Sean Connery! Most of it has been spent playing golf. And why not, when you think of it? What's the point of working hard and making money if you're not going to enjoy yourself?' That sugar-coated version was far from the truth. Tired of inactivity and golf-sated, Connery told Bannen he just wanted to get back to work, get his teeth into some projects that meant something. 'Two things absorbed him,' said Bannen. 'His obsession was the movie version of *Macbeth*, which he thought could be majestic. The other was a theatre play which he wanted to direct, which surprised me since he had professed himself finished with theatre.'

*I've Seen You Cut Lemons*, written by Ted Allan Herman (whose play, *The Secret of the World*, Connery had previously been announced to direct) became the full focus of Connery's creativity.

Assigned – at last – as director, he cast Diane in the lead, playing opposite old friend Robert Hardy.

'We started rehearsals at a church hall in Putney, not far from where Sean and Diane lived,' Hardy remembered. 'It was, of course, a joy to be working with them because I admired them both for their separate talents – but I must say I accepted the play against my instincts. It was too complex a work, the odds were heavily against it even remotely succeeding.' The play was a two-hander – just Hardy and Cilento as Canadian brother and sister – which investigated at close-hand the frustrations and passions of two people descending towards an incestuous involvement. At rehearsals in the church hall Connery was never less than positive-minded, but Hardy is not so sure about the director's vision of likely success. 'Sean knew how tricky it would be, but he had a flair that forced the best out of a performance. Once he'd started, there was no turning back.'

More than anything else, Hardy was impressed by Connery's passion. 'It's a condition not uncommon in our trade, where stars of great international acclaim like Sean decide to go back to their roots, though I doubt if he saw himself in the long term as a director. He just then felt the need to do it, to rebel against the frivolity of other areas of the business, to work *at the heart* of the craft. It was not an ego exercise for him. It was a learning venture.'

Prior to the play's opening at Oxford and then going on tour, Connery asked Hardy to stay for a week at his Putney home for further rehearsals. Hardy found 'a big, empty house, quite attractive but with the bare necessities of furniture, though also some interesting paintings. We rehearsed hard during the day and talked long into the night. In the end, I think it helped our performances. And, God, given the material, we needed all the help we could get.'

Every morning Connery allotted a time for Hardy to utilise the house 'think tank', a zinc-lined fully enclosed sentry box which occupied a corner in the upstairs study. 'Sean believed sitting in there, totally shut up, concentrated the mind and conserved nervous energy. He used it, and claimed it worked. For myself, well, I didn't rush to install one in my own home.'

*I've Seen You Cut Lemons* opened in late November to bad notices. The month-long tour took it to Newcastle and Manchester, thence to the Fortune Theatre in London where 'it hit the deck, but *good!*' Hardy was not surprised. 'I'd jumped in, eyes closed, nose held tight, feet together. I had the gravest reservations from the start, I suspect all of us had.' After five days in London the play was handed the Black Spot. Connery expressed only mild disappointment to his cast. 'When word came that we were to close Sean responded in the same positive way he had right through the setting-up. He didn't, like many directors, disappear. Backstage he gave us our little talking to. He said it wasn't our fault, and so on – all the kind things one can possibly deploy at such a sad time. The alternative attitudes and phrases are limited, of course. But Sean took it genuinely well. He tried, he failed. I think we had all done our best with very, very tough material.' Most critics felt the elaborate scaffold-design set by Sean Kenny dwarfed the players, and, like Hardy, that the play itself was too bizarre. Connery received some lukewarm compliments, but every review, implicitly if not explicitly, called him back to James Bond.

The disappointments stacked up. The radical movie *Macbeth* might have been next, but Roman Polanski suddenly announced his own version, backed by *Playboy* finances, and Connery's second major artistic departure was shelved.

Dennis Selinger's insistence on more commercial work to build on Bond finally paid off when Connery accepted a new American movie project to be directed by Sidney Lumet. Of all the directors Connery had worked with, Lumet exemplified the qualities he most admired – discipline, efficiency in bringing the work in on time, depth in the script. *The Hill* enshrined Connery's happiest professional memories so now, even before reading *The Anderson Tapes*, he was ready for recommitment. Selinger was especially pleased because *The Anderson Tapes* was to be a fun caper movie aimed at a wide audience, as opposed to the usually lofty Lumet fare. 'It was the kind of renewal he needed,' said Selinger. 'Plus I think he needed to laugh a bit at himself at that time.'

Shot on location in New York to the tightest of schedules, *The Anderson Tapes* was a resounding hit, rocketing Connery back into the American top ten box-office draws for 1971, a feat that seemed unreachable after *Shalako*. Once again, Lumet and Connery drew the best from each other and the same Roger Greenspun who had condemned *The Red Tent* in the *New York Times* rejoiced in 'Sean Connery's laconic, attractive, beautifully subdued John Anderson in a movie where the quality of professionalism appears in rather lovely manifestations.' Despite this, Greenspun accurately pinpointed the fact that *The Anderson Tapes* – a linear treasure heist yarn – was no more than 'a minor story'.

In March, three months before *The Anderson Tapes* premiere, a press release out of the blue announced that Connery had been talking again with Broccoli and Saltzman and a startling new deal to reprise James Bond had been reached: Connery would return to the mink-lined harness for a fee of $1.2 million, plus a percentage of the gross. Every penny earned would go to the newly formed Scottish International Educational Trust, whose chairman was Sir Samuel Curran, Vice Chancellor of Strathclyde University and among whose trustees were distinguished names like Iain Stewart and racing champion Jackie Stewart. The personal bait for Connery, it was stated, had been the bonus offer of United Artists' support for any two films of his own choosing, to be made after this single, final Bond.

Connery's closest friends were stunned. Ian Bannen said, 'He never told me he was even thinking about it. I read about it in the papers. Did it seem out of character for him to reverse the pledge he'd made a couple of years before? Well, put it this way: it had nothing to do with [George Lazenby's] failure as Bond. It could never have happened the year before. Sean had things to work out of his system, and the exercise strengthened him. He resumed Bond, I believe, with two equally important motives – to help his charity and to restore his market position.'

It was a transformed Sean Connery who, late in February 1971, signed with Eon and David Picker, UA's Bond fan-in-residence, to make *Diamonds Are Forever*. Gone was the pale-faced tension just the word 'Bond' had induced, the urge to row with Saltzman and Broccoli, the lion's mane of thinning hippie hair, the confusion of purpose. Gone too was the pretence of permanence in the relationship with Cilento. It was change, all change.

At the High Court trial two years before Connery had given his address as Curzon Street rather than Putney, a sidetrack of some significance to those who knew him. Now, he was open in his feelings about the marriage. He told friends it was over, that he had real respect for Cilento, but they could never be compatible. He bought a flat overlooking the Thames at Chelsea Embankment, in a block where Hitler's ambassador von Ribbentrop had once lived, and removed all his possessions from Putney. It was a whole new lifestyle. Casual acquaintanceships with women friends were more actively pursued, and Connery unapologetically told an interviewer, 'Sex is still important to me.' Nothing more was confided. Nothing more would be said. His private life, as he always insisted, was nobody's business.

Contrary to the consensus of jaundiced jibing, the recent Bond, *On Her Majesty's Secret Service* had not, without Connery, fallen on its face. True, in the series to date it was the slowest earner at the box office. But then *You Only Live Twice*, its predecessor with Connery, marked a decline from *Thunderball*. Furthermore, the kind of invidious comparison fledgling George Lazenby was subjected to advanced a reputation for the film which related not at all to its achievements. Far and away the most human Bond story, rich in pathos and irony, *OHMSS* surefootedly took its place alongside *From Russia with Love* as a triumph of British cinema – and stimulated Connery's appetite for challenge.

As eulogy and lament for all that was best in Bond, indeed in 60s' cinema, *OHMSS* would, everyone knew, take some beating. Moreover, its storyline effectively completed a Bond cycle: Richard Maibaum had started *Dr. No* with the raw material of a boisterous, not-too-far-from-juvenile fist-fighter policing the lions' lairs of the world. By *OHMSS* Bond was weathered and weakened – a weary man given to melancholy, finally settling for the emotional shield of marriage. Guy Hamilton, who had been signed by Eon to make this new Connery-Bond, was immediately aware of the need to construct a brand-new James Bond persona.

'I was initially under the impression we were going with a new actor after *On Her Majesty's*,' Hamilton said. 'John Gavin was a possible star, and there were others. Myself, I suggested an affable gent called Burt Reynolds, but the producers said no, he's only a stunt man. So, I worked on the script a little in London, and then Tom Mankiewicz [the writer] was called in to redevelop this Bond character. So, off to America we went – we knew America was to be our setting, having considered France and a few other places – and got down to some hard rebuilding. After *On Her Majesty's*, which for me was slow and had lots of overage [overtime expenses], we needed a fresh, tight type of story. By the time I was told Sean had signed with David Picker and Eon, we had our script finished and it was quite a departure from the old Bond Sean was familiar with. Above all the others it was larger than life, zany. Sean came out to America in April and we had just a day or two with him before we started shooting, and he looked over what we had and agreed it was good. He suggested alterations – attitudes and a line here or there – but fundamentally he agreed that this Bond must be exaggerated and expanded after the kind of saturnine presence that had gone before in *On Her Majesty's Secret Service*.'

*Diamonds Are Forever* was the first American Bond, ostensibly based at Pinewood but, because most of the shooting was in Nevada and California, utilising Universal Studios in Hollywood as its main base. In part, Eon's selection of America was motivated by the promise of maximum media cover. And the strategy worked. On the heels of Connery's arrival at Las Vegas came the old bandwagon, journalists from everywhere (even Japan again), this time fattened by dark gossip that had surrounded the enigmatic personage of 'Bond' in retirement. Connery was unusually amenable, prepared to talk to most about anything; but there was speculation among the discerning about the seriousness of his comments. Though his views about the decline in Bond script values were well known, he announced, straight-faced, that *Diamonds* was 'the best script I've ever had' – curious, Ian Bannen thought, 'because, let's face it, the thing emasculated the [Bond] character as never before'. Questioned about future prospects in light of the bonus two-picture deal that went with Bond he stated, 'There's no doubt that Bond made me a success, and made it possible for me to do other things. But I won't stay an actor, that's for sure.' Directing *Macbeth*, even in competition with Polanski, might be the way forward; but to the few journalists who were old sparring friends he confided that his current fulfilment came not from movies, but from his business investments and his hopes for the Educational Trust. In a candid conversation with Peter Evans he admitted that *Diamonds* was an 'act of enriching exorcism' which would help his charity, help his businesses and, with luck, perk his career. He did not, he stressed, wish to make for himself 'another fortune – I don't want that kind of maniacal power'. Essentially this Bond was a catalyst. 'With this picture I'm finishing part of my life. I will have accomplished quite a few things, and bought a bit of breathing space to look at my life and decide what I'm going to withdraw from, reach for, what I really need.'

Guy Hamilton found Connery very relaxed and clear about his acting future. He had laid down laws about this Bond with David Picker: the shoot must not run longer than 16 weeks; if it did a penalty of $145,000 per week would be added to his salary. His principal purpose was to move on, to broaden his horizons and perhaps find more intelligently conceived popular films like *The Anderson Tapes*. Clearly proud of Lumet's movie, he arranged a special private viewing, pre-premiere, in Las Vegas during the warm-up weeks of *Diamonds*. Chorus lines from all the big Vegas shows were invited, on equal footing with the marquee stars. Though Connery was obviously feeling some disaffection with Bond, at the same time, the obvious high quality of *The Anderson Tapes* had demonstrated that he was still on peak form, regardless of the muddle of *The Red Tent*, and he was clearly chomping at the bit to get going again.

As on *Goldfinger*, Hamilton's refined technique of knowing what he wanted to shoot and going unwaveringly at it satisfied Connery. 'With a limited number of days,' Hamilton said, 'one can't "have a bash". One has to clearly perceive the thing. All our problems were worked out before we shot a foot of film.' Saltzman and Broccoli prudently steered clear of the set and Connery was put up in the presidential suite of the best hotel in Vegas. 'Golf was his only outlet,' said Hamilton. 'We almost had it written into our contracts that we had this one day off per week to take a helicopter and fly to one of the great courses nearby. Sean unwound there. As for gambling, he didn't do much – threw a few dice maybe, tried the one-arm bandits. Basically he was there for the job, and his sights were set further away.'

Rumours about a romance with Jill St John circulated but both stars assiduously avoided compromising off-the-set photographs by dining in private. St John had originally been assigned the part of Plenty O'Toole, a peripheral character devised by Hamilton, who would be Bond's only minor fling beyond the heroine, Tiffany Case. Hamilton then decided she was wasted as Plenty, but just right for the 'brassy, hard-nut Tiffany'. Some rejigging ensued and Lana Wood, raven-haired sister of Natalie, was cast as Plenty while St John took the bigger role.

'The chemistry between Sean and Jill was undeniably interesting,' Hamilton reckoned. 'And that was important to me. One of my interminable gripes about Bond concerns the women. I've always felt Sean especially needed a strong co-lead, a woman who could answer up to him, or appear equal in talent. Jill was quite unique, because she got what he was all about, she *read* him well, so we could put *personal* chemistry on to the screen.'

After nine weeks in America, cast and crew made for Pinewood and the location work in Europe. Connery remained cheerful, though tired from the unrelenting schedule he had set himself. At Pinewood he looked slighty bored, slightly overweight. His toupee was streaked with grey and his eyebrows bushier than usual. He looked, journalist Tony Crawley commented, like 'Bond getting set for his pension'; yet he remained placid enough. As time ran out the schedule tightened and Hamilton speeded up. All journalists were ejected and an atmosphere of closed-door production descended. UA was only too happy to support Connery's no-compromise concentration. Having forked out more than a million of the seven-millon-dollar budget for him, there was a reluctance to open the chequebook again.

A record of the last days of filming indicates the pressure:

Thursday (London):

| | |
|---|---|
| 0715: | Car collects Connery from home for transfer to Pinewood. |
| 0830: | Filming of Metz laboratory sequence commences. |
| 1600: | Filming wraps. |
| 1800: | Transfer Connery, St John, Saltzman & Hamilton to Heathrow. |
| 1955: | Fly to Frankfurt. |
| 2055: | Arrive Frankfurt. Press conference. |
| Midnight: | Break. |

Friday (Frankfurt):

| | |
|---|---|
| 0700: | Make-up & wardrobe call at hotel. |
| 0800: | Filming on set [Lufthansa jet] at airport. |
| 1400: | Filming complete. [Connery and St John lunch aboard jet] |
| 1650: | Depart for Amsterdam. |
| 2030: | Press conference in Amsterdam. |
| 2200: | Break. |

Saturday (Amsterdam):

| | |
|---|---|
| 1200: | Connery's call – after lie-in and late breakfast. |
| 1215: | Filming Bond's drive to rendezvous with Tiffany. |
| 1630: | Daylight shoot finished. |
| 2100: | Night Shoot. Film Bond scenes outside Tiffany's apartment. |
| Midnight: | Break. |

In John Boorman's words, brilliance often arises from adversity; but in the case of *Diamonds Are Forever* an unblended script of disparate elements made the task impossible for Connery and Hamilton. Only three chapters of Fleming's novel formed the basis of the movie and clearly much more could have been use-fully adapted. Instead, a cocktail of Barnum–Vegas razzmatazz and unctuous humour inflated the windbag story where Bond, masquerading as a diamond smuggler, cracks Blofeld's latest plan to use laser-weapon satellites to hold the world to ransom.

Though the film finished on schedule in August, on time for the announced Christmas release, the pressure fractures were so evident as to be laughable. The kind of continuity errors that had a stunt car driving down a narrow alley on two wheels, going in balanced left and coming out tilted right, amused uncritical fans but reviewers were less gullible. *Commonwealth* magazine pined for authentic Fleming, while welcoming Connery, the essence of the series' success, back: 'The scriptwriters Maibaum and Mankiewicz, along with director Guy Hamilton, seem unsure why they are making another Bond feature just now. Their one fresh idea is to throw in some self-parody, not much relief from almost two hours of Bondage but all the film really has to offer.'

By the time such reviews were circulating Connery was too deeply involved in other matters – the promotion of *The Anderson Tapes* and preparation for yet another grand new departure – to be bothered. David Picker and Eon weren't much alarmed either. *Diamonds Are Forever* opened simultaneously in New York and London at Christmas and established box-office records. Film history was made when £6 million was grossed in 12 days worldwide. In London alone the movie took more than £34,000 during its first week at the Odeon, Leicester Square. 'The theatre telephone has been permanently blocked,' *Films Illustrated* reported, 'and police have frequently been on the spot to cope with fisticuffs started by queue jumpers.'

Hitherto critics and cynics had agreed: Bond crested with *Thunderball*, in which he was the neo-establishment rebel-hero of the liberated 60s. But in *Diamonds*, despite the gaffes, despite the jadedness and backtracking, there was still enough magic to raise the ghost. Nobody doubted that this extraordinary box-office success was not entirely due to the alchemic contributions of Sean Connery.

Declared box-office leader for 1971, the movie world once again lay like a carpet at Connery's feet. Older and wiser, he could now reshape his image in whatever way he desired, with guaranteed studio backing. Unfortunately, to smash type, he turned, too soon, to an offbeat classic.

# 14. MICHELINE ON COURSE

It was, for Connery, the best of times and the worst of times, these mellow days after *Diamonds Are Forever*. The press allegations that the Educational Trust funds was a tax dodge device – which had naturally upset him more than a little – were exploded by the patent advance of the cause. Connery's insistence on having *The Anderson Tapes'* European premiere in Scotland brought £5,000 into the Trust and the Troon golf benefit totted another £17,000. This on top of the hefty $1 million that had already begun to assist young artists in need and, more ambitiously, had padded the back-bone of a new social and industrial experiment of Sir Iain Stewart's. A new town in Scotland called Glenrothes in Fife, population 30,000, expected to rise to 75,000, was the site of investment. Money from the Trust, it was announced, would finance a training college for trade unions and management within the estate, the main object of which was to break down the barriers which disrupt industry. A seminar at Glenrothes in which the plan was forged created so much interest that the Labour Party and the Tory government sent representatives north to examine Stewart and Connery's visionary concept.

While waving his socialist-nationalist colours, Connery was eager to extend open arms to anyone with a business scheme that might benefit the Trust: 'If a good idea comes to us I don't give a damn whether it comes from a Tory or a Communist.' Lest anyone doubt his priorities he expanded: 'I'm in favour of fragmentation. There'll always be national differences and skirmishes. So Scotland should pull away somewhat, after hundreds of years taking second place to England.'

While business apparently boomed – he was also now part-owner of a London garage – he was also finally readying himself for the project he'd chosen as the first of the UA-guaranteed two-some, a film version of John Hopkins's stage play *This Story of Yours*, which had been a Royal Court success in 1960. To develop it he formed a production company, Tantallon Films, and scouted for further properties. Everything, through his business, political and arts life, was suddenly tinged with activity, optimism, hope.

But at home there were regrets and heartbreaks. Sombrely preparing for divorce from Cilento he reflected on 'years of failure. What we had to do was step back and see just what we were doing to each other, to our lives, and the lives of our son and daughter. Our careers were incompatible, not us. You were offered a part you wanted to do but suddenly there are a hundred questions to settle: What is she doing? What is he doing? Who will look after the kids? Can they come? Who will look after the house? Interminable.' The split was amicable, with Connery arranging reasonable financial support through his own bank. All that really concerned Diane and himself, he made clear, was the effect of the break-up on the children and 'making sure the future works for them ... fortunately they know the situation, they're great'.

Hot on the heels of the divorce agreement came the shock news in a phone call from Neil that Joe was dead. Less than four years before, Connery had finally urged Effie and Joe out of Fountainbridge – and then only because the brewery had started demolishing next-door properties. They had settled in a pretty gadget-equipped house in the quiet Edinburgh residential district of Newington, a considerable distance from the good memories. In retirement Joe had been endlessly restless: some days he went to the movies, often to see his son on screen, on rainy days he stayed in bed. 'He'd never been really sick a day in his life,' Neil said. 'Right up to the end he looked fine of fettle. It was custom for Mum and Dad to join myself and family for Christmas lunch. But that year Dad had phoned and said he'd a touch of flu, and wouldn't be coming round. I offered to bring food to their house, but he said no, he wasn't hungry. A few days later he was hospitalised for tests ... then a doctor called me aside and spilled it out. He said, "Your father's got cancer, and he hasn't too long to live." At the time I just couldn't believe it. He was only sixty-nine, it seemed impossible.' Once informed, Sean wanted to arrange the best medical care for Joe, if necessary moving him to London. But the doctors advised that no better treatment could be found anywhere: there were no options.

Within weeks, in March, Joe succumbed. In an unfortunate mistake, the duty night sister phoned not Neil but Effie, now living alone, to break the news. Neil was appalled. 'It took mother from midnight till two in the morning to ring over the word – she was so distressed. The hospital had blundered with phone numbers and it was very upsetting.' Roderick Mann, interviewing Connery a short time after Joe's death, found him 'much quietened down'. Connery attributed the change to the events of the last year, especially his father's death: 'That was a great stopper for me. More than I can explain. I never thought it would happen. The Masai tribe say that you're not a man until your father dies. They may be right, but if it's true it is a pretty stiff price to pay.'

Joe's funeral interrupted production work on *The Offence*, the movie version of *This Story of Yours*, that UA had grave doubts about underwriting. Ian Bannen, Sidney Lumet, Trevor Howard – all old friends of Connery's – were signed by Tantallon Films, steered by producer Denis O'Dell. 'It was a cracking play,' Bannen said, 'but it presented real problems in terms of commercial cinema. All the actors working with Denis and Sean loved it, but it would be foolish to say we expected it to have anything like a Bond impact.' Writer John Hopkins, famous for BBC's *Z-Cars*, worked closely with Connery on every aspect of the script preparation and pre-production, switching his title from the theatrical *This Story of Yours* to *Something Like the Truth* and finally – unsatisfactorily for many, said Bannen – *The Offence*.

Bannen remembered: 'We rehearsed it like a stage play, very tightly, then started a fast shoot at Twickenham. Sean was worried about only one aspect of the production: time. He wanted to bring the thing in in twenty-eight days and save money. Otherwise, he was pleased with Hopkins's script and all the technical and acting people he had around him. There was a family feel, which was good, and I thought it one of his finest performances ... though in those last scenes I suffered his true-to-life playing!' (Bannen, as the suspected rapist Baxter, is beaten to death by Johnson in a graphic scene: he was heavily padded beneath his clothing.)

Connery detailed his strategy to journalist Tony Crawley: '*The Offence* was *the* reason for going back to the Bond films. The premise was to make a picture that people [like Lumet and Bannen] could *participate* in, in every creative way. It had a sort of downbeat theme but the last forty minutes of it, quoting John Huston, are some of the best he's ever seen. It was the study in the disintegration of a policeman and the collapse of his mind brought about by the terrible things policemen are exposed to, and a really destructive marriage. Sidney made a fantastic job of it, but I think he got a bit European on us.'

*The Offence* was a rogue movie, styled and performed miles from the mainstream of current cinema. A daring choice for a star actor at any time, but downright insane, on the face of it, after so big a popular hit as *Diamonds Are Forever*, Connery seemed to take fiendish pleasure in indulging himself at the expense of UA, declaring later that he had never believed the movie would make a profit. United Artists had allotted $1 million to the movie – which came in $80,000 under budget – but did finally see profits eight years after its release.

Though Connery defiantly pretended indifference, he had always been hopeful that *The Offence* would take money and win artistic acclaim. As with *The Anderson Tapes*, he arranged a special showing at his business offices near St James's Place, to which he invited friends, industry associates – as well as cleaners and porters from the building. 'I tried to find out how people would react,' he said. 'The film's story, I know, is probably difficult to take. The cleaners and porters all said they liked the acting, but were not too forthcoming about the subject.' For Bannen, everything was right, barring the title. 'In Italy or somewhere I saw it go out as *In the Mirror, Darkly*, using the Shakespearean reference, and I thought that was more appropriate. *The Offence* spelt out grimness.' In retrospect, Connery judged the film fifteen minutes overlong, though he accepted Lumet's right to finish it as he pleased. 'At the end of the day my only complaint about it was UA's distribution, or lack of it. There was no faith in Sidney nor me. Nothing. They did nothing for it and released it through the toilet.' (The film was never distributed in many leading European markets, like France.)

Critically *The Offence* fared well. Sydney Edwards of the *Evening Standard* liked it, and Connery. Marjorie Bilbow admired the 'well-constructed script and finely controlled acting. When any two characters are locked in spoken combat the film is both moving and intellectually stimulating.' But critical plaudits didn't appease those with vested interests in Connery. 'I think the fear might have been that Sean would persist in trying to mock Bond in the rest of his work,' suggested Dennis Selinger – though Connery personally reassured him that he was only interested in building a sound foundation for wider acceptance.

After *The Offence* Connery flew to Spain to unwind and take in some golf, but he brought a mountain of script treatments with him, leaving Selinger in no doubt that he was intent on working on a prescription to build on Bond. 'Above anything he was interested in finding a comedy,' said Selinger, and Connery himself went on record cataloguing his priority choice: 'The only movies I never miss are the *Carry Ons*.' Spy stories didn't interest him; John Hopkins had written another film for Tantallon, based on the adventures of the explorer Sir Richard Burton; but the second $1 million from UA would not cover such an expensive film. Connery had also contracted Germaine Greer for a script, but her story about Australian Aborigines was read and abandoned. Connery quite liked Greer but found that 'her mind works on that outer cog. I feel the Aborigines were there thousands of years before us and they seem to have survived, so let them get on with it.' Politics in movies, he said, left him cold. 'Basically he saw himself as an entertainer first and foremost,' said Selinger. 'He respected the political filmmakers in the same way he respected all the old theatrical thespians, but he felt they were another breed, really. In his eyes, he was more a man of the people, if that doesn't sound too pretentious. He really had a grasp of his craft. It was just a question of getting off his arse and *doing more*.'

At this frantic time of reorientating, Connery's personal life took a happy turn. At a golf tournament in Morocco he met a tousle-haired blonde artist called Micheline Roquebrune, an avid golfer and multilinguist, and found an important friendship. Born in Nice and brought up in a wealthy family in North Africa, Micheline was 38, with three children and a failed marriage behind her. On the day of their meeting, Connery won the competition he was playing in, Micheline won hers. The shared passion for golf was the binding force of that early friendship. Very soon afterwards Connery pursued her and told her, 'I'm very serious about this. I don't play games,' which appealed to Micheline, who found herself inescapably 'attracted to his masculinity and his honesty'. They were inseparable during their first summer together in Spain, but friends doubted the relationship would survive Connery's determination to stay single. 'His feelings about marriage were very mixed,' said Ian Bannen. 'From week to week he contradicted himself. Now he wanted more children, now he wanted total freedom.' Connery himself told the press: 'I don't seem to have the equipment for marriage in terms of the contract as it exists today. But I'd like more children. And of course I'd want them to be by a woman who would bring them up properly. Who knows what will happen?'

For a year, in the eyes of the press and public, almost nothing happened. Over Christmas 1972 Micheline and Connery grew closer, but when he returned to Britain to launch *The Offence* he played his cards close to his chest and gave little hint of the lifestyle changes already on the horizon. On the spur of the moment he accepted an offer from adventurous director John Boorman, based in Ireland, to lead his futuristic fantasy movie *Zardoz*. Burt Reynolds, the director's first choice after their superb pairing on *Deliverance*, had cried off because of a hernia rupture, but Connery was overjoyed to be asked anyway. 'I located him on a golf course in Spain,' said Boorman, 'and sent out the script. Sean doesn't shilly-shally. He read it over a weekend and agreed to do it immediately. He was in Ireland, sitting down with me for script talks within a couple of days. He was extraordinarily imaginative, supportive and assured. I knew instantly I got him at the right time, and I bagged a bonus.'

*Zardoz* almost defied description in its surreal, mythic concept. Its strange, voyeuristic story of a far future world where inhabitants of the bubble-covered Vortex cherish the secret of eternal life owes much, Boorman reckoned, to his six years in America, where he directed hits like *Point Blank* with Lee Marvin. 'It was about immortality being a fairy tale,' he said. 'And America is the land where one sees this obsession with imagined permanence, this desire to perfect life and extend it for ever.' After the success of *Deliverance*, with which Boorman won an Academy Award nomination, he had approached Warners to finance *Zardoz*. Because of his demand for total artistic control he was turned down. Columbia also rejected *Zardoz*. Finally Fox agreed a deal – 'not great, but one accepts and adapts oneself to restrictions in this business. For the artist, the consolation has to be that greatness often comes from adversity. In *Zardoz* we ended up producing on a shoestring, but the pressures brought out the best in everyone, especially Sean. It was no hardship for him, and in collaborating with us to overcome the budgetary restrictions he became almost an authorial presence, which was quite indispensable.'

As Zed, exterminator by decree, Connery plays the balancing spirit incarnate of nature, who breaks into the time-locked Vortex to confound the immortal elite and reintroduce the threat of their morality. He has come from the polluted, ravaged world beyond the Vortex, and appears at once as god and demon to the Vortex people. Consuela (Charlotte Rampling), among others, is eventually swayed by Zed's promise of natural ageing and death, and joins him in escape from the bubble world.

'No one part of the filming was harder than any other,' said Boorman, 'because it was an enormously difficult film to do, with the special effects and the creation of a believable alternative universe. Because there was so much running round, it was physically exhausting for the actors, particularly Sean, who was half-naked all the time. The final sequence, however, caused a stir. It involved a long, messy make-up sitting in order to show Sean and Charlotte growing older and older, till they die. Sean was very good and patient, but after the first laborious sequence we found the film stock was faulty, so that necessitated a complete rerun. Sean was less philosophical about sitting through the make-up process again, but he held up. And we shot the sequence again, and it turned out fine. Then some young boy we had at the studios accidentally exposed the film, destroying it. So I came to Sean and told him. His reaction was hilariously frightening. I mean, he *took off*! The poor kid was cursed to death. "Where is he?" Sean demanded to know. "If I get my hands on him I'll break his fucking neck!" And this boy was scuttling round the studios for days, whispering, "Where's Connery? For God's sake, have you seen Connery?"' More seriously Boorman relates, 'Sean had no patience with people who behaved unprofessionally. His goal was fulfilling the ambition of the movie, fast and competently.'

Connery's Zed, given the dazzling distractions of photographic and directorial wizardry, was masterful, and inspired Jan Dawson in the *Monthly Film Bulletin* to wax eloquent about the ferociously concentrated energy which presents the character as 'both a physical and moral force and does much to dispel one's doubts about the apparent loose ends in the philosophical tapestry.' Dawson also saw the film as primarily 'visionary – its images speaking both louder and clearer than its occasionally pedantic dialogue'.

As with *The Offence*, Connery found the stimulating artistry and relative critical success of *Zardoz* satisfaction enough, though again he was mildly disgruntled by the bad box office. *Zardoz* he judged rightly to be ahead of its time, but he did not regret a moment of the ten weeks he had spent in County Wicklow making the picture. On the contrary, Ireland had galvanised him into reorganising his domestic life. Before *Zardoz* premiered he was flying back from Spain to arrange the sale of his Chelsea Embankment flat and finalise divorce proceedings with Cilento. 'My decision to sell was a pollution thing,' he told the *Express*. 'After spending all those weeks in Ireland and then being in Spain, London seemed pretty ropy when I came back: all those car exhausts spewing out muck.' Allusions to another marriage were evident: 'Who knows? Permissive society or not, it's a rare bird who'll stay with you year in and year out if you don't marry her.' And a telling secret emerged: in London he had started Spanish language lessons, attending classes in a school above Dunbar & Co. The fact that Spanish was Micheline's second language was significant to many.

A sense of anti-climax suffused the next films Connery hurried into during the winter and spring of 1973–4, though their popular targeting was unquestionable. *Ransom*, for Finnish director Casper Wrede, was a pedestrian affair in which Connery played a security chief in Oslo pitting his wits against a terrorist group led by Ian

McShane, which is holding an aircraft and the British ambassador against the release of six political prisoners. The plot incidents, ranged like bean cans on a supermarket shelf, were eminently forgettable, the direction bland. Connery was efficiently heroic, stiffly assured – but little else. Snowbound Oslo seemed more exciting to Wrede than his actors' potential. Actor Chris Ellison felt, 'Wrede wasn't living up to whatever one might have expected from the man who made *One Day in the Life of Ivan Denisovich*. There was no real sense of a hand directing us. We, the cast, figured we were on an average movie, with average chances.' Schedule overruns introduced delays and tensions. The snow melted too soon, and thousands of tons of salt mix had to be brought in for continuity, adding further delays. Connery pretended to grin and bear it, but in fact his patience, says Ellison, wore thin. Minor altercations brightened the lives of snow-blinded actors longing for London. At one stage Connery threatened to walk off the picture because the canteen food was so bad. On another occasion his wit, honed by adversity, lit the gloom. At a private showing of *Ivan Denisovich*, attended by the cast principals and Wrede himself, no one knew that Alexander Solzhenitsyn, author of the book, was seated at the back of the theatre. As the film ended Solzhenitsyn stood up and applauded. In turn, everyone cheered the great man. Connery watched the squat, bearded figure approach, with its high-domed forehead fringed with stubbly black hair. As the Russian drew almost into earshot Connery cracked, 'He's got his fucking head on upside down!' Wrede didn't appear to hear, or pretended he didn't. As for Solzhenitsyn – 'the Scots drawl probably saved Connery,' said Ellison.

In April Connery returned to Elstree Studios to embark on Agatha Christie's *Murder on the Orient Express*, a 30s' crime thriller immaculately dressed and costumed by Tony Walton. Sidney Lumet was the unusual choice of director, and, as expected, Connery attained his near-best under his old friend's control.

As Colonel Arbuthnot of the Indian Army, en route home with his lover (Vanessa Redgrave), Connery becomes a suspect, along with a dozen others, for the vicious murder of Ratchett, played by Richard Widmark. Hercule Poirot, played to definitive perfection by Albert Finney, finally discovers the unlikeliest of conspiracies to murder a man responsible for the death of a child many years before. Though the film was a sizeable hit – 'a splendidly frivolous gift wrapped in glittering silver foil and tied with a big satin bow', said *Screen International* – Connery's nuanced performance shrank to cameo-impact under the sheer star-weight of a film jam-packed with Ingrid Bergman, Anthony Perkins, John Gielgud, Michael York and a dazzling array of other headliners. In a BBC radio interview during filming Connery assessed his recent career frankly, expressing no disenchantment. He recognised the fact that most people still linked him with Bond, though Roger Moore had already taken over the mantle with reasonable success in *Live and Let Die*, and agreed that some of his post-Bond work had disappointed. Work satisfaction was monumentally important to him. But he was learning to enjoy leisure without guilt. Future plans, he said, were vague – though that admission seemed not to bother him.

Though officially still domiciled in Britain he had taken residence in Monaco, was applying for citizenship to ease tax pressures, and had swapped his farm in Spain for a large villa, the Casa Malibu, on the coast near Marbella. In retrospect it was a process that was leading up to his second marriage. According to Bannen, Connery's 'close friends, if they could be described as "close", were golfing people like Tommy Cooper, Bruce Forsyth and Jimmy Tarbuck. Eric Sykes saw a fair bit of him too, and they played together regularly in Marbella.' To all intents, he was married to Micheline already, though he was loath to discuss any intimate business with any journalist, friendly or otherwise. Gigi was sixteen now, and going her own way in Diane Cilento's footsteps, but Jason and Micheline's younger son, Stefan, were settling at the Casa Malibu. Within a year of the divorce from Cilento, Connery was snugly back in a family unit, drawing fresh strengths from the stability of a peaceful home.

In the autumn he started work in Almeria's Cabo de Gata, comfortably close to Micheline, on John Milius's *The Wind and the Lion*, earning his biggest cheque since Bond and his finest chance to achieve wide audience appeal. Privately he was happier than he'd been in a long time but, fearful of any gossipy intrusions, he presented a stony uncooperative face to the press. When the *Daily Mail's* Ann Kent visited him on location she discovered a sober, defensive man who 'gives you his "that's another stupid question you asked me" look'. He did, however, confide some surprising news. The lawyers working to sort out his affairs in Britain had disentangled him from *all* his business concerns. 'It's the easiest thing in the world to start a business empire,' he groused, 'but it creates a chain reaction of secretaries, minutes, meetings ... it just never stopped. I found I was a mogul without a structure to support my empire. Every decision had to be mine and it became too much. Now I am dropping everything except the Trust and my film interests.'

Many old buddies were surprised by the suddenness of the volte-face. Increasingly, through his 30s and early 40s, Connery had prided himself on his ability to turn over a quick buck. Increasingly in the press he was the 'businessman-actor', and it was popular knowledge in the City that most of his investments, properly structured or not, had turned good. The warm friendship with Sir Iain still flourished ... So why the sudden departure? Ian Bannen believed it boiled down to priorities: 'There are only so many hours in the day, and Sean is not a part-timer.'

Micheline's setting up home with Connery, coinciding with his abandonment of business concerns, assumed some importance in light of *The Wind and the Lion*. For Bannen, 'There were clearly some guiding hands steering him back to popular cinema. Diane's influence, during their time together, was huge. I'm sure, in her own savvy way, Micheline had as much of an impact as Diane or Selinger.'

John Milius, famous for telling the cinema tales of *Dillinger* and *Jeremiah Johnson* (which he scripted), designed *The Wind and the Lion* as a mass-market swashbuckler, applying, by *Photoplay's* reckoning, 'all the elements essential for big screen entertainment: romance, drama, large-scale battles, pageantry and, above all, heroes'. In spite of the clutter, Connery's Berber leader Mulay El Raisuli, holding America to ransom by kidnapping an American woman (Candice Bergen) and her children, towered like a colossus, a character creation of Bondian dimension. Marjorie Bilbow saw it as 'relax-and-enjoy-it gusty entertainment to be taken no more seriously than a game of cowboys and Indians', while Vincent Canby in the *New York Times* contemplated what was possibly 'the most sappy movie ever made, as well as one of the shrewdest'.

By the time *The Wind and the Lion* opened in May 1975 Connery was at work on another 'local' picture, the John Huston epic, *The Man Who Would Be King*, shooting across the Med from home, in North Africa. For it too the signs were good. In the way of the movie business, though Milius's picture had yet to be judged at the box office, word had it that Connery was focused, ergo hot again, and his fees were up. The small aberrations that succeeded *Diamonds Are Forever* were as good as forgiven and the fan mail was pouring in once more. The sideline business distractions were gone, the bachelor drifting was over. Dennis Selinger was happier, and Connery and Micheline had reason to smile. In May, coinciding with the release of *The Wind and the Lion*, the couple finally tied the knot in Gibraltar.

# 15. HITS

*The Man Who Would Be King* was a watershed in many respects. Crucially, it marked the end of critical assessment of everything Connery did in terms of transmutations of James Bond. In the film, playing adventurer Danny Dravot who becomes king of a remote Himalayan tribe, Connery finally outpaced Bond and created his richest character. In work terms, the movie was the milestone of altered outlook. With it he began an intensive spate of varied, non-stop mass-targeted projects that has lasted to today – a Selinger-and-Micheline-inspired unflagging campaign that has yielded quite a few superb movies and huge box-office business. Connery clearly recognised the dividing line. 'The definite swing', he told *Men Only*, started when Joe died. 'It really hit me. I changed offices, agents, accountants, lawyers, secretaries – even my wife!' Micheline became comforter and guide, but Connery still harboured resentment about a variety of wrong decisions over the last years. Bit by bit, from the serenity of life with Micheline and work with the much-admired Huston, the lingering bitterness was vented. Those few journalists who got past amiable film PR man Brian Doyle heard Connery's bald account of wasted years. Staying loyal to Britain, for starters, had cost him dear. On reflection, the colossal taxes he had paid for ten years enraged him. Only very lately did he realise the need to 'get out from under the umbrella of parasites headed by people like Healey – and if not him Barber, when he was Chancellor'. He expressed no admiration of British accountants either. 'People have said I'm worth three or four million pounds,' he told writer William Hall, 'but that's rubbish.' He went on to outline losses in shares and anticipated the likelihood of being 'finally worth a million' once all affairs in Britain were sorted. His future, he made clear, would now be films, films, films.

*The Man Who Would Be King* was a $7 million version of Kipling's youthful yarn which John Huston had originally developed more than twenty years before in hopes of getting

Bogart and Gable together in rebel-ridden India. 'It kind of sat on a shelf,' Michael Caine said. 'First Bogie died, then Gable, and John didn't know what to do with it. Then, after all those years, John brought it to Dennis Selinger, saying he wanted Sean and me, because we were the big British names and I suppose he thought that would be nicely fitting for Kipling.' Selinger was more excited by the script than anything he had read in years. He contacted Connery and Caine immediately, confident that 'this was an important picture for Sean, something of real substance that could give him one hell of a spurt'. Connery liked the idea of working with Huston, and with his friend Michael Caine. The added attraction of Morocco location work, next door to Micheline, was also persuasive. Fees were negotiated – not great, said Caine, but not bad by contemporary standards for actors trailing the Hollywood elite of Redford, Hoffman and Newman: 'We got about a quarter of a million, which seemed OK but ended up sour.' Part of the deal also guaranteed a percentage of the net profits for Caine and Connery. Allied Artists, the producers, didn't pay, and the actors later sued, winning a further quarter of a million dollars each. (Allied Artists' countersuit for $22 million, claiming libel, 'would have completely destroyed us', Connery said: the suit failed.)

Filming began in the foothills of the Atlas Mountains, in an atmosphere of harmony. 'Sean had married Micheline shortly before,' said Brian Doyle, 'and he reluctantly decided to announce it to a Scottish journalist during the film. In a matter of hours, of course, Fleet Street had it and there was a mighty fuss that didn't please him. It was like Bond all over. He would say before a press conference, "Look, no questions about Bond, OK?" But that only incited them. That's all they wanted to talk about. And now he found it all a bore again, and he let it show. He was really for the most part quite pleasant with journalists, but the myth of the surly, difficult slob was perpetuated, based on scraps.' Connery severed with Bond bluntly in a chat with William Hall: 'I say no to a reprise because I don't feel a great passion for it myself. If it was something that would give me a zing then I'd do it.' No mention of Kevin McClory or the upcoming collaboration with writer Len Deighton was made; at this point in time Bond was a fringe irritant, no more. He had other fish to fry.

After two weeks of meticulous rehearsals under the African sun, the cameras were ready to roll. 'One of the things that worked right was the relationship Sean and I had as Danny and Peachy,' said Michael Caine. 'It was based, if you like, on the way we got on. There was humour in the script, but we wove in our own. Back at the hotel at night, or just before shooting during the day, we'd work out together some bit of business and go to John [Huston] and present him with it. More often than not he'd accept it, and say, Yeah, that's better than the script, do it. For instance, there's the little soldier routine we do at one point, marching into the palace, one-two, one-two, all haughty disdain – that was Sean and me injecting a bit of our schoolboyish selves.'

Huston was also impressed by each actor's confidence in the other. 'We decided we'd play to camera, emphasising each other's best lines, so in that *we* orchestrated all the movement. And Sean was particularly good at that; anything physical, anything to do with grace of movement, he was terrific. He was great, a *great person* to work with, not only an actor. He had no time for the appurtenances of success, none of your whose-dressing-room-is-biggest? I think the biggest hit element in the movie had going for it was the *genuine fun* of the whole escapade.'

Shakira, Caine's wife, was in the film too, and with Micheline, they made a happy foursome after hours. There was much laughter and Huston thought the experience rewarding beyond expectations. Six years later, when the director was critically ill and believed to be dying, Caine and Connery visited his bedside. 'It was uncanny,' Caine said. 'He recognised us all but he called us Peachy and Danny. He'd loved those damned characters so much, he'd lived with them in his head for so long that he couldn't let them go.'

Huston, assisted in the writing by Gladys Hill, had considerably expanded Kipling's short story, embodying the author as narrator in the parable of two former army sergeants, half-literate, striking a 'contrack' to cross the Himalayas and become the first Europeans to set foot in wildly primitive Kafiristan, where they will set themselves up as kings. Duly succeeding, they ultimately lose their hold over the tribesmen by revealing their humanness. In the *Monthly Film Bulletin* Tom Milne drew comparisons with Orson Welles's planned production of Conrad's *Heart of Darkness*, which was thematically similar. Though Welles would doubtless have explored the parables more fully, Milne opined, Huston 'does bring the conflict ignored by Kipling (sympathy for the underdog combined with support for imperialist authority) into the open. Here the film is beautifully served by the performance of Sean Connery and Michael Caine, very funny as twin incarnations of typically endearing Kipling ranker-rogues, identical in their sharp-witted, foul mouthed opportunism.'

From the moment the film opened in December its success was evident and it eventually grossed $11 million in the US market, making it easily Connery's best non-Eon performer. This definitive success, totally removed from Bond, excited Connery's energies in yet more ambitious efforts. After the briefest holiday spent water-skiing from his own beach at Marbella with Jason and Stefan ('actually I find the sport quite boring, give me golf any day'), he signed for Richard Lester's tragicomic *Robin and Marian*, to be shot entirely on the Plain of Urbassa (doubling for Sherwood Forest) near Pamplona – a favoured Spanish site Lester had used in *The Three* (and *Four*) *Musketeers* the year before. 'Filming in Spain was suddenly important to him,' said Selinger. 'It reflected his new mood, this settling down thing. He had decided on a new life with Micheline and he'd had enough of Britain and so it became a key factor: if a producer wanted a better than average chance of Sean taking his project, then it had to be shot in Africa or Spain. I don't think Hollywood was much on his mind, as such. He was big enough everywhere, I suppose, and he had no love for the bullshit of LA anyway. So these new movies were like a little cottage industry. It was working at home, in your own front garden.'

*The Wind and the Lion* and *The Man Who Would Be King* had been made back to back, so by the time Connery encountered Lester's film he was unusually tired. Still, he perked up when he read James Goldman's novelistic script. He was also stimulated by the prospect of exploring a new relationship with Lester, whose avant-garde daring immortalised the Beatles on film in *A Hard Day's Night* and *Help!*. For his part, Lester was inspired by Connery's recent work and eager to cut new ground. 'Not having worked with Sean before I can't say I imagined at all what his reaction [to the initial approach] would be,' Lester said. 'He wanted to see the script, naturally, but his response revealed no tiredness. He took it, read it and the reading sealed the deal. He was as enthused as I had been four years earlier when the idea was first put to me.'

*Robin and Marian* started life years before when Columbia executive Peter Grüber came unannounced to Lester's Pinewood office with four white cards on which were scribbled synopses of potential films. Riding high on the Beatles' hits, Lester had an embarrassment of choices, but Columbia's chief David Begelman leapt the field, offering carte blanche. 'I wasn't especially looking for anything at that time, but I jumped on the *Robin Hood* idea. I told Gruber that that was a picture I wanted to make and if he could go away and fix the deal, I was in.' A few months later Goldman's commissioned script – 'beautifully done, and scarcely tampered with at all in the shooting version' – was submitted, and Columbia made its formal offer. Lester first considered casting Connery as Little John, a part eventually played by Nicol Williamson. 'I thought that that might have been fun, off-centre casting – but then the notion of Sean taking on Robin Hood began to seem very appealing, and it just took root in my brain and grew and grew. That quality of innocence Sean can portray was the notion that set the wheels going.'

Competition from other *Robin Hood* productions-in-planning threatened Lester's movie. Polish producer Wieslaw Kliszewicz was in discussion with British thriller director Sidney Hayers to shoot a version starring Patrick Mower in England. In Hollywood, Mel Brooks was at work on a *Robin Hood* television series. Undeterred, Lester gave himself the challenge of 'the consummate version', and to that end secured the participation of Audrey Hepburn, agreeing to return to the cinema after seven years' absence, to play Maid Marian. That coup effectively silenced the competition and proved decisive in winning Connery. 'Sean was obviously delighted and flattered to have Audrey aboard, but he was also very high on Goldman's script,' said Lester. By Connery's own account, he was attracted to 'a provocative story about death and dying. I had to find out what kind of man *is* Robin? Considering his later days will be something new for cinema.'

Micheline approved, as did Selinger. But, said Ian Bannen, not everyone in the industry was excited by this dark new script. As Bannen recalled, 'There was a story going round that raised a smile. Apparently, some senior Fox executive heard about the Lester film and said, "So Sean's making a picture about Robin Hood dying? That'll be interesting. How long will it take for him to die? Because it took ninety minutes in *The Offence*."'

Lester completed his film in an astonishing six weeks, entirely on location. 'I don't think I made many mistakes with it,' he said, 'but I regretted Ray Stark's [executive producer] decision to change our working title. Our title was *The Death of Robin Hood* and it should have been left as such. In changing it we were inviting the kind of mindless trick a lot of critics have of evaluating your new movie by the last one you made. *Robin and Marian* sounded like a comedy. It might have been a Beatles movie, for heaven's sake. To me, *Robin* was not comedy yet studio people kept asking me, Where are the jokes? Yes, it had humorous moments. Almost all movies do. And Sean is an actor who looks for humour in all his roles, to humanise his characters, which is intelligent strategy. But *Robin* was a straight movie, all of us saw it like that – and because of the connotations of the changed title it prompted the wrong reaction.'

Nonetheless *Robin* was sufficiently strong for Connery to complete the hat trick of critical successes begun with *The Wind and the Lion*. Despite kind critiques, however, the film failed to ignite the market, earning just $4 million in its US rentals, less than half the takings of *The Man Who Would Be King*. The heart of the story, Connery later concluded, was wrong for America. American films favour fountain-of-youth heroism. But Lester's movie showed Robin in decline, returning disillusioned from the Crusades, wearily forced to do battle again with the Sheriff of Nottingham, played by Robert Shaw. Maid Marian as portrayed by Hepburn was now abbess of a priory, under threat of imprisonment by the Sheriff, and the catalyst of the story. The fated love affair ended with Robin gravely wounded in Marian's arms and a tragic, unsentimental resolution. Vincent Canby in the *New York Times* noted the well-intentioned gloom while conceding that Hepburn and Connery saved the day: 'Their screen presences are such that we are convinced that their late August love is important and final.'

Connery, in hindsight, queried Lester's basic approach: 'There were elements that hadn't been foreseen,' he told a press conference a year later. 'Principal of which was the Catholic Church response. She [Marian] was guilty of committing many sins – by committing suicide, by killing me and by living in sin.' Another difficulty for Americans particularly was that 'their philosophy is very much in terms of *solving* problems, and that the good guy should never be over the hill, never in a state of deterioration'.

This American failure didn't unsettle Connery because the movie, more than anything he'd recently done, won him the admiration of people whose opinions he valued. John Boorman and John Huston admired it. Robert Hardy considered his contribution 'a personal best' and took the trouble to write to Lester when he couldn't contact Connery. Pauline Kael of the *New Yorker* was effusive in her praise: 'Sean Connery – big, fleshy, greying – is the most natural-looking heroic figure. He seems unrestrained, naked, a true hero. He is animal-man at its best.' Fred Zinnemann said, '*Robin and Marian* was the movie that drew my attention to Sean. There is one word too rarely applied in evaluating actors: authority. In that movie Sean showed total command – of his skills, of the plot. It was the kind of sensitive authority that haunts you.'

Though Connery seemed focused on hit-making movies, he had not, clearly, abandoned his fondness for art house films. After *Robin*, Lester emphatically wanted to work with him again – 'as quickly as possible, as soon as I can lay my hands on the right script' – but Connery went immediately for an unorthodox small-budget feature with no distributor in place, called *The Next Man*, to be directed by Richard C Sarafian.

Sarafian's film vision was enshrined in his arcane 1971 hit *Vanishing Point*, but *The Next Man* strained for the mass market. What Sarafian called 'a humanitarian plot', was presented as a high-risk thriller, obviously bent on utilising Connery's marquee status. Here he would play a visionary Saudi Arabian politician manoeuvring a pact with Israel for the distribution of gas profits to the Third World; sexy Cornelia Sharpe would be the Bondian sub-villainess out to thwart him. The movie's failure seemed inevitable. Preachy in tone but thin on narrative, it fell between stools and looked charmless. Its greatest sin, for many, was the lack of authentic political resonance. Vincent Canby slammed the makers as people 'whose talent for filmmaking and knowledge of international affairs would both fit comfortably into the left nostril of a small bee'. On US distribution, the movie barely earned a million dollars and – a first for Connery – found no willing distributor in Britain. (*The Next Man* was finally screened in Britain on the ITV network in January 1982.)

Sarafian and Connery were appalled by the universal failure of the film. In the search for a kind of cinéma-vérité accuracy, locations skipped from London to the Bahamas, Ireland, Germany and Morocco, pumping the budget past $4 million. No expense had been spared on research and rewriting. The obvious faults of the film were skirted by Connery and when one journalist wrote that Cornelia Sharpe, with her 49 costume changes and token nude scene, was only cast because she was the producer's girlfriend, Connery blew his cool. He phoned the journalist, he later told Roderick Mann, and threatened to push her words down her throat. 'What did she say?' Mann asked Connery. 'Nothing,' Connery replied. 'She was speechless.'

This quality of loyalty, never less than impassioned, had always won Connery friends in the industry. Even those directors who stopped short, for whatever reasons, of employing him, held him in high regard. John Schlesinger, whom Connery himself had approached in 1971 for a part in *Sunday Bloody Sunday* – Peter Finch was already cast, so Connery was turned down – frequently loaned out his Beverly Hills home to him. Others, like Boorman and Guy Hamilton, relished his company. Still, Guy Hamilton said, 'Sean's friendship comes at a price. He is not essentially a social animal, though once admitted to his circle, people are inclined to stay there. But he is afflicted by the gypsying that takes hold of many actors, and he is afflicted by the moods of an artist. So his friendship can feel inconstant.'

In Hollywood, during the gloomy aftermath of *The Next Man*, Connery dined and drifted with Michael Caine, the writers Jackie Collins and Stanley Mann and the handful of expatriate intimates he trusted. 'The truth is he wasn't a great guy for advisers and all that stuff,' said Caine. 'He was your typical canny Scot. Nobody's fool. Every time he reached a career dead spot – or a hot spot – he took time out, a day here a day there, to reconsider and *question* himself: Where did I go wrong? Where do I go from here? I think Sean is *the* great gut-instinct career planner. He hides it, but it is true.' Smarting from the poor press for *Robin* and *The Next Man*, Connery was momentarily disdainful of Hollywood. Spain, he told Caine and others, was the dearest place on earth to him, Hollywood was 'only worthwhile for the best beef and lamb in the world', and Britain – well, Britain had its political, cultural and business values confused. He told Roderick Mann that he regretted not having been able to attend the premieres of his last three movies in Britain but 'the tax laws just won't allow it. If I stay in Britain for more than ninety days I'm subject to those crazy taxes. It's self-defeating, the government is making a big mistake. [The tax laws] only serve to discourage major film-making in Britain. No big star will agree to risk a movie there that might conceivably overrun and land him in it. It's unfortunate, but I personally just don't want to know.'

Back in Spain, far from the potential penalties of London and LA, Connery welcomed the plum of Joseph Levine's European mammoth, *A Bridge Too Far*, a $25 million reconstruction of operation Market Garden, General Montgomery's daring attempt to end the Second World War in a single coordinated thrust. Richard Attenborough was the director, and the prestige ring of the endeavour, along with the quarter-million-dollar fee, was a salve for Connery's frustrations. He was, in fact, the first of a dozen major stars to be signed and he was enraged when, three weeks before shooting commenced in Holland, he read a newspaper account of Robert Redford's negotiated $2 million fee. Connery's response to this discovery revealed his perception of his own market value. 'At first I thought it was a mistake,' he said. 'Then I learnt it wasn't. Now, considering the size of my part in the picture, the salary I'd agreed on seemed fair. But when I found out how much others were getting – for the same amount of work and with no more acting ability – it became unfair.' Connery's role was that of Major General Roy Urquhart, who commanded the Rhine bridgehead at Arnhem. The part was substantial, equalled only by Anthony Hopkins, playing Lt-Col Frost, the fighting hero of Arnhem Bridge. Incensed by what he suddenly saw as LA perfidy facilitated by his absence from 'the Hollywood set', Connery met with Levine and demanded a better fee. 'It had nothing to do with egotistical arrogance or greed,' Ian Bannen said. 'I know Sean. One of his slogans after Bond was, Pay me what I'm worth. Naturally he gathered that since Levine priced Redford so high, he deserved more. No smooth-talking horse-trader, however well disposed towards him – and Levine he regarded as a mate – would deny him his worth.'

Levine agreed to increase Connery's salary by 50 per cent and the production started at Deventer, 40 kilometres north of Arnhem, comfortably less than two hours by plane from Marbella.

The logistical problems of mounting *A Bridge Too Far* were more complex than anything Connery had previously observed, Bond notwithstanding. A production crew of 300 was deployed, more than one hundred actors were cast, period aircraft, tanks, guns and munitions were purchased from all over the world. Unlike Bond, however, Connery could hang back a little, his centrality in the production eased by the equal focus on the starry heavyweights around him. While Attenborough toiled round the clock at Arnhem, Connery did his best to carve out free time though, for once, the golf fell by the wayside. 'When I'm working this hard I miss the golf, but I try to find ways to get round that.' The consolation, on *A Bridge Too Far*, was the nobility of the endeavour and Attenborough's and Levine's intelligence. Unlike Zanuck's approach with *The Longest Day* (also based on a Cornelius Ryan book), where the story-telling was episodic and the star names seemingly scattered at random, Attenborough, Levine and the screenwriter William Goldman carefully composed an almost intimate storyline, where star 'faces' served to punctuate and, in their easy identity, clarify a complex background history.

*A Bridge Too Far*, premiering on 15 June 1977, proved a happy experience for Connnery, as for Attenborough, but its $20 million gross in the US didn't appease writer William Goldman, set, as it was, against a backcloth of negative critiques. In Goldman's view, the poor reaction reflected American appetites for fantasy heroism of the John Wayne type, not the detailed realism depicted by Attenborough. Still, with international rentals and, given its historical authenticity, an assured long shelf life, it was evident that the movie would clear its $35 million budget ($15 million of which went on actors' fees) and was work to be proud of.

After the laborious months in the grey chill of Holland rehabilitation in Marbella seemed on the cards but the experience of misjudgement during the deal-making on *A Bridge Too Far* had chastened him and Connery made straight for Hollywood as if to reaffirm his status at the core of the industry. 'He seemed to grab the first big studio script he could find,' said Bannen. And on 31 October 1977 he swooped into the muddy mire of Warners' *Meteor* – a $15 million flop – directed by Ronald Neame, all about the attempts of an American and a Russian scientist (Connery and Natalie Wood respectively) to divert an earth strike by an off-course asteroid. Elaborate special effects delayed the completion of the movie – which didn't open till the autumn of 1979 – but Connery wasn't bothered. Before a quarter of the picture was shot at MGM Studios the gloom of defeat was afoot. 'It was one of those movies where you could see they had to try hard,' said Ian Bannen. 'When you have to *try* that hard, you know there's something amiss.' The expat community he usually sought out found Connery tired from three years of unbroken work, but philosophical. He stayed again at Schlesinger's house, but this time had the company of Micheline and the children. When he wasn't working he often sat late into the night, sipping beer or red wine and wallowing in nostalgia. En route for this trip the family had stopped off in Britain, where he had treated Micheline and the boys to a saunter down memory lane. He had collected Effie and driven to Fountainbridge to look over 176 before the wrecking cranes moved in. To his surprise, he himself mirrored something of the boys' reaction. Fifteen-year-old Jason found the place only 'interesting'; where Stefan, two years his junior, thought it awful. 'I wanted them to see it,' Connery mused, 'but it really was a dump. A terrible place. No hot water, gas mantles on the landings ... ugh.'

Micheline, who had had the comforts of a wealthy French–African upbringing, was horrified: 'What a dreadful place!' was her verdict. But Effie just smiled and hugged her son and whispered that it was really quite nice, and unchanged.

In the Hollywood Hills, in the spring of 1978, Connery ruminated on the grey harsh past. Watching Micheline working with her oils and easel, painting Shakira Caine, the children, the scenery; dining with old pals like Ian Bannen and Richard Burton; snatching an hour's golf in therapeutic sunshine ... In many ways, remembering Fountainbridge, the new, serene life was hard to accept. He certainly had more than he'd ever dreamed of. The ups and downs of his Bond fortunes were over. By his own strategising he had made the million he'd intended when he quit Britain for good – and well more. His career was stable, his services in demand, his company sought. So much had changed. And yet ...

'In himself he remained basically the same,' Michael Caine said. 'There was always a bit of the decent working man about him, like the time we were at a club in Los Angeles and this crowd of loudmouths started to heckle the performer on stage. Sean wouldn't have it. He didn't call the manager or anything. He just did the bold thing and had a go at 'em. Very brave. But, you see, he himself wasn't offended. It wasn't about his night out being interrupted. He was upset for the performer on stage. He just couldn't take those rowdies, so he gave them a dose of their own medicine, just as he would have at the dancehall in Edinburgh forty years ago.'

The spell of reflection was broken by Michael Crichton's offer of *The First Great Train Robbery*, a witty Victorian caper that greatly appealed. Literary value apart, Crichton's intention to shoot not on a Hollywood stage, but on locations in England and Ireland, won Connery's commitment. After signing, he discovered that the greater part of the studio work was planned for Pinewood. Since this would compromise his British tax allowance status, he withdrew, necessitating a rethink for Crichton, and a resiting to Ireland's National (Ardmore) Studios.

Before filming started in the summer of 1979, mulling over Crichton's revised screenplay at Schlesinger's house, Connery once again demonstrated his principles of loyalty. Ian Bannen was staying for the weekend and he suddenly invited him aboard. 'It was two o'clock in the morning and Sean threw me the script and said, "See if there's anything in it for you. I can't see it, but have a look and if you can find a part, let's do it."' Bannen perused the screenplay and declined. 'Sean was a very astute reader,' said Ardmore director Sheamus Smith. 'His intelligence was obvious and he had a conversational range that reflected the kind of great intellect that one associates with a genius raconteur like, say, Peter Ustinov. He read all the time when he was in Ireland. Whenever I saw him he had a book in his hands, not some trashy paperback, always something substantial. And his way with scripts was remarkable. They were constantly coming at him at that time and he would glance over [an offered script] and establish instantly whether it was right for him, or whoever else. He was never brash when one submitted something for his evaluation, and he was never hesitant. It was always insightful and decisive.'

*The First Great Train Robbery* was a good choice at a good time in Connery's career. Packed with images resoundingly redolent of Victorian life, it told the story of the incorrigible crook, Pierce (Connery), who devises a plan to steal £25,000 of bullion being shipped on the Folkestone train to the troops in the Crimea. Aided by his mistress, played by Lesley-Anne Down, and an accomplice, played by Donald Sutherland, Connery steals the four keys necessary to open the safe in the episodic spine of the movie. The thefts required hair-raising carriage-top stunts on the moving locomotive and Connery, refusing a stunt double, delivered his best action moments since James Bond. Sheamus Smith recalls Connery's enthusiasm for the stunt work – and his horror when, accidentally, he overshot himself: 'Micheline wasn't around for all the shooting, and had she been, there would have been trouble over the main stunt sequence that is the movie's highlight. Sean wanted to do it, but he was under the impression, as was Crichton, that the train which was an original 1870-built steam engine, couldn't travel any faster than twenty-five or thirty miles an hour. He did the sequence, and staggered off that train top, completely winded. When the helicopter photography pilot landed to congratulate his daring he mentioned that no other actor he knew would risk his neck at crazy speeds on a rattle-bucket. Sean said, "No, it was only thirty miles an hour, or so." But the pilot told him otherwise: "My instruments don't lie, mate," he said. "At times there you were doing more than fifty."'

After location shooting in Counties Meath and Cork, Crichton moved his cast to Pinewood for two London sequences, carefully limited so that Connery would not spend too many days 'under the umbrella'. Sheamus Smith followed on to watch progress and saw that Connery demonstrated 'remarkable stamina. One found it impossible not to admire the gusto he put into the picture. When Micheline wasn't around he kept his head down at the golf. He ate well, enjoyed good grub, and drank mostly wine. I got the feeling here was a contented man, ideally suited to the rigours of a tough career.' Confusion of identification with Bond no longer troubled this mellow Connery. Smith recalls 'one awful, rainy afternoon, late lunching with him at Pinewood's restaurant. The manageress came in, having picked up her children from school. Sean was off duty, wearing a scruffy anorak, bearded, without his toupee. But the kids instantly recognised him and came darting over, asking, "Can we have your autograph, Mr Bond?" Sean paused – and grinned. He seemed delighted to be recognised and cheerfully responded to these children with their awestruck faces.'

Crichton's film was a small triumph, mixing pure escapism with visual sumptuousness, and presenting a fitting epitaph for cinematographer Geoffrey Unsworth, whose last film it was. Gordon Gow in *Films and Filming* crystallised the magic of the movie when he applauded the 'charm [that is] uppermost in this breezy film'. Looking back on Connery's recent career, *Films Illustrated* called him 'the most improved British actor of the decade' and the general critical response was enthusiasm for what the future held. 'He wanted to direct,' Sheamus Smith said. 'Everybody knew that

that was a desire he'd long held. He genuinely adored acting, and the parts were there for the taking like never before, but it was clear that acting would never be enough for him.'

'I haven't made too many mistakes,' Connery told a French press conference in 1981, 'but I made one with *Cuba*.' Late in 1978, just weeks after finishing Crichton's film, Connery signed on to Richard Lester's new project, a love-and-war story about the last days of Batista's Cuba. By any reckoning he was due a break but aspects of his last movies bothered him. Before he saw a frame of it he felt *Meteor* was a dud. This misjudgement annoyed him, as did the growing signs that United Artists had no intention of heavily promoting *The First Great Train Robbery*, a movie he believed in. *Cuba* was an urgent compensation device. But in *Cuba* he blundered, settling for the two things he was always disdainful of – an unfinished script in the hands of an unsure director.

'Confidence is an actor's lifeblood,' Robert Henderson had once lectured him. 'Take it away and you've got an actor in trouble.' Connery's choice of *Cuba* was to take him from the smoothest, happiest plateau of his career to the brink of disaster.

# 16. MISSES

A considerable amount of Connery's undoing with *Cuba* was his own fault. Ever since the Bond days he had resisted long shoot commitments on movies, believing a tightly controlled, fast schedule created the emotional intensity which made for interesting screen results. The film most wasteful of his time had been the penultimate Bond, *You Only Live Twice* – a memory which rankled. As late as 1981 Connery was still cribbing that 'that thing took six months of my time, after two or three postponements, which meant it was almost a year out of my life. And if one film takes six months and the people who are supposedly producing it are so stupid they cannot programme it properly, then it leaves no room for flexibility [to make other movies].' Dennis Selinger's tactical scheme of rapid-filming had shown itself worthy over four productive years, and now Connery was emphatically agreeing that 'the more diverse the parts you play, the more stimulating it is and, in turn, the wider the experience, so there's even more you can play'. But speed-of-light transition from role to role entails real dangers, the very least being the on-screen exhaustion which showed itself during the mid-60s; at worst, muddled mishmash caused by rushing the fence.

Richard Lester had been eager to work with Connery since the day *Robin and Marian* wrapped. Motivated by loyalty principles similar to Connery's, Lester believed he had 'come close to something really special' with *Robin*, but had failed commercially. Determined to make up to the actor he much admired, in 1977 he commissioned his friend Charles Wood, 'a gifted character creator' who had worked on ten Lester films, to write something special for Connery. Inspired by conversations with producer Denis O'Dell, a mutual friend who had spent some stranded weeks in Cuba during the Castro takeover in 1960, the director chose this 'truly historic period' as the basis for what would be the Connery mega-epic of the 70s. During Lester's phone call outlining the proposal,

Connery expressed enthusiasm. He thought the originality of the concept striking. It seemed, he said, 'extraordinary that no film-makers had examined the Cuban revolution in twenty years'. Once engaged, and trustingly fond of Lester, Connery was in. Once in, he was hurrying. The first treatment Charles Wood submitted he liked, and though he felt uneasy about the unfinished first draft, he felt far more unhappy about the prospects of *Meteor* and the damage that might do. Working fast, he negotiated *Cuba* with Denis O'Dell. On the strength of his recent achievements, his asking price had rocketed to a million dollars, and this fee was agreed. Then he gave Lester a deadline: the film must start while the weather was right in southern Spain, which would double for Cuba. The period of September–October would be the perfect time.

But by October Wood's script was still not ready. 'It was constant re-evaluation and constant rushing,' said Lester. 'In the script, I felt we weren't reaching the proper balance between foreground characters and background history. We were risking falling between a romantic story involving uninteresting people, and a documentary-like survey of a ridiculous, fascist, sin-ridden Mafia-controlled city undergoing a tidal change in a three-day revolution. The pressure to get rolling was ferocious, but I was terrified of trivialising it.'

Connery claims he postponed shooting twice because the script was not satisfactory. Eventually, 6 November was announced as a start date. 'But that was a date dictated by the weather,' said Lester. 'It was just unrealistic, and again it was cancelled.'

Logistically, for Lester, the film was a nightmare. As on *Robin*, there would be no studio work, just ten weeks at 78 locations, ranging from the famous old cities of Jerez de la Frontera (where the sherry comes from) and Cadiz to picture-postcard Seville. The crew, organised under a plethora of assistant directors, numbered 160, their job being to utilise multiple camera techniques in order to speed up the shooting and vary choices of sequences for editing. 'It was a case of leaving no stone unturned in making it well, and making it fast,' said Lester. 'But with that many moving pieces, you just know something will go wrong.'

Finally, Connery's patience was spent. The umpteenth draft of the script was deemed acceptable (though Lester maintained reservations and was still scribbling amendments till the last minute) and filming started on 27 November. Connery's personal first choice of a love interest was the singer-actress Diana Ross. But she had dropped out in the last weeks, to be replaced by coquettish Brooke Adams, whom everyone agreed was a fine actress, albeit one who looked prepubescent alongside Connery. Lester cast her, he said, before he'd even met her.

The opening of *The First Great Train Robbery* in Britain a few weeks into shooting did nothing to cheer the panicked mood on location. United Artists had, as Connery anticipated, spared much on promoting *Robbery*, even though the notices were excellent. Since UA would also distribute *Cuba*, Connery interpreted the signs as ominous. On the set he was gruffer than usual, refusing all entreaties to join a party of British journalists specially flown out for informal drinks after work. 'But there were no tantrums,' Lester insisted. 'Sean is too seasoned and too professional.' Good relationships with fellow actors Jack Weston and Brooke Adams were formed and, day by day, problems were tackled and overcome. 'But it was such an uphill run,' said Lester. 'Those problems, script apart, were just too numerous to keep up with. They ranged from the difficulties we had borrowing military hardware from the Spanish government, which was taken back at the last minute. And then the key airplane, the only one of its kind in Europe, crashed on us. On top of that, the train for the last big sequence blew up *on the first take* ... It was too much, and we got bogged down.'

By January the rumours of chaos on *Cuba* were rife. Allegedly *two* different endings were to be shot and *Screen International* reported that 'Lester can often be heard speaking about fear. It seems that when he wakes up he is terrified of what lies before him. He worries about all the things that might go wrong.' In Spain, meanwhile, Lester insisted he kept up a brave face. 'Yes, the open-ended script was a problem, but it was no cause for alarm. It is lovely when films have their own organic growth. You let it develop and sometimes marvellous things happen.'

During filming, said Lester, Connery never once complained of developments. 'I'm not a director who runs rushes, so he saw nothing as we went along and in that way there was nothing to be discussed.'

Throughout the filming, in fact, the two men spent little time together. Connery's focus instead was on golf, and on driving home whenever possible to Marbella, taking the wheel of his own Mercedes. Quinn Donohue, the publicist, urged him to cooperate more fully with the press but his regular reply, bundling golf clubs into the car at wrap time, was 'Give me a break, eh? I've done my bit.'

*Cuba* came in on schedule and on budget, a laudable accomplishment in the eyes of those who knew. Connery finally saw a rough cut, but didn't reveal his feelings to Lester. 'Only later did it come back to me that he wasn't happy,' Lester said. 'He never said it to my face, but he was cross and he held me responsible for everything that went wrong.' Lester emphasised that he has no regrets about making the movie, notwithstanding reservations about the forced schedule. 'The movie works on a superficial level. The character interplay, all that is there. But the profundity I envisioned went out the window. There just wasn't time to get it.'

*Cuba* had Connery looking more Bondish than he had done since *Diamonds Are Forever*. His hairpiece was thick and neat, the Gable moustache cropped to insignificance on his leaner, fitter face. But the story of a former British Army major – Connery – hired by Batista's people to teach the troops counter-insurgency as the storm builds in Havana resonated with indecision and, viewing it today, decades later, still feels incomplete.

For Connery, *Cuba* was a total waste of time. Unforgiving, and admitting no blame himself, he dubbed it 'a fatal error ... a case of patchwork'. In his opinion, he stated grimly, Lester 'hadn't done his homework'. Lester was understandably aggrieved and doubted the breach of friendship was repairable: 'I haven't heard from Sean about that picture, but I take it his feelings are very strong. After our good times on *Robin and Marian*, it feels sad to have reached that point of departure.'

A shock of disillusionment, or tiredness, rattled Connery after *Cuba*. Its consequence was the first long period of inactivity since 1972. Some speculative projects were announced – a possible role in James Clavell's *Tai-Pan*, to be directed by John Guillermin for Filmways Productions (originally announced to star Steve McQueen); another possible in *Shogun* for ABC TV – but all dissipated, lost under an apparent blanket of business reshuffling. After a row with ICM in Los Angeles, Connery quit Dennis Selinger and ICM's management advice. As replacement, Michael Ovitz, then in the ascendance at Creative Artist Associates, the new premier agency, took personal control of Connery's movie affairs.

In the spring-cleaning that followed, Connery unearthed astounding miscalculations, bad judgements by himself, bad advice and unwise investments throughout the 70s. He told the *Express* journalist Victor Davis that while founding the Educational Trust and seeking ways, with Sir Iain Stewart, to improve the industrial atmosphere between men and management, he had mistakenly assumed himself to be rich. The regretful irony was that when he was writing over his $1 million-plus to the Trust, he himself was almost broke. 'Thanks to mishandling, the fortune had turned out to be all figures and no substance.' Having rebuilt his nest egg during the relentless Selinger era, he swore that this time he would oversee everything personally and trust no manager, agent or business partner entirely. 'Nowadays I handle contracts myself, and I have a good lawyer. I think it was Erica Jong who said the difference between making a lot of money and being rich is a good lawyer.' In West Los Angeles he purchased a large apartment, and in Iowa a 600-acre pig and cattle farm. 'His intention,' said Caine, 'was to resettle a part of himself near the hub of the film world. On *A Bridge Too Far*, for example, he had suffered the remoteness of Marbella. Everyone else was raking in their millions while he was naively playing golf, thinking, "Oh, they won't try to swindle me ..." Sean always had that interest in the American scene. He and I both learned that you had to reside there and play their game if you wanted the international reputation, and the cheques.'

Much as he guessed, Connery was in trouble, reputation-wise, when *Meteor* finally opened in November 1979, followed just weeks later by *Cuba*. The panning both movies received reverberated through the industry, amplified by the story of poor takings on *The First Great Train Robbery*, whose progress around America was funereal. Connery sprang into action, publicly blaming United Artists for its weak-spined promotion of *Robbery*. He didn't need Ovitz to speak up for him – 'after all, it was me who made the film' – but went directly to the publicity and distribution departments at UA and demanded explanations. 'No satisfactory explanation came. United Artists owe me a bit, but I suppose I owe them some too. I never did make that second picture for them, after *Diamonds Are Forever*. Still, it was inexcusable what they did with *Robbery*.'

For Columbia, half interestedly, he promoted *Meteor* with Natalie Wood, pushing its earnings up to a respectable $6 million, a multiple of six on the *Robbery* gross. But it was a relief to get away from the grind and out to the new farm he had purchased in Iowa, where he resolved to put Stefan and Jason to work for a spell, 'to toughen them up'. Commuting to his West LA apartment, he was happy to hang out again with Michael Caine and 'talk about anything except the bloody business'. Dining with his friend Roderick Mann, he would not be drawn on the failures of *Robbery*, *Cuba* or *Meteor* – nor the hot air talk of playing Daddy Warbucks in the upcoming movie of *Annie*, offered to him by producer Ray Stark. Yes, he liked the idea of hoofing in a musical again, and had taken singing lessons to loosen up the vocal chords last fully tested in *Darby O'Gill* – but that was as far as he would go in committing himself. Instead, he wanted to chit-chat and, as always lately, his idle talk was about the fortunes he'd wasted. Did Mann know, for instance, that the Chelsea Embankment flat had been sold for £60,000? Much too little: it was worth £300,000 today. But it wasn't all bad news. Dunbar & Co, the City bank, was still flourishing, still important to him, and he still held 80,000 shares. Plus 'shares in a number of banks in the Mid-West'. Mann noticed, as others had, that the driving principle was a balancing act of business and movie-making. Success in one area, said Mann, was still as important as success in the other.

It was Peter Hyams, the celebrated new whiz kid director who had scored a big popular hit with *Capricorn One*, who at last urged Connery out of what Caine called 'this new mini retirement'. His movie-in-planning was *Outland*, an undisguised reworking of *High Noon* in outer space. Connery was thrilled by 'the story, the whole story and the setting of it and how it was to be designed'. Hyams's plan was to shoot in Hollywood. But Connery's make-or-break bargaining card was a request to film (to a controlled schedule) at Pinewood – 'partly because the technical facilities are so superior there – *Star Wars* was made at Pinewood – and also because I haven't fully made a film there since 1974'.

While waiting for the start date Connery snuck in a few days' worth of cameo playing in Terry Gilliam's *Monty Python*esque *Time Bandits* – a breezy bag of jokes, awkwardly interlinked but full of invention, which told the story of a boy's odyssey through holes in the fabric of time. As King Agamemnon, Connery was, predictably, the heroic colossus at the axis of the film, battling with the Minotaur till saved, by chance, by the boy (Craig Warnock). *Time Bandits* was convenient because it was shot in Morocco, next door to Aloha Golf Course and the stress-saving opportunity to bang a ball about with racing driver James Hunt, now in retirement and living nearby.

'It was a period where his social life had become very important to him,' said Ian Bannen. 'His personal journey had been some-thing like the Beatles', who had really sacrificed their youth to their fame. Sean saw it in a similar way. He kind of missed his 30s. And now he was trying to catch up.' James Hunt saw Connery at play principally as 'a man's man', but, like Bannen, he too observed Connery's 'deepening spiritual relationship with Micheline, which was like a stabilising rudder while all the tough business stuff was going on'. Micheline's great quality, the friends believed, was her ability to share Connery's daily routines while allowing him the space and privacy he craved. 'Her devotion to him was beyond question,' said Michael Caine, 'but she never cramped his style.' At the ritzy Marbella Club hotel, where Loren and Bardot stopped off whenever they were cruising through, Connery was now a frequent visitor, usually in male company. Jackie, wife of high-living Prince Alfonso, the hotel owner and casual friend of the Connerys, com-mented, 'Dozens of the most beautiful women dally and flirt with him, but he doesn't give them the slightest chance.' Micheline, quite clearly, was the ideal mate. Golf continued to unite them, though he baldly confessed that he preferred male competitors, which just made Micheline laugh. 'I like to win too, that's the trouble,' she told Caine. Together they played his favourite golf courses, she off handicap seventeen, he now off a confident nine. The relationship thrived, Michael Caine believed, because it was founded on deep, abiding mutual respect. Connery's brazen honesty Micheline loved, and her personal confidence was such that it didn't at all bother her when Connery said, 'I couldn't possibly be with someone night and day. Whatever your situation, you should be parted for a lot of the time. I'll tell you why: if you've been away acting, painting, whatever, it's that marvellous exchange when you get back together that counts for so much.'

After 16 months of film inactivity Connery was enthused by the prospect of bringing *Outland* to Pinewood, his movie alma mater. But he was upset too that the usual games of tax penalty avoidance were facing him again. Because he had insisted on visiting St Andrews and other Scottish courses for BBC TV pro-celebrity golf matches over the last four years, his allowance for work days in Britain was reduced. Hence, despite the fact that through his efforts millions of American dollars were coming into Britain with *Outland*, he found himself commencing the movie under the kind of time pressures that had flattened Lester and *Cuba*. Ian Bannen believed, 'It really fucked him off. He hated the injustice. He is a very black-and-white man who has felt at times abused by the system. He always paid his dues and he has contributed millions to the UK economy. His Bond movies reinvented British international cinema, but a lot of the time he felt penalised.'

*Outland* was an inherently complicated production that looked likely to swallow every minute of Connery's permitted 90 days, so at weekends he was forced to fly out of Britain aimlessly, returning for work on Mondays. This 'nonsense handicap' drained him. He told anyone who would listen that he had proudly given employment to a hundred Pinewood technicians and he resented the 'paradoxical law that makes it difficult for a man to work as hard and often as he chooses to do. They [the government] seem to be more flexible with the villains who break the law.' The ninety days' earnings concession should be reshaped, he told Hyams, with a distinction made between personal investment earnings, and the kind of money-generating endeavours people like himself and Caine facilitated. Caine, Burton, Roger Moore – all of them should be encouraged to bring what work they could into Britain, and then be taxed on their earnings for each individual production.

Peter Hyams listened, but concentrated on the production with the rigid discipline Connery admired. 'I like his working to pro-gramme,' was Connery's report from the coalface, and Hyams in turn expressed his huge appreciation for 'an actor so consummate that he can convey a breaking heart without his head moving an inch to left or right if the technicalities of the scene forbid it'.

The modus of *Outland* was fresh and adventurous, even for the realm of sci-fi. In telling his parable-like tale of the manipula-tion of labour in a futuristic mining base on Jupiter's moon Io, Hyams used a new camera system called Introvision, and all Fred Zinnemann's tricks from *High Noon*. Where Gary Cooper was the moral marshal single-handedly confronting corruption and cowardice in the Wild West, Connery was O'Neill of the Federal Security Service, doing the same on Io. Some late sequences of *Outland* mimicked *High Noon* visually, but Fred Zinnemann took exception to the publicity campaign launched by Warners which traded on the connection. 'It was ill-advised,' Zinnemann said. 'I saw *Outland* and naturally observed similarities in isolated incidents. But the pictures were *totally* different in content and meaning.'

Connery himself, as he had done before, tripped into the hyperbole. After filming he was, he said, 'most conscious of the *High Noon* aspects' and that Hyams had not tried to disguise the fact that his picture was a tribute to Zinnemann's. 'What was clever,' Connery said, 'was setting it in space, a new frontier town. That was what appealed to me in the first place.' Connery pushed the *High Noon* promotion for a variety of honest reasons, not least of which was his desire to work the box office and regain lost ground. 'But he truthfully believed in it,' said film writer Tony Crawley. 'He set out to promote it more actively than anything he'd done in years because he said it was a novel and worthwhile space venture, a new cinematic departure. He greatly admired what George Lucas and Spielberg had been doing in their sci-fi movies but he made a big point that here (in *Outland*) was a space movie *he* could understand. His kind of futurology.'

Connery said: 'Space fantasy generally doesn't appeal to me. In the end I get lost among all those laser beams and hurtling spaceships. But *Outland* is a logical extension of human technology.' He also appreciated Hyams' skill in 'dealing with human issues in a world of technology run amok'.

Connery's creative input in *Outland* was on a par with *The Offence*. He participated with Hyams in set design and vetted all the actors, deeming it should have 'mainly people with good faces [who] have a certain look about them, rather like Western pioneers'. He'd sought Colleen Dewhurst for his assistant, but when she was unavailable, accepted Hyams's choice of Frances Sternhagen. Introvision, a complicated camera effects technique related to simple old back projection, intrigued him and he involved himself in one way or another in most departments of the production at Pinewood, frequently working unsolicited overtime.

Connery's pride in *Outland* was evident when he enlisted immediately for two more major films, one American and one European based. The main attraction, in these instances, was the directorial names. First up was *Wrong is Right* (later retitled in Europe), directed by Richard Brooks, whom Connery knew socially and whose work – sometimes dramatically successful, like *In Cold Blood*, other times bizarrely indulgent – Connery admired. Brooks's reputation was an oddball one ('boisterous', John Boorman called him), and Connery didn't hesitate in asking to preview the screenplay. Brooks agreed, and went further, requesting, to Connery's delight, his collaboration in redrafting the overlong 208-page script.

During the rewrites in New York, Fred Zinnemann made his approach. Zinnemann, a cinema legend in Connery's eyes, had greatly admired *Robin and Marian* and wanted Connery for the lead in a long-term pet project, a story of Alpine mountaineering called *Five Days of Summer*.

It was mid-1981 and though Connery was beginning to experience the upswing of new demand in important quarters, there remained some muted frustration. In the opinion of a producer associate Connery was doing OK financially, but hadn't managed to break any records over the previous few years. His best run had been around *The Man Who Would Be King*, since which he had continued to appear in a number of lofty, classy pictures. He did want an Academy Award, or respectable recognition, at any rate, but, not surprisingly, his fee status was probably as important. So, when nothing seemed to be particularly exciting in his life, he seriously looked at Bond again.'

Approaching the twentieth anniversary of his breakthrough in *Dr. No*, it seemed the right time to recap. Being at Pinewood again, he told friends, had given rise to happy nostalgia. It was there, on Stage D, that James Bond had first introduced himself to the movie world. From there the journey to wealth and wisdom began. And yet, all these years later, he had to admit he had never actually sat through an entire completed Bond movie – other than those demanded of him at the few premieres, and the two Roger Moores he had sneaked in on. Once in LA, he told Roderick Mann, he did arrive home after a night on the town with Richard Burton and Michael Caine to find *Dr. No* running on TV. He took a beer from the fridge, kicked off his shoes and slumped in a chair to watch it alone. He liked it well enough ... but fell asleep halfway through. For the admirers, Connery-Bond was an institution, the epitome of hedonism, the enviable face of high living. For Connery, Bond was confused memories, old hopes, triumphs, frustrations.

Box-office anaemia struck *Time Bandits* around the time of the European premiere of *Outland*, arranged by Connery for Edinburgh again, with proceeds to the Trust, in August. In Europe, especially, *Outland* did well, aided by a fan press that loved sci-fi and admired Connery as the stoutly moral hero. In America, by contrast, it earned its way (a decent $10 million in receipts, comparable with *The Man Who Would Be King*), but was critically slaughtered as an anachronistic, jaded fable that paled alongside the spectacle of *The Empire Strikes Back*.

By now Connery was in Switzerland, toiling with Zinnemann, but he interrupted the shoot to help promote *Outland*. To producer Alan Ladd Jr's chagrin, Connery allowed only three press interviews in Edinburgh. Then it was back to the Bernina Mountains, round the corner from St Moritz, for five months of snowbound labour. Ladd didn't complain too much: his new company was funding *Five Days One Summer* as well.

For Zinnemann, a double Academy-Award-winning director with a 30-year record of excellence, Connery was 'never less than remarkably professional. He was not difficult, had no star ego, no moods. One felt he had only one objective – to get on with the picture and do what was best for it.' Typically, nothing of the creeping insecurity that was the legacy of so many recent poor choices revealed itself to Zinnemann. As a young man Zinnemann's favourite pastime was hiking through Europe's mountains; for countless years he had tried to stage this cherished project. 'Sean was my first and only choice of actor because no one else could undertake the hazardous exercise required, and yet was mature and yet again *could* act,' Zinnemann said. After the Richard Brooks film wrapped in June, Connery had immediately started mountaineering training at Pontresina. From there it was plain sailing. As with Brooks, Connery requested script participation – a precondition on all his movies now – and Zinnemann found no problems in agreeing. 'Sean was constructive,' he said. 'The story was one I'd read, in a short story form, thirty years before, and it needed quite a lot of development and imagination to make it work for cinema. We had a very fine young writer, Michael Austin, but Sean had many many thoughts and concepts, ninety-five per cent of which were worthy of assimilation.'

Betsy Brantley, the North Carolina newcomer cast to play the young woman obsessively in love with the married doctor twenty-five years her senior, posed problems. 'Obviously there are difficulties when you place an actor of Sean's experience opposite a girl without the range, like Miss Brantley,' Zinnemann said. 'I can best explain the problem by referring to the second film I ever did, which had to do with a detective and a senile dog. The detective had trouble learning his lines and needed seven or eight takes. The dog, on the other hand, was only good for one take – then he ran away to hide. All this had to be done in four weeks. So one learns to gear oneself against such disparities and make things fit. Sean was as helpful with Betsy Brantley as could have been expected of him. He's a very fine actor, and he didn't let me down.'

The stresses of coping with arduous, freezing rock climbs and inexperienced actors were pushed aside again when, three weeks after Edinburgh, Connery attended the Deauville Film Festival on a $15,000 expense chit from Warners, to beat the drum about Hyams's film. *Outland* opened the festival and attendants were later treated to a retrospective of Connery's earlier films, coincidentally side by side with a Lana Turner retrospective. Turner showed up to queen over the event, and even dined with her former close friend. They were pictured together brushing shoulders, grinning wide, but neither would comment on their controversial and mysterious past. 'Through Turner's stay and her packed press conflab,' wrote Tony Crawley, 'she gave the kind of glitzy performance that can only be described by one of her film titles: *Imitation of Life*.' Connery, for his part, was life itself – an accurate embodiment of all that had been whirling round him professionally and personally these last tough months. He was curt but courteous, impatient but grimly dedicated, voicing concern but brave-faced throughout.

To discerning onlookers at the Deauville press conference it seemed that here was a star actor who was floundering, but hanging in.

# 17. FIGHTING BACK

At Christmas 1981 Sean Connery came home for his first serious break from work in almost a year to ponder the question that had been on the lips of half the world's movie-goers for nine years: would he don the Savile Row mantle of James Bond again? Home, 'the sanatorium rancho' by his wife Micheline's definition, was the place to be after the rigours of Switzerland. Balmy in December as a good May in Britain, with hibiscus and lime trees to spice the air, San Pedro de Alcantara, next door to Marbella, had the peaceful spirit of a quiet fishing village all year round. The Casa Malibu, the Connerys' immaculately neat villa there, had increasingly become the haven and hideaway in the troubled times. By the early 80s the Connerys had an embarrassment of choices of places to call home. Apart from Spain, there was the luxury apartment in LA and the house on the golf course at Lyford Cay in the Bahamas. But the Casa Malibu, designed from scratch by Micheline and now encompassing an outhouse bungalow where Connery worked in his moments of seclusion, was always first choice for privacy and rest.

That Christmas Connery's mood was rocky. Sheamus Smith spoke often to him and described him then as 'restless'. John Boorman knew why: the potential of reviving James Bond was challenging and troubling him.

There were other distressing distractions. A court action by a former ally, trusted film accountant Kenneth Richards, greatly upset him. Richards sued for monies he claimed Connery owed, totalling more than £100,000, and an ongoing 2 per cent of 13 films Richards had worked on, which, with court expenses had Connery's countersuit failed, would have amounted to a massive sum. Richards lost his claim, but Connery was shaken by his misreading of a key professional associate and by what was, not only on the face of it, a close fought battle. A measure of his anguish about the November row was reflected in a *Daily Telegraph* headline – CONNERY NEAR TO TEARS AS HE WINS BOND FILM FIGHT – and the concurrent splay of articles that spoke of his torment and delight. 'It was certainly an ordeal,' Connery confessed just before Christmas. 'Something I don't want to go through again. It's much better on the film set.'

But on the film set, since *Meteor*, things weren't all rosy. *Meteor*, *Cuba* and to a lesser extent *Time Bandits* had all proved major disappointments. All fared badly at the box office, *Meteor* worst of all, with a recorded loss of $15.8 million two years after release. In his attempts to reorientate, Connery had taken great care in choosing *Outland* and *The Man with the Deadly Lens* (the retitled *Wrong is Right*) but they too faded quickly from view. Fred Zinnemann was the obvious potential saviour, but *Five Days One Summer* attracted weak notices and weaker business (less than $1 million in US rentals), despite its smooth playing and memorable scenery.

By Christmas Connery sensed a professional cul-de-sac. 'He ran aground,' Ian Bannen believed. 'There are stages and ages an actor goes through. Sean was past fifty and, maybe in somebody's view, past his prime. So he was poised for a different *kind* of role. I think it all becomes quite muddled for a lot of actors around that time. I think Sean is no different. He wasn't a young man. He wasn't a granddad. What exactly was he? How would he cast *himself*? It was a conundrum.'

According to Bannen Connery was 'especially disappointed' by *Outland*. 'He prizes his instincts, you see, and he had seen the success of *Star Wars* and accordingly believed that space age *Outland* would make a fortune. I believe it continued to matter to him that he succeeded with a very wide audience. He had set himself that standard, and now it wasn't working so well, and that upset him.'

Connery understood the dilemma of age. He understood too how professional inertia is insidious and potentially fatal, how rock-solid superstardom frequently gives way to petrification. Richard Burton in his heyday could be farmed out to junk, Richard Harris to parody his own manic raucousness, Olivier to all comers. A star is not for ever.

Through December, Connery found himself particularly reappraising the question of Bond, the career cornerstone he loved to hate. Various Bond projects had been pushed his way over the last few years and he had always distanced himself. Now, in the face of an apparently viable new Bond project that did not involve Cubby Broccoli, he was tempted to reconsider. Could Bond restore his flagging market appeal? Certainly, without doubt, 007 could hike Connery's going rate. The deal on his last Bond, *Diamonds Are Forever*, had never been matched: $1.2 million from United Artists, plus a percentage and a choice of two further movie projects. Connery's recent fees had been nearer half a million, often somewhat less. Apart from elaborating the super-draw profile, what could 007 offer Connery in compensation for the risks and difficulties – at 52 years of age – of revival? $2 million? More?

The businessman in Connery was stirred by the factors working for a return to Bond at this time. Above all, the proposed new project, offered by producer Jack Schwartzman, was in direct competition with the Cubby Broccoli–Roger Moore Bonds. The course and purpose of the recent Moore Bonds was manifestly confused and audience indulgence was waning. In 1979, *Moonraker*, undistilled kids' fizz, grossed massively by turning tail totally on trademark Bond. Its 1981 successor, *For Your Eyes Only*, limped through twelve months without showing a remotely Bondian profit. But still Roger Moore could cruise on *Moonraker* and demand, as he did, $4 million for the upcoming Broccoli venture, *Octopussy*. This was instructive to Connery. If Moore was good for $4 million while the pre-sold Bond market was moving uncertainly, couldn't Connery bat against that figure?

What of the quality of the new Bond property, though? 'Quality never came into it, not in the purest sense,' Ian Bannen opined. 'In my view, Sean was crazy to give up Bond in the first place. When he quit he was riding high, but he could have gone higher. He could have cruised. He could have done a Bond a year and said, To hell with it. Great, it's done, now I can go on and do Shakespeare or whatever I like. He could have played the game.'

But Connery had never treated Bond lightly. At the start, he had addressed it as he addressed *Anna Christie*, all the classics. Bond remained for him a class act to be proud of. In conversation with friends he spoke with delight about the multilayered scripts, the extraordinary production values, Terence Young's canny knack with women and guns. 'Never a braggart, even when drunk,' as Ian Bannen attested, he was very aware that those early Connery-Bonds minted a brand-new cinema genre. The great frustration, hard felt and often bemoaned, was that so few understood how much application and art went into the invention of Bond.

Schwartzman's Bond had all the indications of quality. Schwartzman himself seemed to be the kind of producer Connery liked to deal with: by reputation forthright, ordered and a fast decision-maker. He had been associated with Lorimar, producers of the TV hit *Dallas*, and – best recommendation for Connery – had masterminded Peter Sellers's subtle swan song *Being There*. Schwartzman's essential intention was to remake *Thunderball*, the rights of which, with *Casino Royale* (spoofed-up and seemingly spoiled for ever by Charles Feldman and Jerry Bresler in 1967) did not belong to Cubby Broccoli's Eon Productions. The circumstances that brought about the availability of *Thunderball* rights are today still in debate. When Kevin McClory sued Fleming for copyright infringement on the original *Thunderball* storyline, part of the settlement gave McClory the movie rights. These he later shared with Eon in a fund-sharing deal to make the 1965 hit movie. But specific in that arrangement was the condition that all rights to *Thunderball* would revert to McClory after ten years. This remarkable clause either demonstrates the shortsightedness of Eon or the bargaining strength of McClory. Whichever way, as Bond sailed soundly into the 70s, the Irishman was left with a solid gold property – the script and characters of the most widely successful of the 60s Bonds. Early in 1975, when Connery was in America overseeing post-production on *The Wind and the Lion*, McClory presented his first revival idea. Connery demurred. But McClory wasn't discouraged.

'He asked would I be interested in contributing in any way,' Connery explained later, 'with all the experience that had been gained in the six previous ones I'd done. I thought about it and said, "It depends who you've got writing it."'

The novelist Len Deighton, living in tax exile 50 miles from McClory's County Kildare home in Ireland, signed into a development deal with McClory and Connery was finally appeased. It was agreed that Connery, Deighton and McClory would co-write a new Bond. Connery flew to Ireland and moved into Straffan House, McClory's sprawling country mansion. 'Sean was keen,' McClory said. 'Bond was still in his blood because, after all, he *made* Bond. But then, in the 70s, we kept it a close secret because we knew how Broccoli might jump.'

After a year's staccato work, a full-page advertisement in *Variety* in 1975 announced production preparations for McClory's *James Bond of the Secret Service*, a Paradise Film Production, with an office address in Nassau. A superfluous recommendation – 'One of the most exciting screenplays I have ever read', signed Irving Paul Lazare – suggested ominous overkill. According to McClory, Connery was 'rampant and ready to play the role once a studio deal was in hand' – but suddenly McClory and Paradise Films fell silent. The cause, quite simply, was Eon's wrath. Many believed McClory had hit a brick wall in seeking a distribution deal, that no studio saw a remade *Thunderball* as a safe earner. McClory answered the gossips by reminding them that the original *Thunderball* was the biggest ever Bond grosser, taking $27 million against a budget of $4 million. 'And the laws of cinema are like the laws of gravity,' said McClory. 'What worked once can and does work again. You reinvent the wheel, it's still the wheel.'

Connery himself defended McClory's financial planning: 'So many people were wanting to contribute to that picture with funds and what have you. There were no problems financially. But I was under the impression that it was totally clean. Free from any litigational problems. When we started to talk quite seriously about the possibility it became so complex. Ouch, the lawyers came out of the woodwork by the hundred. The legal factors were harder to face than making the film. Then the publicity started to work on it and I said, "That's enough! And I walked away."'

Walking away entailed some anguish because 1975 was, for Connery, the ideal time to contemplate a return as Bond. At 45 he was still fit and fast enough to appear credible with Berettas and in the boudoir. And the clutch of interestingly diverse and artistically successful pictures he had just made distanced him sufficiently from a too-ready character identification whilst allowing the challenge of developing Bond with some continuity. Roger Moore, then commencing his third Bond for Broccoli, was consolidating a personal following, just enough to whet Connery's competitive appetite. 'Professionally there's no more fierce competitor than Sean,' said Michael Caine – and Moore's challenge was, then, the happiest of motivations.

But Eon and United Artists, the Bond series' distributors, would allow McClory no leeway. Clearly they recognised Connery's power, resurrected at any time as Bond, to scotch their films. Court action began. Arthur Krim, head of UA, allowed that McClory had rights but insisted that nothing other than a verbatim rehash of *Thunderball* was permissible. McClory counterclaimed, detailing his broad speculative screenwork with Fleming back in 1959, before Bond ever hit the big screen. *Thunderball* was not his only Bond screen treatment. There was *Latitude 78 West, Bond in the Bahamas* and others – any of which could legitimately be used as the basis for a McClory Bond film.'

It was a borderline case but McClory's intentions were eventually seen to be honourable and legal enough, and Broccoli's intentions designed – for understandably commercial considerations – to obstruct and delay. Early in 1980 an Appeal Court decision in America cleared the path for McClory and in July, while ICM in LA was negotiating *Outland*, British newspapers announced that Connery had at last signed a contract to return as 007 'for a small salary, most of which will go to charity'.

In reality Connery had signed nothing. McClory had his clearance to do a Bond but, exhausted from wrangling, was beginning to offload. Already he had invested and lost a considerable sum in defending his Bond rights. Enter Jack Schwartzman, fresh from the triumph of *Being There*, with a favourite writer, Lorenzo Semple, Jr, formerly of *Batman*, latterly *Three Days of the Condor* fame. Protracted talks followed before a deal was settled upon, late in 1981. Schwartzman inherited the Fleming–McClory concepts and the Deighton–Connery script and hefted the lot on to Semple's desk. Around the same time Schwartzman, in McClory's wake, decided only one actor could revive this Bond: Sean Connery.

Before the respective producers' signatures had dried on what was then widely known as the *Warhead* contract, Schwartzman had Connery in renewed negotiations. Connery's first response was wary but encouraging enough for Schwartzman to hustle together a distribution deal and independent investments that allowed him to offer Connery $2 million. Two million dollars was not enough.

Without doubt Connery paced himself alongside Roger Moore's fee negotiations with Broccoli over Christmas. Broccoli incurred Moore's expensive anger by scouting for a possible new Bond – Superman Christopher Reeve was considered as, reputedly, was Broccoli's daughter's boyfriend, an unknown American actor. Moore continued to up the asking price for *Octopussy*, finally settling for $4 million – ample to cover his daily consumption of Monte Cristos at $10 a smoke and jet-hop commuting between Gstaad and the main family home at Les Hauts de St Paul near Nice. Connery now had a hard target to bat against. Schwartzman continued his careful courtship, signing a favoured director of Connery's, Irvin Kershner, in April.

'Sean might appear to be playing games with this,' Ian Bannen said in the spring of 1982, 'but you can bet he's involved on every level. He knows they need him. But he knows he probably needs this too. He'll have the measure of everything working for and against him. He'll be aware of the Broccoli plans, and every aspect of Schwartzman's finances.'

To understand Connery's procrastination one is drawn back to his resentment of what he regarded as Broccoli and Saltzman's meanness. In 1981 a conservative estimate put Connery-Bond movie earnings at around $250 million. It is unlikely that Connery, the acknowledged life's breath of the series, had netted a fiftieth of that. *Never Say Never Again* was a chance, in his view, to right a wrong.

For Connery, who had gone on record confessing he was 'more troubled losing ten dollars on a golf match than losing thousands in business', the manoeuvring for position was also, importantly, an issue of ethics. John Boorman believed that 'the joy of profes- sional sparring' played its part too: 'He knows this business inside out and he is properly cynical about it. I think he took great fun from standing up to certain people and certain demeaning, dehumanising situations, and winning out.'

The preliminary contract to do Schwartzman's movie was signed in Los Angeles by Connery on 18 May, a few weeks after *The Man with the Deadly Lens* opened. Location shooting was slated for the Bahamas and Ireland but this was changed when the Irish government closed its Ardmore Studios late in the summer. Kershner flew to Britain and booked alternative studio time at EMI Elstree, not many miles down the road from Pinewood where the Bond saga had begun and where, on 16 August, Roger Moore knuckled down to 16 weeks on the rival *Octopussy*.

Kershner, Schwartzman and Connery refused to comment on the actor's fee but Connery was clearly happy. John Boorman spoke to him about the upcoming challenge and later said, 'I won't say Sean's madly looking forward to another go at Bond, but at the same time he's looking forward to the five million dollars it will earn for him.'

Once decided, Connery threw everything into the Bond come-back. 'It was unequivocal commitment,' Ian Bannen said. 'A lot of the driving force, I believe, was Micheline. It was she who came up with the movie's title, *Never Say Never Again*, which was brimming with wisdom. I'm sure Sean loved the ironies. She groomed him for it. She even trimmed those bushy eyebrows again. It wasn't a wishy-washy effort. It was: Now, let's show Broccoli and those bastards how to do the *real* James Bond.' With echoes of the Malgrem dance-movement studies of the Cilento days, Connery engaged Peggy Spencer, the BBC *Come Dancing* judge who trained Nureyev for Ken Russell's *Valentino*, to develop an exercise plan that would increase his agility, and teach him the tango he'd abandoned thirty years before in the Palais de Danse.

Reactivation brought him back to Scotland, too, for happy reasons and for sad ones. In the run-up to Bond, Lord-Provost Kenneth Borthwick asked him to participate in a film to promote Edinburgh tourism. Andrew Fyall, in his capacity as Edinburgh's Director of Tourism, led the production and was flattered by Connery's generosity. The budget was £100,000, mostly funded by the British and Scottish Tourist Boards, but Connery refused a fee. 'He started by agreeing to do just a voice-over, then gradually dominated the whole production,' said Fyall. 'It was utter commitment, from seven a.m. on location at Edinburgh Castle, till seven p.m., when he took the crew out for dinner. He was a gem to work with.' For the film Connery returned to broken-down Fountainbridge as he would do, again, in 1991 for Fyall and Ross Wilson's STV documentary. The time was well spent and the resulting intimate film received excellent notices and book-ings for screenings at the Commonwealth Games in Brisbane in the autumn, as well as in Melbourne, Auckland and Sydney where Connery was, and remains, among the best-loved interna-tional stars. The film premiered at the Edinburgh Film Festival, coinciding with the conferring of an honorary doctorate from Heriot-Watt University that deeply moved Connery. Connery abandoned his golf at Gleneagles to accept the award. Old pal John Brady said, 'I know it touched him. He never got the educa-tion he wanted, because of the circumstances of his childhood. That sort of honour recognises his intelligence and the intelli-gence of his achievement as an actor, which is no small thing. I mean, how many actors are given doctorates like that? It doesn't happen to the folks from *Coronation Street*, does it?'

But it wasn't all good news. On 27 September location filming of the new Bond started in Villefranche, near Nice in the south of France. Connery appeared content, in the words of journalist Margaret Hinxman of the *Daily Mail*, 'shooting his cuffs with deceptive nonchalance'. Though Schwartzman and Kershner's presence was conspicuous, it was clear to Hinxman that Sean Connery was in command on this movie. Co-star Barbara Carrera said, 'It was Sean's picture, Sean's choices all the way.' One of Connery's first decisions was to avoid banter with the media, the great bugbear of Broccoli–Saltzman Bond. Even at this late stage Broccoli was still attempting to stop the film, now in partnership with the trustees of Ian Fleming's estate, and Connery was worried. Despite his best shot, though, Broccoli's legal arguments failed. In London Mr Justice Goulding rejected Eon's request for an injunction on the basis that it would be unfair to hinder a film so far advanced. The judge acknowledged the plan for a further

High Court action but rejected Sam Stamler QC's plea that a deferred victory for Eon would be pointless, 'merely closing the stable door too late'. Effectively, Broccoli's opposition was over.

Hinxman was the first and last of the journalists allowed access to Connery. He told her: 'Bond is an interesting character. There's a lot more I can do with him. I'm fifty-two. There's nothing particularly daring about playing your age. I've done it before, in *Robin and Marian* and *Murder on the Orient Express*. It's absurd to cling to what you were in your youth. It's the difference, say, between Burt Lancaster and Kirk Douglas. Lancaster plays his age, looks his age and has given some memorable fine performances on the screen. Douglas strives to stay young. But he seems gaunt, a shadow of his former self. It's a little sad.'

To many, there was something a little sad about Connery – who otherwise embraced middle age – attempting to recreate superman 007 in an era that danced to the youthful testosterone of Travolta and Stallone. Sure enough, Connery was light-footed as ever, but it was hard to miss the thickening of his features and the age-emphasis of an awful, Fred Astaire-like wig.

After France, *Never Say Never Again* moved location to the Bahamas where McClory's Paradise Island home, Pieces of Eight, became Bond's native base. Here the brooding atmosphere was augmented by foul weather. After a week of monsoon rain Connery was edgy. Richard Schenkman, the founder of the international James Bond fan club, visited and observed, 'Irvin Kershner was under a black cloud and was trying to save a schedule knocked all to hell. Connery's glib humour and creative interest can quickly turn to vociferous anger if he thinks people, including the director, are being inefficient or uncommunicative. He blew up when he realised that ten minutes of rehearsal time had been lost because Kershner hadn't told everyone that he had changed his mind about something.'

Kershner, meanwhile, remained stoical. He had grown to admire Connery while directing him in *A Fine Madness* and that admiration was unshakeable: 'He had done some wonderful things in movies – *The Man Who Would Be King*, for instance. Unlike so many American actors of his status, he isn't afraid to take risks and that deserves support.'

With the perspective of time, Connery himself admits that *Never Say Never Again* was a no-win gamble that probably shouldn't have been undertaken. Initially McClory, then Schwartzman and Warner Bros' publicity department, offered the earth. What they delivered, in the shadow of *Thunderball*, was featherweight. The 'event extravaganza' Warners promised premiered in New York on 7 October 1983, and in London a fortnight later. First returns were excellent and the general press write-ups bland but good. But when the dust settled, the post mortems were dire. *Films and Filming* condemned the 'tide of improbability and a slack script'. In the same article Brian Baxter lamented the updating of Connery-Bond, deriding his appearance in bicycle shorts and boiler suits. 'For myself I would be a lot happier to see the *real* actor develop. Anyone who has waltzed so successfully through masterpieces like *Robin and Marian* and *Marnie* should not need to tango. Let's say never again.'

*Never Say Never Again* lost the box-office war against Roger Moore's *Octopussy*. By 1990 the US rental grosses on Connery's picture were listed as $28 million. *Octopussy* had taken $34 million. These were suitably grand Bondian figures, but they paled against other big hits of the 80s. The relative failure of Connery's revised Bond seemed apt: the movie really did display chronic weaknesses and misjudgement, much of it down to Connery. He told Marjorie Bilbow: 'I had script approval as well as casting approval, director approval and lighting cameraman approval. The idea of lighting it with a first-rate man like Dougie Slocombe gives it so much prestige and substance.' In fact, most notably in the camerawork, the movie falls far short of competent. Slocombe's photography bizarrely minimises the beauty of the French and Caribbean seascapes and the camera framing, which is consistently tight in the TV manner, gives a feeling of low budget to the most flamboyant scenes. There are also plot problems – a critical Bond ally in France never properly identified on camera or in dialogue – and evident bad acting. Elsewhere, the movie's music (by Michel Legrand) is undramatic and the set design, so distinguished an area in the history of Bond, suggests a kind of Sunday supplement phoniness.

Connery saw the mess he was in but steered clear of artistic analysis to focus the bad faith business aspects which hit home once the movie hit the theatres: 'There's nothing I like better than a film that really works, providing you don't have to deal with all the shit that comes afterwards in getting what you're entitled to. But when you get into a situation where somebody who is totally incompetent is in charge, a real ass, then everything is a struggle. There was so much incompetence, ineptitude and dissension during the making of *Never Say Never Again* that the film could have disintegrated. It was a toilet. What I could have done is just let it bury itself. I could have walked away with an enormous amount of money and the film would never have been finished. But once I was in there I ended up getting in the middle of every decision. The assistant director and myself really produced that picture.'

Micheline told journalist Pat Tracey that the movie had been 'a nightmare' and that Connery would never re-do Bond for love nor money. 'That was the last time,' she said. 'He's too old now. And I am glad that Roger Moore is quitting too. He has been marvellous, but no one can go on for ever.'

# 18. ENTER OSCAR

Five million dollars better off but spiritually exhausted, Connery reacted to the trauma of Bond by withdrawing into another semi-retirement. For almost three years he refused all scripts and vanished from the public arena. According to Micheline, the reason was 'the upset' caused by the less than honest management of the Bond revival. 'Sean has such high ideals. He is always being shocked by people. I have tried to teach him cynicism. Don't be shocked, I say, the world is like that.'

But there were shocks in store. In the autumn of 1982 as he worked on Bond Effie suffered a stroke in Edinburgh and was admitted to the Infirmary in a critical condition. Connery left location to fly to her side and was saddened by what he saw. A friend said, 'She was the rock at the core of his childhood. No matter what, the fame never touched her. He thought her invincible – and now she was fading away. Joe was gone – so much had changed in his existence in the 70s. Neil was still in Edinburgh but Sean was never *that* close to him. So I think he felt something slipping away.' Micheline and Neil were never close friends but Micheline always acknowledged the key role Effie had in Connery's affections. When it was clear that Effie's active days were over, Micheline grew even closer to Sean. He was jaded and she was there for him, either at home when he needed her or on the golf course when he needed her. Micheline and the boys gave him the family security that was so important to him at the time. Connery's relationships with stepson Stefan and son Jason grew warmer though he was hardly a conventional dad. There had been a definite distance with Jason, the reason being that he didn't want Jason to become overdependent, to assume the role of a rich man's son. Jason's progress in acting briefly horrified Connery, finally delighted him. After schooling at Gordonstoun, Jason first trod the boards in *Aladdin* in Perth before graduating to minor movie playing alongside his mother Diane in Australia. Later success in the UK starring in HTV's *Robin of Sherwood* brought bigger film roles and, ultimately, perhaps inevitably, the role as James Bond's creator in *The Secret Life of Ian Fleming*, an American TV movie that attracted wide attention. 'I've never felt in competition with my father,' Jason later said. 'And he's never made me feel I get work through him, or that I have to prove myself to him. There are a lot of unhappy people with famous parents, but he's never made me feel uncomfortable about who he is. I'm proud of who he is.'

Connery arranged the best medical treatment for Effie, who would linger for a few disabled years, visited daily by Neil who fed her soup and kept her abreast of family news. Andrew Fyall said, 'Sean rang me constantly with messages for the doctor, or for Neil. He may not have been on the spot, but he was close to everything that was happening. He adored her, but there was nothing more he could do.' When Effie died, on 2 April 1985, she was cremated at Mortonhall on Edinburgh's southside and Connery joined a close family group for what Fyall described as 'a traditional Scottish wake' at the North British Hotel. 'There were lots of old Connerys there,' said Fyall. 'Distant uncles mostly, and the younger generation was really just Neil's daughters. There were no celebrity guests. It was a very personal sadness that touched Sean deeply.'

The blows fell thick and fast. The disillusionment of *Never Say Never Again* fortified Connery's determination to wring whatever he could from Broccoli and Eon for past services unrecognised. In the summer of 1984 he unleashed his worst, filing a federal action against Broccoli, Eon, Danjaq SA and MGM/UA for unreturned profits on *From Russia with Love*, *Goldfinger*, *Thunderball*, *You Only Live Twice* and *Diamonds are Forever*, amounting to at least $1.25 million. Connery's companies that took the action accused Broccoli and his companies of 'fraud, deceit, conspiracy, breach of contract and causing emotional distress'. Damages sought amounted to $225 million. The hearing early in 1984 in Los Angeles revealed much of the intimate background of Connery's early Bond deal-making. For *Dr. No*, it emerged, he had been guaranteed 1 per cent of all gross monies in excess of $4 million received by backers United Artists. For *Goldfinger* it was 5 per cent, with an additional 5 per cent on profits for *You Only Live Twice* outside UK, Ireland and North America. Connery also claimed he was entitled to, but received nothing, from the vast merchandising of his face and image as James Bond.

The case was thrown out by District Court Judge David Kenyon on the basis that the defendants' action did not constitute a violation of the Securities Exchange Commission. Connery had no comment to make but Broccoli professed himself 'pleased' while his lawyer, Norman Tyre, announced that his client had not made any plans on whether to sue for false accusations.

A very low-key Sean Connery re-emerged on movie screens in the final aftermath of the 007 debacle in two broadly differing movies. Stephen Weeks's Arthurian mess *Sword of the Valiant: The Legend of Gawain and the Green Knight* earned him $1 million for six days' work and generated no excitement at all. In the States it was hardly seen and even its subsequent video distribution proved a failure. The film had been through various hoops of development over ten years and the muddle of the script and quasi-moral message show why. The *Monthly Film Bulletin* called it 'an unsatisfactory crossbreed of *Robin Hood* and *Monty Python*'. The recovery plan was Russell Mulcahy's *Highlander*, another costume part, this time a grand $12 million feature shot in Scotland that had more, perhaps, in common with *Zardoz* than anything. Connery seemed briefly enthused – though friends attributed the Scottish distractions, not the work, to the smiles on the set. Connery's publicity profile was next to non-existent, but Russell Mulcahy welcomed 'a pro', who 'loved the costumes'. If the film's publicists hoped to galvanise Connery as the project matured, they were bound for frustration. Connery obviously liked the role of Juan Sanchez Villa-Lobos Ramirez, the time-travelling immortal who is Christopher Lambert's spirit guide in his own immortal quests, but saw no reason to analyse it. His best contribution was: 'The dramatics take care of themselves if you get it right. The humour you have to find.'

Denied the tub-thumping, *Highlander*'s publicists could only watch wistfully from afar as Connery helicoptered across Scotland from golf course to location, or larked about on Loch Shiel with co-star Lambert and Micheline, lustily enjoying the role of tour guide, expounding the legends and beauties of his beloved Scotland. In his one longish but insubstantial interview of the time Connery seemed unfazed by what he himself judged to be professional mistakes, and resilient in his independence. 'I somehow never fit into the scene in the United Kingdom, or Hollywood, or Spain, or anywhere for that matter. The only group I ever belonged to was the Navy. Rightly or wrongly I've always made my own decisions. But given today's climate, to be in demand for so wide a spectrum of parts means I must be doing something right.' Second billing to Christopher Lambert or anyone else didn't bother him in the least. 'I am also an actor unconcerned with age. I do not have to stay within the confines of the leading man label.'

'Sean has never had that vanity per se,' said Guy Hamilton. 'But his *presence* leads him in a certain direction. After Bond was passed he had to replace him. He isn't complacent in any area of his life. So I would say that the urge to score big again kept him on his toes – and continues to keep him edgy. I imagine that drives him subconsciously day and night.'

*Highlander* had cult success but was seen by the highbrows as an unmitigated failure. 'A mess,' *Sight and Sound* reckoned, though Connery passed unscathed. In the US the film was released in a much shortened version, which helped repair some of the plodding historical point-scoring in the original. But the *Monthly Film Bulletin*, among many, saw through the ruse: only on the surface, said the *Bulletin*, is the film 'periodically exhilarating'.

Once it was clear that Connery intended to bury Bond and reestablish himself as an actor, everyone who knew him expected role choices as radically varied as possible. The cynics insisted that if he got a good deal from Broccoli he would simply give up and play golf for the rest of his days. But Connery told Michael Aspel: 'I couldn't just play golf. My God, I'd kill someone.'

His next film choice – immaculately timed – was a gruelling test: the austere, excellent *The Name of the Rose*, based on Umberto Eco's modern classic. From the start Connery gave it his all, displaying a candour and commitment beyond the norm. When *Rolling Stone* visited the freezing Roman location in February 1986 it reported with surprise that Connery was more socially active with director Jean-Jacques Annaud's team than anyone had previously seen him. After an exhausting week traipsing over the wind-lashed Roman hills, clad only in the coarse smock of the fourteenth-century Benedictine monk-detective he was playing, Connery was in no rush to go to any golf course, nor did he hide himself in the comforts of his suite at the Savoy Hotel. *Rolling Stone* reported: 'Tomorrow, Saturday, [the crew] will all get together for a feast at the local trattoria, a tradition with this group. Even Connery will perform magic tricks, tell jokes and cheer as Annaud dances a fiery flamenco ...'

Connery was, in fact, elated by the quality of this subtle, brilliant project. It was *the* tonic. Eco's book, serpentine and elusive in its linguistic adventures and semiotic discourse, thrilled him and challenged that aspect of his intellect formerly fed by the likes of Henderson and Cilento. He flitted and prowled through the book, constantly teasing new dimensions from his character, Brother William of Baskerville, who is appointed to investigate a string of grisly murders at a remote monastery. The character is multi-faceted and Connery especially enjoyed the subplot device of his relationship with a young novice, Adso, played by 16-year-old Christian Slater. Adso narrates the movie as an old man reviewing his youth, and Annaud and Connery enjoyed the best of working relationships with the new star. '[Adso] is the student and Sean Connery is the teacher,' Slater told *Rolling Stone*. 'It's pretty much what's going on here in real life.'

Annaud reported Connery relentlessly pursuing the truth of the part and 'inspired' by the thoroughness of the production's homework. The shooting script, for example, was the *fifteenth* draft, on which four very experienced writers had worked. Connery's greatest pleasure, it appeared, was maintaining the reality of authentic medieval life. Not only was the actor studying ritualistic and hierarchical accuracy but he was disciplining his own every move – 'how close you stand in relation to each other, how much obeisance to give, who sings who talks ...'

There was further motivation for Connery, Sheamus Smith

believed, 'in the deprivations and awfulness of the locations which took him back to his own lean, mean days'. Connery might have been reminded in some oblique way of Fountainbridge when he proudly detailed life in a monk's outfit, thermal underwear and moonboots: 'All those rats you see underfoot are real. They had them ready in polythene bags, hundreds of them. I was walking on a carpet of rats. I killed about fifteen of them in my sandals and bare feet. I was sorry about that, but there was nothing I could do about it.'

In every way *Rose* was the opposite of the reprised Bond movie, and its purity and thoroughness wrote a blueprint for Connery's future movie outlook. As Annaud tells it, the movie was prepared with an enormous, sensitive passion. There were no cheap concessions to commercialism, no half measures. In the beginning, Eco himself had resisted the idea of a Hollywood-big movie. RAI, Italian television, initially owned the rights but Annaud – with a Sorbonne degree in the Art and History of the Middle Ages and Greek behind him – met Eco and persuaded him that an international, large-scale production was essential in terms of maintaining fidelity to the book. 'When I was a kid I was impressed by the magic of castles and old churches,' Annaud said. 'There was something very romantic about those old stones, their smell, the humidity.' Eco swooned, the deal was done and Annaud commenced the daunting task of reconstructing 'a fully honest' Middle Ages. The movie's interiors were shot at the Kloster Eberach, near Frankfurt, a twelfth-century home of the Cistercians unchanged in eight hundred years. Exteriors proved more difficult and no match for the monastery and tower described in Eco's book could be found in Europe. Annaud then employed Dante Ferretti to construct a real Romanesque church with a 210-foot tower, mostly cast in real stone. The props, too, were mostly real artifacts which, Annaud claims, helped the confidence and posture of the actors. Attention to detail was relentless: all the casting was 'authentic'. 'In the Middle Ages people were malnourished, semi-crippled, with disastrous skin conditions in some cases.' Therefore backgrounds were filled with real people, local farm-folk, hand-picked special extras. During the shooting day Annaud even forbade the wearing of foot-warmers and socks, despite the often sub-zero temperatures 'because people sit differently when they are cold'. Later Connery called this 'over-realism'.

Annaud confessed that the movie's $16 million budget might easily have doubled in Hollywood but there was no way this film could be made with integrity in LA and he was satisfied to take the half-price fee he was offered to do it as it was done.

*The Name of the Rose* garnered wonderful plaudits worldwide throughout 1986 and restored Connery's confidence and good humour. The *Monthly Film Bulletin* applauded Connery's Brother William as 'a quite remarkable construct'. *Photoplay* called the movie, and Connery, 'masterful'. Others concurred and the movie became that rare beast: an honest intellectual endeavour that scored at the box office.

For twenty years stalwarts across the industry had predicted an Academy Award for Connery. In 1982 John Boorman openly mused on the reasons for the Academy's neglect: there was no denying that Connery had produced supreme characters beyond Bond, in hugely diverse movies like *The Offence* and *The Man Who Would Be King*: 'But then many other notable achievers got left out. Cary Grant, Burton, lots of them.' Lewis Gilbert wondered if Connery wasn't his own worst enemy in his projection of invincibility, what journalist Neil Sinyard called 'the face of heroism in an anti-heroic age'.

True to his guns, it was for his portrayal of conventional, square-chinned heroism in Brian De Palma's gangster movie *The Untouchables*, Connery's first real Hollywood picture in five years, that the elusive Oscar nomination finally came. In the film Connery played a street-wise cop called Jimmy Malone who is guardian angel (but second-billing) to Kevin Costner's Eliot Ness, the scourge of Al Capone. De Palma, whose bloodshedding reputation was made with hits like *Carrie* and *Dressed to Kill*, approached the project with his usual thunder and re-created 1930s Chicago with the aid of 400 guns and 50,000 rounds of ammunition.

Michael Caine had starred in *Dressed to Kill* and highly commended De Palma to Connery. What doubtless appealed to

Connery too was the pedigree of David Mamet, the Pulitzer-Prize-winning screenwriter. Mamet grew up in Chicago and was schooled across the street from the spot where the St Valentine's Day Massacre occurred. As a child he fed on the stories of gangsters, and of Capone's terrifying power. But the facts of gangsterdom, Mamet came to believe, weren't enough for great drama. 'That something is true,' he said, 'doesn't necessarily make it interesting. There wasn't any real story [in Ness and Capone]. So I made up a story about two good guys: Ness and Jimmy Malone.'

True or not, De Palma left no stone unturned in depicting the terrors of mob rule. 'The photogenic qualities of gore are very apparent,' one reviewer wrote, though others criticised De Palma's historical exaggeration. The plot centred on Fed 'untouchable' Ness's efforts to eliminate Capone and the mob. Ness seems bound for success in the movie but in reality he never met Capone, never killed his enforcer Frank Nitti (as he does in the movie) and never succeeded in stemming the rackets. Nonetheless, the day-to-day activities of agents like Ness were painstakingly depicted, coached for accuracy by a surviving 'untouchable', 85-year-old Al Wolff.

On the face of it, *The Untouchables* was Costner's picture. But during the previews journalists signalled it as a breakthrough for Connery. In the *Sunday Mail* Dermot Purgavie spelled it out. He acknowledged Mamet's fine screenplay and the brutal ingenuity of De Palma but 'It is the informed performance of Sean Connery, judiciously working for a percentage of the profits, that carries the film . . . and he is widely expected to get an Oscar for his portrayal of the cautious cop who keeps a sawn-off shotgun in his gramophone, a bottle of whisky in his stove and a medal of St Jude, the patron of lost causes, in his pocket.' In the same week, the influential Pauline Kael likened Connery's performance style to Laurence Olivier's.

In many ways Connery's tutor role in *The Untouchables* echoed his part in *The Name of the Rose*. Here, once again, he was the oracle, wisdom incarnate, the old moraliser. In *The Name of the Rose* he triumphs. Here, poignantly, he dies – though his wisdom is delivered and absorbed.

The heroic tragedy of *The Untouchables* decisively won the Best Supporting Academy Award for Connery. Prior to the ceremony Connery refused to participate in anticipatory interviews but was, said Caine, 'very anxious'. When he won, 6,000 industry guests rose to their feet *for two ovations*. Compere Cher, in a controversially see-through chiffon-and-spangles gown, had dominated the celebratory evening till that point. But when Connery's win was announced the walls of the Shrine Auditorium came down. 'It was something I had never seen before,' Michael Caine said. '*Two* ovations – it just doesn't happen.'

There were plenty of worthy high flyers in the other awards categories that year – Michael Douglas took Best Actor for *Wall Street*, Cher Best Actress for *Moonstruck*, Bertolucci Best Director for *The Last Emperor* – but Connery undeniably held centre stage. At Swifty Lazar's party afterwards, with Micheline by his side, he told NBC with touching modesty: 'I don't know why they gave it. I suppose it was recognition for a body of work.'

There were those who lamented Connery's Academy Award, declaring it second rate, insisting – nobly and probably rightly – that he belonged at the peak: as Best Actor. Certainly his consistent lead performances over the years easily outranked newer players like Costner; but, as he himself averred, there is a pecking order in Hollywood, a definable 'club', and it is famously difficult for infrequent visitors like Connery to break through.

Though Connery ranks today as one of the few always bankable Hollywood imports, his forays into West Coast movies have been few. Some years ago the actor Robert Hardy said: 'I cannot see Sean and Hollywood settling down as long-term partners. There is a rebel element within him that will not fit, I think. It is such a pity, in ways, that the theatre didn't hold on to him, because the method of his approach is not lightweight or conventional and it befits quality drama.' John Boorman agrees: 'Sean's trouble – and his advantage – is that he remains inside the system while living outside it. He is his own man at whatever cost. He will never be an actor who conforms to the Hollywood way and he will always suffer for that.'

Connery isn't shy about denouncing the limitations of 'the system'. Whilst embracing Michael Caine, Roger Moore and Kevin

Costner as 'good friends', he criticises freely when he feels it is due: 'Actors like Costner are very much tied to American audiences. But I've been making films all over the world for the last thirty years and I have a very strong international [fan] foundation. Outside the United States there isn't an actor who gets better exposure or success ratios in any country than me.' ('When you are with Sean you learn pretty quickly your place in the galaxy,' Costner once told the *Sunday Times*.)

After the Oscar, inevitably, Connery was flooded with American offers. He took his time in selecting the best, and exercised a new tactical planning that would bring him into a position of greater executive power within the Hollywood system – a position he had been seeking since the Bond heyday.

A succession of large budget pop movies was quickly rejected, including Neil Jordan's humourless comedy *High Spirits* (Peter O'Toole replaced him), and Terry Gilliam's *The Adventures of Baron Munchausen*, a Pythonesque muddle that eventually starred Robin Williams. Connery's criterion of choice has always been interesting. It is, Michael Caine said, 'directed, as for most of us, by the wider social and business demands of the time'; but it is also, in Connery's case, deeply instinctive. From time to time he has steered clear of surefire mega-movies that turned into pap: he turned down Mel Ferrer's invitation to star opposite Audrey Hepburn in *Wait Until Dark*; he also rejected Tony Richardson's *The Charge of the Light Brigade* (replaced by David Hemmings), and roles in *Boom!*, Charlton Heston's *The Last Hard Men*, *Ladyhawke*, *Air America* and *Sleeping with the Enemy*. Now Connery opted to stay in Hollywood and apply his instincts to the biggest submission of script offers since the Bond era. He worked hard and fast, making four major films over the next two and a half years – his longest unbroken American spell. First up was old pal's Sidney Lumet's multigenerational black comedy *Family Business*. Here Connery again prematurely courted old age in portraying Dustin Hoffman's father (and Matthew Broderick's grandfather) in what was essentially a 60s-style crime caper aimed at the mass market. Connery played Jesse, head of a half rehabilitated hoodlum family from Hell's Kitchen, who joins with his grandson in a bungled heist, against his son's wishes. Writer Vincent Patrick adapted his own novel and Lumet imparted what significance he could to sideline commentaries on class and age conflicts and the dichotomy between morality and the law. But ultimately the story died in its forced levity. Connery's own comedy performance seemed theatrical, tired even, and did little to revive the glow of *A Fine Madness*.

Connery wasn't stopping for analysis. With a grand plan clearly in view, he was determined to maximise the opportunities afforded by the Oscar, utilising the buckshot theory of parts-playing first postulated by Dennis Selinger in the early 70s. This time round Michael Ovitz of Creative Artists Associates was the navigator egging him on. Ovitz negotiated superb deals on three other high-profile Hollywood movies in rapid succession: Peter Hyams's *The Presidio*, Steven Spielberg's *Indiana Jones and the Last Crusade* and John McTiernan's *The Hunt for Red October*. All these movies were in the mass-appeal category, all lavishly budgeted and peppered with American stars. All brought Connery huge fees, dramatically enhanced as they were by the Oscar success. Ian Bannen said: 'Those few movies earned Sean maybe ten million dollars clear. No one ever called Sean a dumbo – right? Well, look at his position. He'd been thirty years trying to get there, to the top of the Hollywood hill. When Bond happened he was either too tired or too distracted or maybe too immature [to capitalise on it]. The kudos of the Academy Award was a little like the impact of Bond, on a smaller scale of course. But this time round Sean was older and wiser. He knew what was possible, and he wasn't about to miss out on any angles.'

Living out of his three-bedroom condo in West LA (but dodging home to Spain when he could) Connery knuckled down to relentless months of seven-day working weeks initially, it seemed, to no great advantage. *The Presidio*, like *Family Business*, failed him. A straightforward murder mystery in which Connery plays a US Army Provost-Marshal engaged to assist the San Francisco police in finding the murderer of a military policewoman, the movie staggered through 50s-style B-movie red herrings to lose itself in the same kind of arcane subplotting that grounded Hyams' earlier *Outland*.

Only in Spielberg's new *Indiana Jones* did Connery appear to make headway. The Jones series was already vastly popular on the basis of Spielberg's first two movies, which had been landmark box-office successes. Later Spielberg confessed the influence of his boyhood devotion to James Bond. As a teenager growing up in Arizona, he said, he had 'revered' Connery's 007. When it came to planning his third Indiana saga, Spielberg 'suddenly sparkled to the notion of using seminal Bond as a foil for Indiana's Harrison Ford'. But when a meeting was set up, at Spielberg's request, between himself, producer George Lucas and Connery, first impressions were not good. Spielberg proposed the middle-aged professorial-type character he had in mind for Indiana Jones's father. George Lucas, Spielberg's partner in the project, wasn't too sure. There seemed little flesh on the idea anyway, Connery later stated, and when he asked to read a first draft script Lucas nervously refused him. In Connery's opinion, that initial meeting was a waste of time and he left Spielberg's suite 'feeling there was a reluctance on the part of George for me to play the part'.

Steven Spielberg admits that Lucas was wary. 'George wasn't thinking in terms of such a *powerful* presence for Indiana's father. His idea was for a doting, scholarly person, played by an older British character actor. But I had always imagined Sean Connery. Without a strong, illuminating presence, I was afraid that Harrison Ford would eradicate the father from the movie. I wanted to challenge him. And who would be the equal of Indiana Jones but James Bond?'

Connery was vacationing in Marbella when Lucas finally forwarded the script. He hated it. 'It was all very serious and there wasn't any jazz in the part. So I told them, It's not for me. Steven couldn't understand why, so I went to America to discuss it. My idea was to base a lot of the character on Richard Burton, the nineteenth-century explorer. He had been quite selfish and intolerant. So we called in Tom Stoppard to rewrite the part that way and he came up with things like the dialogue where Indiana said to his father, "You never talked to me," and the father replies, "You left home at nineteen, just when you were becoming interesting." And also the business of the father and son sleeping with the same girl, which is a good gag.'

Stoppard was the glue that made it work – though his name did not appear on screen; only Hollywood resident Jeffrey Boam was credited. What emerged was a joyous, absorbing shoot in familiar Spanish desert locations that Connery found 'more fun than I've had in a while'. Especially gratifying was the growth of his character. What started as a few incidental pages in Lucas's fat script grew to occupy half the story. On its release, audience response validated Connery's remoulding. 'It gave him particular pride,' said Ian Bannen. 'In Bond he dominated and Indiana Jones was a phenomenon like Bond. Harrison Ford had made it his own by copying Sean. Sean likes to compete. So he competed with Ford and he blew him right off the screen. Nobody could ask for more.'

At this high point Connery suddenly faced the greatest shock of his life. During the summer he was in good spirits, commuting to Spain, golfing in Scotland, counting his luck. He was, in the words of the *Sunday Times*, one of the most sought-after actors in the world: 'the star who grew and grew'. Steven Spielberg, said *The Times*, judged him 'one of only seven true movie stars alive'. The friendship with Stoppard that grew from the Indiana Jones collaboration was flourishing and Stoppard had asked him to star in his own upcoming directorial debut, a film of *Rosencrantz and Guildenstern Are Dead*. Connery was keen and CAA was happily negotiating when the blow fell.

For some time Connery had been suffering a dry throat. Often, in the din of a loud scene during *Indiana Jones*, his voice had failed him. When the movie wrapped, he warily consulted a specialist at UCLA Medical Center. 'The doctor stuck a probe down my throat and said, "Oh-oh, there's some trouble here,"' Connery later said. 'They found three little white dots on the right side of my larynx. Like most people, medical matters are a mystery to me and a lack of knowledge makes matters worse.'

Connery was, he said, 'absolutely terrified' by the results of the check-up. He had seen old friends like Jack Hawkins die before his eyes, agonisingly worn down by throat cancer. On *Shalako*

Hawkins had been seriously disabled and, despite the game show, all his lines had to be dubbed by Charles Gray. Now the UCLA throat specialist was advising that the 'angry patch of tissue' was probably benign but needed investigation. Connery's options, he was told, were a biopsy with laser surgery, or he could sit tight and hope a prolonged rest of his vocal cords might repair the problem. Connery wasn't satisfied. 'Sean was always a bit of a hypochondriac,' said Michael Caine. 'You don't dare ask how he is because you're soon in the picture: "I've got this stiff arm and my back has been killing me and, funny you should mention it, I haven't been feeling too hot ..."'

Connery consulted several other specialists, then opted to try thirty days of rest and silence. *Rosencrantz and Guildenstern* was the first casualty of the crisis. In his terror of the possibility, however remote, of cancer, Connery decided to keep the situation from the media. He instructed CAA to withdraw confidentially from Stoppard's movie, now just three weeks away from filming. Stoppard, his agent, the producers, the fellow actors, were stunned by the unexplained reversal. Stoppard was livid, believing Connery's resignation reflected annoyance with the small fee on offer. The movie's budget was just $4 million. Connery had agreed to accept $75,000 – his lowest fee in decades. But now he was crying off. Stoppard's agent, Gordon Dickerson, strove to get explanations from CAA, to no avail.

On 13 January 1989, Dickerson announced Connery's withdrawal, dodging: 'There has been a problem over conflicting dates ... it's now up to the producers to solve.' Robert Lindsay, Sting and Jeremy Irons had been booked to star opposite Connery, whose role was the Player King (the roles were eventually filled by Gary Oldman, Tim Roth and Richard Dreyfus). As Dickerson wriggled and CAA hedged, the legal manoeuvres started. Then Connery abruptly decided to buy himself out of the movie for a penalty $300,000. 'Tom was annoyed, and he behaved badly,' he said later. 'But he got it all wrong. I could have fought it out in court but who needs another lawsuit? So I just paid my way out.'

In LA, CAA denied media gossip that the star was ill, but within weeks the British tabloids carried the scream headline CONNERY

CANCER SCARE. 'Once those inaccurate rumours started circulating, I couldn't deny them. I didn't know what was going to happen until I went back to UCLA a month later,' Connery said. 'It was depressing. I have to admit the effect on me [of the gossip] was just awful.'

Distressed, Connery flew back to Spain with Micheline. The word 'cancer' haunted their days and nights. 'Other things in your life take second place,' Connery later said, 'and whatever you are doing, that nagging worry is always at the back of your mind.'

In the privacy of the Casa Malibu all he could do now was sit on the terrace and watch the sea, and wait.

# 19. UNTOUCHABLE?

'It was a pill,' said Connery wryly. 'I had this pen which I wore around my neck. And every time I wanted to say something I wrote it down on the back of old scripts. I wrote hundreds of pages and I should have kept them, because it was so crazy. It was lots of non sequiturs, like you never knew the question. Like there would be "How the fuck do I know?" Anyway, I printed up these cards saying "Sorry, I cannot speak. I have a problem with my throat. Thank you." And everyone would look at the card and say, "Why, what's the matter?" . . . And then I would write out what I wanted to say. Half the people would take the pen and write their answers back. You realise very quickly the world is full of idiots.' Micheline underlined the anguish: 'You should have seen the *way* he was writing . . .' Connery confessed: 'I cut right through that paper.'

Rigid with fear as he was, Connery rejected depression. He cut himself off from many people – it was something he shared with Micheline, Stefan and Jason and it wasn't something he wanted dragged round. It was a very debilitating thing – how could he answer people? By showing a card saying *I cannot talk*? He had to bite the bullet and try to keep smiling.'

Connery returned to LA to bad news: 'I was told that the month's silence hadn't worked and I would have to have the biopsy anyway. You can't imagine how I felt. The terror returned. But I got three opinions before I settled for this supposed expert who is the top man in UCLA. It was very hard to make a calm judgement in such circumstances.'

He finally had one bout of laser surgery in LA, but the results were inconclusive so he checked into London's Royal National Throat, Nose and Ear Hospital under the alias of David Martin. The *Sun* and the other tabloids had him rumbled overnight and, rather than face the fray of journalists camping in the street, Connery checked out just hours after cancer specialist David

Howard performed another minor laser operation. One more minor procedure followed before Connery was at last given a clean bill, with a recommendation of six-monthly screening tests.

Connery got his final clean bill in LA in April and opted to stay there when *The Hunt for Red October* was offered to him. Klaus Maria Brandauer, his old adversary from *Never Say Never Again*, had been signed by Paramount to play the hero Soviet skipper who defects in the film version of Tom Clancy's bestseller, but had dropped out at the last minute to accommodate a German movie in Europe. Connery was offered $4 million – his biggest cheque since Bond and, perhaps, justification for doing Bond after all. He dallied, taking careful medical advice, before agreeing in late April. The movie was already six weeks under way, with hotshot John McTiernan at the helm, before Connery joined the cast at Paramount Studios on 22 May.

During the in-between weeks Connery spent frequent hours in LA with Dr Lillian Glass, a former Miss Miami and university lecturer based at a Beverly Hills clinic, who specialised – for $95 per half-hour session – in speech therapy. Glass's regulars included Dolly Parton, Rob Lowe and Mickey Rourke and she addressed herself, in Connery's case, to restructuring his voice. Glass said, 'Sean came to me every day for weeks after the operation to remove the nodules ... The story that he had cancer was a lie. He is a very healthy man. It's his bad habits that caused the trouble. I could find examples of these in the early James Bond films when he said "My name is Bond ... James Bond." His voice sounded as though it was clenched in a ball. It sounded sensuous, but it was very damaging. Now his voice is even more sensuous because it is open and flowing.'

Connery's refusal to discuss his throat problem created a lingering mood of suspicion on the set of *Red October*. There was talk of his illness everywhere but the actor kept himself to himself. The first confirmation the cast and crew had of Connery's role in the movie came when, in late April, shooting the Washington crisis sequences, the image of the skipper of the submarine *Red October* flashed on to a monitor during a government briefing scene. Sean

Connery's face was superimposed on the skipper's body. When Connery eventually arrived on set to play defecting Soviet Captain Ramius, all eyes were on him, wondering, prying. Connery countered with a solid, disciplined performance that won everyone's admiration and silenced gossip. Sheamus Smith observed: 'He was hoarse, that's for sure. You see it in the screen cut. The voice is quite different, lower, more gravelly. He also doesn't *boom* like he usually does, in the tense moments.' Connery responded: 'It's the first time I've been able to do a movie without losing my voice.'

*The Hunt for Red October* was a flawed but very compelling movie whose timing was unfortunate. Tom Clancy, the author, published his technically heavyweight account of a Soviet defection in 1984, prior to *glasnost* and *perestroika*. The book was a publishing sensation, not least because Clancy gave it to a little-known academic publisher, the Naval Institute Press of Annapolis, instead of one of the leading commercial houses. The Naval Institute had helped Clancy in preparing the book and the 116-year-old establishment expected nothing other than a modest popular success. But *Red October* proved a runaway bestseller, its appeal vastly heightened by the dramatic political changes in Moscow. The Institute made a killing (and scored again almost immediately with Stephen Coontz's *Flight of the Intruder*). Though the Institute disputed ownership with Clancy – and prompted him to go elsewhere with his follow-up novels, *Red Storm Rising* and *Patriot Games* – the author was paid handsomely by producer Mace Neufeld for movie rights. The plan was to develop the novel's American CIA agent Jack Ryan (Alec Baldwin in *Red October*) as a series character. Clancy was overjoyed but suspected, rightly, that *Red October's* topicality might present problems. The speed of change within the Soviet Union and Eastern Europe that would see, within a year, the fall of the Berlin Wall and, shortly after, the collapse of Communism and the USSR as a political entity, made the movie an anachronism before its completion. Though it had its undisputed qualities – Connery's dark determination as Marko Ramius being uppermost – its aura belonged to the 70s. The *Monthly Film Bulletin* called it 'old-fashioned' and expressed profound disappointment in director McTiernan: 'Although he has demonstrated with the empty but actionful *Predator* and the marvellously tooled *Die Hard* that he is one of the best action men around, he can hardly do much with this overlong, humourless suspense picture.'

*Red October* served Connery well enough. 'It gave him back his vocal confidence,' said Sheamus Smith. It also provided a shot in the arm for the Scottish Educational Trust when the movie had a Royal Premiere on 17 April 1990 before Prince Charles and Princess Diana, with proceeds divided between the Prince's Trust and Connery's charity. Subsequently the movie played to excellent box office everywhere, slipping into profit within weeks of its opening.

Russia had always played a subtle, vital role in Connery's professional life. As Bond, he challenged its might during the Cold War. In 1969, filming *The Red Tent* there, he had developed a fascination for a nation he found 'mysterious, misdirected and confused'. On *Red October* he was intrigued by conversations with Soviet émigré extras like Herman Sinitzen, who played one of his naval subordinates and was also responsible for the recruiting of 25 former Soviet residents for the movie. Sinitzen had worked for Intourist, and had resided in LA for nine years, working as an interpreter for the LA court system. His and others' descriptions of new Soviet life riveted the always-eager-to-learn Connery. Now, on the heels of McTiernan's film, he had again the chance to visit the country and see the effects of *glasnost* first hand. Connery jumped at the opportunity to do Fred Schepisi's *The Russia House* not just because of its Leningrad and Moscow locations, but because the story was a thoroughbred, adapted by Stoppard from John le Carré's novel. Some saw his eagerness for the project as a gesture of conciliation towards Stoppard, who was allegedly still smarting over his directional debut letdown. But Connery wasn't saying so. For Connery, the inducement was, pure and simple, 'the landmark opportunity of making an American movie in Russia'.

Director Schepisi describes his first scouting trip to Russia, which came after months of delicate diplomatic negotiations: 'It was incredible because I was there when they were making historic changes in the country. You could feel the excitement. There was uncertainty and worry. I thought John le Carré's book was a real look at *glasnost* and the end of the Cold War, and a look at the people who should know better. [The story was about] the spymasters of East and West [and they] are the people who should appreciate that the Cold War is over ... but they seem to want to perpetuate it to keep their jobs going.'

Cooperation, none the less, was forthcoming and the movie started filming – co-starring Roy Scheider, Michelle Pfeiffer and Klaus Maria Brandauer – in Leningrad's Palace Square on 2 October 1989, with enthusiastic local police support. Connery said: 'When I was there before [on *The Red Tent*], you never knew where you were. I had a different driver every day, so he knew me but I never knew him. I'd be standing there like the laundry, waiting to get picked up. The interpreters were invariably KGB people. I'm not saying they are not KGB now, but this time they're younger, very outgoing.'

The shoot was as arduous as any Connery had endured. Unlike the six static weeks on a Paramount sound stage for *Red October*, *The Russia House* leaped all over the place. Connery described the schedule to journalist Baz Bamigboye as flying 'from Malaga to Madrid to Amsterdam, then Madrid again, from there to Warsaw, Leningrad, Moscow, back to Leningrad, on to London, then on to Lisbon ...' The compensation was in the educational value of the locations. After a week in Leningrad, the shoot moved to St Basil's Cathedral in Red Square, then Peredelkino, dacha home of countless writers and artists, then the City of Churches, Zagorsk, then Kolomenskoye above the Moscow River, where the Czars had a vast country estate. Schepisi was greatly helped by his friend the Russian director Elem Klimov, who cut through the remnants of obstructive bureaucracy. Connery and Micheline drank in the sights, visited museums, listened to the local lore, took what they could from what he called 'this momentous experience'. Schepisi circulated a memo to his cast and crew: 'In a small way you are part of history. We are the first people to be making a film, in this way, in this country. The people here are bending over backwards to help us in ways that are alien to their upbringing. They are more than willing. They know that many high-level people are closely observing what is considered a bold experiment. In an era of *glasnost* I believe it is important to make this work.'

Australian Schepisi, whose most significant movie till then had been Steve Martin's self-penned comedy *Roxanne*, declared himself utterly satisfied with Connery, Pfeiffer and *The Russia House* experience. Most others concurred, though Connery later conceded that in some degree the end result proved disappointing.

In *The Russia House* Connery played weary, cynical publisher Barley Blair who becomes involved with Katya (Pfeiffer), a courier being manipulated by a scientist codenamed 'Dante' who is putting *glasnost* to the test by spiriting Soviet nuclear information to the West. Blair becomes embroiled in the moral dilemmas of Katya and 'Dante', but the main thrust of the story is his slow-hatching love for Katya. The movie has a moody, understated movement that lost the youth audience and caused hiccups at the box office (an unsatisfactory $10 million in the US, which failed to cover its costs). *Time Out* defined its problem: 'Although sold as a thriller, the film boils down to a series of scenes in which two people talk enigmatically to each other. In the end, this is a movie that tries to be tense and exciting without a single incident of violence.'

Connery didn't sit around licking wounds. His regular throat tests were encouraging and he continued to push himself, taking small roles in *Highlander II: The Quickening* ('Whizz-bang pop videosque sequel,' moaned *Film Review*) and, at Kevin Costner's personal request, *Robin Hood: Prince of Thieves*, which would be one of 1991's biggest global earners. For a few weeks' work on *Highlander II* Connery was paid $3.5 million; for one day's work on *Robin Hood*, £250,000, all of which he divided equally between the Educational Trust, Heriot-Watt University and the Dundee Cancer Charity.

The year 1990 found Connery as uncompromising as ever in his attitudes to fame and fortune, and private as ever in his specific future plans. Celebrating his sixtieth year, he had wealth and security beyond his dreams but – triumph of all, untypically in the industry – his wit and objectivity remained intact. Old Oscar was something he never spoke of, hardly thought about unless it looked him in the eye from its shelf in the new en suite bathroom

Micheline had designed for him overlooking the sea in Marbella. The industry, he told his friend Andrew Fyall, still fascinated him, drove him, but neither money nor fame per se was enough now. 'He had no time, he said, for the conventions, nor any desire to live out his career to other's prescriptions. He told me he didn't want to slow down, that there were bigger fish to fry, both in his artistic aims, and in business – which, as he talked, seemed to boil down to the same thing.'

Despite the watershed birthday, Connery refused the journalistic ritual of public self-analysis. But in a *Guardian* interview that year he did offer a revelatory glimpse into his personal acting principles: 'I think a lot of American actresses' indulgences are permitted by some producers. Somehow all their neuroses, or whatever they are, come out. They think nobody but they have problems. Therefore we all have to bear their problems, or be tortured by them. This has produced people who are forced into internal ways of acting. But standing on a set for twenty-two takes, looking for "something inside", is not going to be inspirational. I'm against using only oneself as a total instrument of acting. How – if you are a stupid actor – do you play someone intelligent, for example?' Humour tempered the apparent chauvinism. It was reported that, when an American journalist asked him, 'Is it true that sixty-year-old men are more virile?' Connery responded with: 'It's years since I've been to bed with a sixty-year-old.'

Reaching sixty didn't bother Connery because, said Ian Bannen, 'Sean has always been old. I don't mean that in any derogatory way. I mean it in the sense that from the start, when I met him, he had the world on his shoulders. He was not one who went running home to mummy. He was out to fight to the top and do whatever had to be done. He never hid his age. He wasn't one of those Rank types where you read in the official bios that he was born last week. He grew grey, he went bald, so what?' Connery did indeed defy the gloom of ageing. As a young man, in his late 20s when it became apparent that he would go bald as his father and grandfather had, he panicked: 'I remember thinking, my God, what can be done? I'm finished!' But he quickly scorned his own vanity. Barely out of Bondage, he'd made fun of his baldness, relishing talking about it on prime time television. Unlike star players like Richards Harris or Burton who dyed their thinning manes and hollered their youthful yearnings, Connery – in the words of Robert Hardy – 'dashed into middle age'. 'It doesn't worry me,' he said repeatedly. 'It is inevitable, so what can one do but accept it?' He had no interest at all in 'letting eighteen hairs grow a foot and a half long and dressing in trendy jeans'. Instead: 'Being comfortable in your own skin is more important than anything else – and most of the time I feel pretty comfortable in mine.'

Connery entered the pension decade absorbed on a new project scheduled for shooting in the depths of the Central American rain forest. *The Last Days of Eden* (later retitled *Medicine Man*) was hugely important to him because it marked the transition from actor to producer, the crucial artistic-cum-business manoeuvre that he had hinted to Andrew Fyall. Directed by McTiernan, the *Red October* director, the movie was a first venture from ex-Carolco chairman Andy Vanja's new Cinergi Productions and afforded Connery the kind of creative control he had previously exercised only on *Never Say Never Again*. In this instance the social and political relevance of the project, written by *Dead Poets Society* author Tom Schulman, greatly appealed. This was not simply a romantic adventure – though much of the advance publicity indicated a kind of late-life *Romancing the Stone*; this film had a profound statement to deliver, about the destruction of the rain forests and its probable consequences. As senior executive – the equivalent of Broccoli's status on Bond – Connery had script and casting approval and chose Lorraine Bracco from Scorsese's *GoodFellas* as his co-star: 'She was my choice immediately. We needed someone who could be tough, dynamic and have a sense of humour about it. We simply couldn't risk attempting something like this with an actress who was concerned whether her hair was in place, or whether she was sweating. It calls for a certain kind of girl, like Lorraine.'

*Medicine Man*, despite its comfortable $40 million budget, proved an obstacle course. McTiernan scoured the world's jungles for the perfect location for his story of an ageing ethnobiologist who has found the cure for cancer in the rare bromeliads nesting

in the treetops – then loses it. Five years earlier the director had
made his movie name with Arnold Schwarzenegger's *Predator*,
filmed in Borneo's rain forest. He had, naturally, favoured Borneo
for a return visit, but now, on a recce, he discovered the rain
forest severely depleted. 'It was an object lesson in the message we
were trying to put across,' said McTiernan. 'The forests are vanishing: that is the reality of it.' McTiernan scouted in Malaysia,
Equatorial Guinea, Belize, Venezuela and Ecuador before deciding
– then convincing Connery – that the best solution was to import
Brazilian Indians to the accessible remains of a fading jungle at
Catemaco, in Mexico. Here Micheline and Sean were installed in a
modern, but modest bungalow situated on a lake which, at
twilight anyway, reminded the Connerys of home. 'It could be the
Highlands,' Connery told Sue Russell of the *Daily Express*. 'And
there are some wonderful fish in the lake – although everything
has to be specially cooked because of the parasites.'

The weeks in Mexico and later, briefly, in Brazil, were weeks
of discomfort and genuine danger. In the movie Connery plays
Dr Robert Campbell, exploring the jungle's upper growth in
search of plant extracts that will cure cancer. As usual, Connery
insisted on doing his own stunt work, which in this instance
involved being strapped into wire harnesses and levered hundreds
of feet into the sky. Fortunately, he didn't suffer from vertigo. 'I
prefer heights to [going] underwater,' he said. 'At least you get to
breathe.' Parasites, crew desertions and physically taxing stunt
work were, for Connery, not the worst of it. More than anything,
he told Andrew Fyall, the slow drudgery of film-making in the
depths of nowhere, in 120 degree heat and 98 degree humidity,
wore him down.

McTiernan, just 40, suffered the stress of the shoot every bit as
much as his star. With a background in award-winning commercials and three major features behind him, he had the jargon of the
set, the vision and the stamina. But Connery, he admitted, fazed
him. By his own admission McTiernan had 'pussyfooted' around
Connery on *Red October*. Now, by default, he learned that the best
way to forge a bond with his star was by pushing him. 'Not only
could I get away with telling him what I thought,' said McTiernan,

'but he *wanted* me to tell him what I thought. In fact, the only sure way to get him annoyed is if you *don't* speak your mind.'

The difficult conditions made Connery 'chronically grumpy and gruff, and sick of the dubious Mexican food'. Copious amounts of daily vodka kept him immune. In his description of the tribulations on the phone to Andrew Fyall in Scotland, he appeared to be galvanised by his executive-creative role. 'When the actor energies tired,' said Fyall, 'the other aspect, the executive producer role, obviously compensated.' Connery seemed, said Fyall, exhausted but bold: 'I'm quite sure the fulfilment and sense of duty [as executive producer] kept him feisty. He would complain, but it would be leavened with a very healthy concern for the progress of the film in all departments. This felt like new work for him.' In the midst of the location wars Connery told Sue Russell, 'I am not always happy at work, but then who is? I'm certainly happier working than not. And [my profession] has given me a real education, too.'

For the journalists who trekked out to Mexico on the scent of production troubles – the rumours of an allegedly unhappy relationship with Bracco, of ominous rows with McTiernan and interminable crew illnesses – Connery was non-compliant. The only story he was interested in reviewing was the movie's tale, and its moral signals. He was – genuinely – disturbed by the implications of 'this serious and important story'. The statistics were at his fingertips for anyone who wanted to listen: where once there were 9 million rain forest Brazilian Indians, now there were less than a quarter of a million. The human tragedy, in terms of tribal culture and personal loss, was obvious, but the broader issues, said Connery, were disastrous in terms of global well-being. As the rain forests and their parasite species disappeared, so too the unknown, untapped curative potential of a thousand plants vanished. '*An acre of rain forest is destroyed every second of the day*' became a kind of mantra to anyone within ten metres of Connery. 'He made that film out of very real concerns,' said Fyall. 'He isn't an activist in the soap box sense, but when he has a cause he lets it be known. *Medicine Man*, at its heart, was a "cause" movie for him, one of the few he has made.'

Despite Connery's passion, the jungle skills of McTiernan and Schulman's witty script (which was doctored with fresh dialogue by Tom Stoppard and Sally Robinson), the finished movie, premiered in May 1992, failed to live up to expectations, earning only about $20 million on its first run US release, less than half the takings of *Red October* (though still twice the box office of *The Russia House*). For *The Times* it was, astonishingly, an 'aimless movie', a view endorsed by the *Monthly Film Bulletin* who labelled it 'loosely constructed and pointless'.

Outwardly Connery seemed unaffected by the negative press. To his thinking, the movie served its purpose. It was literate, his personal performance was more vocally confident than anything since *The Untouchables* and it earned him one of his biggest cheques – $10 million, plus 15 per cent of the gross. Most important, the degree of creative control afforded by producer Vanja and director McTiernan satisfied his questing artistry and put steam into his amorphous Fountainbridge Films, the infrastructure he would henceforth use to lever power on studio productions and manage his share of gross receipts.

In truth, said Andrew Fyall, by the time *Medicine Man* premiered Connery was cruising on his post-Oscar game plan and too absorbed in prepping his new movie, Philip Kaufman's Japanese-set *Rising Sun*, to be much bothered by media flack. 'When I met him after *Medicine Man* he was underweight from the dodgy food, but his mood was one of satisfaction at having survived. It was an attitude of "What does one lousy film review mean anyway, after all those great years?"'

Fyall was especially advantaged in his intimate access to Connery at this time, because he was the one coordinating the actor's Edinburgh homecoming to accept the Freedom of the City, a throwaway honour in certain provinces, but one famously measured and meaningful in Scotland. Since the death of Effie, it appeared that Connery's ties with his homeland had started to slip. According to a close friend, there had been rifts with brother Neil and protracted, argumentative absences; but in fact the link of mutual affection had never diminished. As early as 1966 Edinburgh Council had debated a civic honour for Connery. In

November 1990 Councillor Eleanor McLaughlin, the Lord
Provost, tabled the motion for the Freeman award on the grounds
of Connery's 'distinguished contribution to world cinema; to mark
his largely unpublicised work in founding the Scottish
International Education Trust ... and in particular to recognise the
respect and high esteem in which he is held by the people of the
City of Edinburgh'. Within the council, inevitably, there were dissenters: during the ballot in chambers on 20 December, 49 voted
for the award, 8 against. At the same time the *Evening News*, in
whose employ Effie had once imagined her son's future, tested
public opinion. Their phone-in poll told the full story: among the
several thousand callers, more than 90 per cent expressed support
for the Freeman honour for Connery. In his conversations with
McLaughlin and with Fyall, Connery expressed his deep satisfaction at the honour. Prince Charles had been proposed for the
award in the middle 1970s, and rejected. The earlier luminaries
glittered from the pages of every history book: Dickens, Walter
Scott, Disraeli, Livingstone and Stanley, Churchill and Alexander
Graham Bell. Only one other popular entertainer – Harry Lauder
– had been graced, back in 1927.

The award ceremony took place on 11 June 1991, during the
making of *Medicine Man*. It was for Connery a symbolic but also a
vividly redefining event that opened a new chapter in his relationship with his homeland. Ross Wilson, the Scottish television
producer assigned to film the ceremony and the concurrent bio-
documentary organised by Fyall, suggests that Connery himself
was surprised by 'the reawakening' afforded by the honour: 'I felt
[in the documentary] we achieved a sketch portrait of the man that
was unusually intimate and accurate ... and I felt we had the
circumstances of his homecoming to thank for that. The roots ran
deep. With some people, they don't. You meet prominent
achievers all the time who give off a feeling of disconnection, that
they are happiest in movement. Connery *appears* to be like that,
but at the Freeman ceremony it became clear as to who he really
was. He is an organic actor, and that means he has a powerful
respect for, and connection with, his origins. The Celts, the Scots,
cherish their own – so the legend goes. And Sean exuded

something I least expected: that despite his bohemianism, despite the gilt of Hollywood and the limousines and the private helicopters to Turnberry, his is a tribal nature. He is not so much an actor as a *Scots* actor. And that attention to roots, the primitivism in him, gives him – gave James Bond – his power.'

On the morning of the award ceremony, while breakfasting at the Balmoral Hotel, Connery read a sour *Scotsman* article written by a journalist who had been refused a private interview. The journalist quoted *Premiere* magazine's assertion that Connery had been paid half a million dollars for Costner's *Robin Hood*, some of which had been divided among Scottish charities. In the last year, the article went on, *Variety* calculated Connery's earnings at £35 million: 'He has chosen to live abroad and every time he steps ashore in Britain, the taxman's clock starts ticking towards that elusive point where he can claim a share of the millions.' Connery was enraged by the article, in equal parts because of its apparent mean-mindedness and because it seemed to imply some betrayal of his nationalist pride. At the major press conference of the day he headlined with a defensive diatribe, insisting that he only agreed to the small work on *Robin Hood* so that the Scottish charities would benefit. 'Another inference was that I don't pay taxes, which is equally untrue. When I moved out of Britain in 1974 I paid nothing but taxes on everything that was frozen in this country. You're not allowed to take money out. And I pay full tax in Britain and America whenever I work, with none of the benefits of living [in either] country.'

Fyall saw Connery's vitriol as evidence of renewed Scots pride and, sure enough, by the autumn, with a national general election upcoming, Connery pulled out all the stops to restate his affinities. Back in 1969 he had spoken of his admiration for the Scottish National Party and the separatists who envisioned an independent Scotland. Now he made himself available to voice-over an aggressively ambitious SNP political broadcast that called for independence within a European Union and, temporarily, caused tumult within the party itself. Fourteen Scottish MPs joined in a public statement dissociating themselves with Connery's broadcast – seemingly because Connery was simultaneously lending his skills to voice-over Japanese liquor commercials – though the SNP's media representatives claimed the party had gained 'at least a thousand' new members as a result of Connery's contribution. The ironies didn't pass unnoticed: Connery was still not officially a member of the party, in spite of his 25 years of declared support. After the Freedom award, however, the anomaly seemed untenable.

In January 1992 the distinguished title of Chevalier de la Legion d'Honneur was bestowed by the French Ministry of Foreign Affairs, but, just days later, Connery appeared just as honoured to be formally signed in as a card-carrying member of the SNP. Fyall, among many Scottish friends, was amused by the circumstances of his formal alliance. More than ten years before, Gordon Wright, an Edinburgh-based activist and publisher, who hadn't known Connery personally, sent him a copy of *Scotland: A Concise History*, written by an ex-chairman of the SNP. Subsequently a pen friendship of sorts began and, in a casual phone conversation, Wright asked the actor why he had never joined the party. 'No one ever asked me,' Connery told him; and Wright set about immediately repairing the situation. On 31 January Connery's membership was processed by the Newington branch of south Edinburgh and by April he was in the midst of controversy on the floor of the Commons. Here was a flavour of the rarefied, dubious media moralism that would attend his future political efforts. In 1965, at the dizzy heights of Bondmania, *Playboy* had featured him in its celebrity interview. In the course of ten pages of erratic biography, Connery – rather Connery-Bond – had stated that 'an open-handed slap' was tolerable in an argument with a woman. Barbara Walters fished out this piece of semi-contextualised arrogance in her televised face-to-face with Connery in the 80s, and *Australian Woman's Weekly* regurgitated it in the run-up to the British general election. Immediately partisan MPs jumped on the bandwagon, implying poor judgement on behalf of the SNP. The party's parliamentary leader, Margaret Ewing, struggled to his defence, stating that, in the old interview, Connery had 'spelled out the unacceptability of violence towards women and also drew attention to the many varied and tortuous ways in which women had been demeaned.' The gist of her remarks suggested that she had been in telephone contact with Connery who, friends say, was appalled by the opportunism and distortion in the floor debate. Connery told *GQ* journalist Diane Shah: 'I was talking [in the original interview] about a slap on the face, and that you could do much, much worse damage to a woman, or a man, by totally demoralising them, by taking away their identity ... I'm saying that if one of a couple is intent on having a physical confrontation, it's impossible for it to be avoided. It's emotional, it's passion. And passion lacks thinking. Therefore, it will explode. And that's all I'm saying, without getting into a three-act play.'

Ian Bannen observed the media storm with dismay. 'I believe Sean was naive about his politics [till then], but then he is not a professional politician – and look at the naivety *among them* when it comes to matters of personal behaviour intruding on public life. Sean didn't think there would be any crossover, because he was a background activist, not a public contender. But he was proved wrong. It didn't frighten him, because you don't scare Sean. But it did make him extremely cautious of where he was going with the SNP.'

In 1992 cultural values, ethnicism and nationalism were in debate all across Europe. The gathering impetus of European integration with the dissolution of trade boundaries, the projected common currency and the epidemic fears of cultural homogeneity, occupied all political discourse and the hearts of most thinking people. The signals for a vibrant new world order were clear. Communism had failed, energy issues defined all foreign policies among the superpowers, the corporate behemoths dictated social and economic policy-making in the West, Muslim fundamentalism, on the rise since the overthrow of the Shah of Iran in the 70s, challenged the hubris of Western supremacism, and the disintegration of the former Yugoslavia provided a murderous casebook of what goes wrong when empire strategies attempt to suppress the tribal spirit.

As Britain rejected a Labour government and clung to a fast-fading isolationist Thatcherism, Connery turned away from the deep complexities of political life. Political philosophers like

Michael Ignatieff argued that the only happy resolution of nationalist hopes – indeed, the only hope for human survival – was a worldwide cultural and political shift to accepted pluralism. Connery had always said as much, but his timing in entering the debate couldn't have been worse. As it was, the slow adagio towards some sort of devolution – for Wales, Northern Ireland and Scotland – was already in motion. It seemed inevitable that separate parliaments and some autonomy would be granted. It also seemed time to return, with focus, to his calling as a film artist.

# 20. RETURN OF THE ROCK

In the summer of 1992 Connery was pleased to return to the gladiatorial forum of Hollywood where, in principle at least, the heroes and villains wore white and black hats. *Rising Sun* was his new venture, based on the novel by Michael Crichton, who had directed him in *The First Great Train Robbery*. Once again, as had almost become expected in the annals of Connery movie-making, the project started in a blaze of arguments. This time, however, the arguments did not involve him.

Michael Crichton's fortunes had changed dramatically since *The First Great Train Robbery*. Having directed five substantial movies, with a career in medicine behind him, in his late 40s he had turned exclusively to book writing, hitting full flight commercially with the Conan Doyle-styled *Jurassic Park*. He had written *Rising Sun* with Connery in mind, then sold it to Joe Roth at Fox, Connery's old studio. CAA, Crichton and Connery's agents, had packaged the movie in the prevailing in-house style, teaming its clients, director Philip Kaufman and co-star Wesley Snipes with Connery and Crichton. The casting of Snipes was the first great departure from Crichton's novel, and that casting had been prompted by Connery. *Rising Sun*, in Crichton's version, was a story critical of the Japanese business and techno invasion of the US. Crichton was unapologetic against accusations of xenophobia and stressed the statistics that proved mischievous Japanese displacement of American market shares. Director Kaufman, however, chose to develop the plotline differently, taking the core elements of the screenplay written by Crichton and his partner Michael Backes, and steering towards a more benign and thriller-orientated script. Connery, playing semi-retired LAPD oriental expert John Connor, guides his younger partner through the protocol of investigating a murder in the world of corporate high finance. In the original script, the partner is white, but Connery was irritated by the 'one-note nature' of the character and leaped at Kaufman's suggestion of the greater resonance, given the motives of the story, of substituting a black actor. Connery then watched Snipes's work on *New Jack City* and approved him. Crichton, with Backes, resigned, claiming fundamental creative differences with Kaufman. 'It wasn't acrimonious,' said Backes. 'We weren't fired. We exited the project because it wasn't going the way we wanted it to go.'

Connery stayed out of the fights, only venturing to *Premiere* magazine that Crichton was 'probably a little too brilliant for Hollywood', a seriously meant compliment couched not to offend Fox and Kaufman. In fact, Connery supported the streamlining and defusing of the original, exercising lessons, perhaps, from the experience of a preachy script in *Medicine Man* and the recent exposure to the super-sensitivity of contemporary social politics.

In June, work began on location in LA and Connery relished what historically he best likes: a clear-headed director. CAA's proposal of Kaufman had pleased him from the start, on account of the unobvious notion of placing the director of delicate existential movies like *The Unbearable Lightness of Being* in charge of a corporate-world thriller. 'I thought it was an interesting notion,' he said, 'because it is a volatile story and Phil is more associated with Milan Kundera and Tom Wolfe.'

*Premiere* reported Connery on location in LA becalmed and commanding: 'A white-bearded Sean Connery climbs the long row of steps leading up to a new skyscraper in downtown LA. He is meticulously flanked by two younger men shouldering a large, portable canvas awning carefully positioned above his head, shielding him from the blazing sun. The young men look down at his feet and gauge their steps to his so all three can proceed in tandem. From a distance, this is an odd sight, even for Los Angeles, and if it weren't for the surrounding architecture and the clothes, you might think it the scene on an Ottoman potentate arriving at a mosque during the sixteenth century.'

Though Fountainbridge Films was just nominally involved in *Rising Sun*, Connery's magisterial presence, both behind and in front of the cameras dominated the movie. Snipes's relationship with Connery was, as Matthew Broderick's, Christian Slater's and so many other young bucks' had been, one of open deference that carries into the screen performance, electrifying the film's mood and magnifying Connery to a stature comparable with the legendary silver screen stars of old. In this extraordinary alchemy, manifest since *The Name of the Rose*, Connery had no peers. Michael Caine, himself a big man, believes that, 'Sean is literally larger than life – his hands, his smile. But there is a dimension you can't define that the movie camera catches, like the old story about a beautiful woman being measured in a matter of millimetres – and that is the kind of mysterious millimetre-gauge that Sean satisfies on film. This has nothing to do with James Bond or marketing tricks. I contend that even if you put Sean on a stage and filmed him reading the phone book, you'd watch till he got to "z". You cannot define that, but when it's there it humbles other actors and it often makes them stretch, which is what it's all about in making movies.'

Connery liked Snipes, found him 'kind of dynamic and attractive. A very good actor, very physical.' Snipes reciprocated with the kind of cool street shuffle projected in Web Smith, the screen character developed for him by Connery, Kaufman and David Mamet, brought in at the last minute for a script polish. Connery was nifty in the 'hood, Snipes observed; as if the impoverished, downtrodden street environment of downtown LA wasn't easy turf for the Fountainbridger. 'He's a very serious man. He doesn't take a lot of shit. At the same time, he's a relaxed guy, he jokes and he plays. I think I'm pretty much the same: have a little fun, live life, enjoy it. Don't be serious all the time. Everything is not a headache.'

At Christmas, with Peter Chernin replacing Roth as head of Fox, there was a renewed wave of conflict about the movie's release date. Kaufman was contracted to release in the spring, but the cut of the film he had was well over two hours long and obviously unfinished. Fox distribution pressed for the release, but Connery stood fast behind his director, yet again demonstrating the authority and clearheadedness of an executive producer. A spring release, he insisted, was 'totally unrealistic to consider'. Fox backed down, and the movie was recut through the summer with the loving attention to detail for which Kaufman is known, and released in the fall of 1993.

*Rising Sun* went into quick profit, easily tripling the box-office takings of *Medicine Man*, and restated Connery's long-held belief that 'meticulous redrafting of the script is the best starting position and the best finishing position'. From the perspective of Crichton and Backes, the movie was a damp squib. 'Taking the politics out of it,' said Backes, 'is like taking Z and turning it into *Zorba the Greek*.' But Kaufman, with Connery's support, had brilliantly straddled the potential ethnic controversies and still retained the essence of Crichton's dark novel. With a real interest himself in eastern culture (his undergraduate thesis at the University of Chicago was on Japanese internment during the Second World War), Kaufman had covered all bases in retooling the storyline. He had, for example, held meetings with prominent Japanese-American organisations to explore their concerns about racial issues, and he had cast Asians as Asians and accommodated much of the spirit of Crichton's first principles. The best judgement of Kaufman's good navigation through difficult waters was given, perhaps, by the Japanese actor Cary-Hiroyuki Tagawa, who portrayed a playboy in the movie. 'I have to give Phil Kaufman credit for taking all the negatives out of the book,' he said. 'He is very sensitive [to racial issues], being Jewish himself, and having experienced anti-Semitism.' Gratified by the trickiest of movies proving popular and thought-provoking, Kaufman concluded with praise for Crichton: 'I think he was just trying to enter into a world that's crucial for us to begin to understand. I tried to enter into that world through Crichton's book, but I know I have taken a little different path into that world.'

Fortified by a massive popular hit, in the middle 90s Connery's re-energised commitment to his career took the form of the eclectic productivity of the early 70s and the post-Oscar period, inevitably paving the way for misjudgements of exhaustion and experiment. Almost all his headline competitors – Bruce Willis, Arnold Schwarzenegger, Robert De Niro, Al Pacino – also produced quickfire and varied performances during this time, but Connery's range, from *Medicine Man*, through *Rising Sun* to *Dragonheart* and *Playing by Heart*, seemed exceptional and often exceptionally risky. Still determined to achieve comprehensive control over his productions, the nomadic bug filled the vacuum between Fountainbridge Films deals. The next two movies, made in South Africa and Florida through the winter–spring of 1993–4, yielded interesting performances in above-average films – Bruce Beresford's *A Good Man in Africa* and Arne Glimcher's *Just Cause* – that seemed more reliant on the gravitas and dignity of the Connery 'legend' than on any nuanced skill. Connery was still obviously applying the highest literary standards to his work (*A Good Man in Africa* was written by William Boyd and the script of *Just Cause* read like vintage Agatha Christie) but the relative failure of both films – the first financially, the second critically – seem more to do with an absence of fire in the characters than in the narratives. In *A Good Man in Africa* Connery played the title character, the movie's common sense axis, who dispenses wisdom to Colin Friels, playing a venal colonial High Commissioner in the fictional African state of Kinjaja caught in a sex-and-politics rat trap. Most reviews were good, but box-office business was strictly art-house class, barely edging past $2.5 million. *Just Cause*, by contrast, opened on a par with *Rising Sun* ($10.5 million in its first weekend), whose thriller modus it also replicated. Released in February 1995, *Just Cause* was justly accused of jumping the rails within its own definitions. The unlikely story of a Harvard law professor (Connery) who is encouraged to take on the complicated pro-bono case of a young man charged with a racially motivated rape-murder, Roger Ebert in the *Chicago Sun-Times* summed up the views of many by complaining about the 180 degree motivational turns of the characters: 'It's the kind of movie where you look at the screen and start imagining the push-pins holding the 3-by-5 cards to the cork board in a Hollywood office, as the filmmakers try to keep the plot straight ... There is no psychological depth, no real motivation, no human values to weigh, just characters jerked here and there like puppets in an arbitrary plot.' Only Connery, as the core of a wobbly movie, said Ebert, was worth watching: 'When it comes to expressing quiet wrath, Connery is like few other actors ...'

There seemed to be a certain wrath or disaffection at the centre of Connery's philosophy in 1995. By the middle of the decade he had pulled up the drawbridge as never before and become nigh unavailable to the media. The irritation caused by previous major media sallies – like the Barbara Walters network tête-à-tête that caused the political furore – had apparently chastened him and he was now unwilling for anything other than the scantiest personal promotion of new movies. In July, a few months after *Just Cause* opened, the impact of the withdrawal was in evidence in the pages of *Variety* which debated the rumours of Connery's alleged demise. 'Eventually the inevitable happens to all of us,' Robert Hofler wrote, 'but Sean Connery is getting a little tired of being reported dead.' The mix-up, Connery grumpily explained, was down to the passing of his golfing friend, the racing driver James Hunt, who died of a massive heart attack at his home not far from Connery's on the Costa del Sol. 'The Japanese translated "James Hunt" as "James Bond", which was then picked up by the French, via South African reports. I have a lot of friends in France and they were afraid to call my wife, [but] eventually one of them did. "Oh I have terrible news," they said. "We hear Sean has died." Micheline said, "I don't think so, he's out playing golf at the moment."'

The week the *Variety* report was filed, Connery was immersed in two new movies significant in their content and revelatory of what Michael Caine calls 'his gradual acceptance of an attribute most of us can only dream of: a mythic nature'. The movies overlapped, though in many senses one fed off the other. Commenced first, during the summer of 1994, was Jerry Zucker's *First Knight*, an updating of the Camelot legend, in which Connery played Arthur alongside Richard Gere as Lancelot. The second was Raffaella De Laurentiis's long-in-planning production of *Dragonheart*, a movie that took the fundamental computer animation breakthrough of Spielberg's *Jurassic Park* and worked it into a near-new art form. In it, Connery played – voiced, to be exact – the last dragon alive, half of whose heart is held to ransom by an errant knight, and whose quest is to stay alive. For Ian Bannen, these movies 'emphasised once and for all Sean's uniqueness. Very very few actors can play the kind of monumental virility [of *First Knight* and *Dragonheart*]. Typically, [that kind of casting] goes to a

John Gielgud or an Olivier type. Very few actors in their late six-ties can project "the monument" *and* the testosterone. In those movies, Sean showed that he had the market cornered.'

*First Knight* opened just weeks before Connery's 65th birthday, an event celebrated quietly by Connery but marked in his native Scotland by SB Holdings, owners of one of the largest worker-owned bus companies in the UK, publicly announcing the grant-ing of a pensioner's bus pass. Connery had the wit to respond with alacrity: 'Many thanks for my bus pass,' he wrote to Peter Shaw, SB's chairman. 'I don't know how many times I shall get the oppor-tunity to use it, but I shall have it clutched to my bosom and I won't venture across the border without it.'

Connery's good mood, according to Bannen, was attributable to the slick professionalism of the production teams on the mythic movies. Jerry Zucker, whose tragic-romance *Ghost* was the fourth highest grossing film in history, managed to execute a lavish, actionful medieval movie with sets at Pinewood and locations around Trawsfynydd in North Wales within a precise four-month shooting schedule for *First Knight*. Connery, whose legendary gripe was inefficient scheduling, was more than appeased. Bannen saw that 'there's a lot of anger in Sean – in fact, anger may be the great key to his power. But for those of us who know him, you get a sense of his mood in the roles he plays. He'd probably deny it, but I believe you can tell when he has a shitty director or producer who doesn't know the deal. It comes through in Sean's expressions on the screen. In movies like *First Knight* you see a kind of contentment behind the eyes.'

With a triumphant opening weekend return of more than $10 million – the same profits-indicator territory as *Rising Sun* and *Just Cause* – *First Knight* paled in many ways alongside *Dragonheart*. Apart from the litmus comparisons of box-office – *First Knight* finally grossed about $38 million in its US run while *Dragonheart* topped $52 million – De Laurentiis's cherished movie was memo-rable as a kind of cartoon celluloid homage to Connery's long career. Laurentiis's partner, the director Rob Cohen, had had a clear image from the word go of ideal casting: 'I had only two names in mind for Draco the dragon – Sean Connery and Sean Connery. Not just for his acting skills, but for the character and moral quality he also brings.' The movie blended live action (led by Dennis Quaid as the knight-nemesis who ends up partnering Draco) with a sophisticated stop-motion animation hitherto unseen. An illustration of its complexity was the Draco animation cost: for 23 minutes of creature computer graphics screen time amounting to 182 individual shots, De Laurentiis and Cohen spent $22 million, more than half their budget. *Jurassic Park*'s T-Rex invention (on screen for six and a half minutes) utilised about 80 moving parts; Draco utilised 1,200 and demanded a personality all of its own. Cohen approached the challenge by immersing himself in the techno worlds of character creator Phil Tippett and George Lucas's Industrial Light and Magic, at Marin County, California – and in an intimate personal study of Connery. 'Sean has an incredible body of work,' said Cohen. 'So I went and looked at everything he did from *Darby O'Gill* through *Just Cause*, then got the editor to assemble a roll of hundreds of clips from laser discs and videos covering Sean in every mood and expression. We categorised every possible emotion: sardonic, amused, sceptical, critical, charming, seductive, angry, whatever. We broke down his emotional life on film and analysed how he used his expressions and mannerisms, and then we applied them to Draco in such a way that Sean wasn't just voicing the dragon, but was actually *acting* the part. When we wanted anger for a scene, we would say, Yes, there's that moment in *Russia House* where he expresses anger, and so forth. It was wonderful, because Sean saturated the film with his presence.'

Connery's work on *Dragonheart* was a phased series of vocal recordings, the first laid down at Chris Blackwell's oceanside Compass Point Nassau Studio, about ten minutes' drive from the Connery home at Lyford Cay, before filming began. The second and third sessions, sychronised with the film, were executed at International Recordings Studios in Rome during time out from *First Knight*.

The six-month span of this work coincided with the postproduction and release of *GoldenEye*, the new-minted version of James Bond, featuring the television star Pierce Brosnan, an unavoidable occasion for reflection. This time round, the circumstances of new

Bond were charged, marking as they did the near abandonment of the series, and the serious illness of the last surviving architect, Cubby Broccoli. *Licence to Kill*, the last Bond, in 1989, was Broccoli's swan song. Its monumental failure, grossing just $33 million, was an inauspicious farewell to the family franchise set up with Saltzman in 1961. Thereafter, MGM/UA, the production-distribution partners, let it be known that they had neither the will nor resources to continue with 007.

Behind MGM/UA's business stance was the reality that the studio which had grown from the creative vision of Charlie Chaplin and Mary Pickford almost a century before was dying. By default the French government-controlled bank Crédit Lyonnais owned the studios and, under US law, was obligated to sell it before 1997. In a last ditch effort to pump up viability, the new controllers John Calley and Frank Mancuso, decided to revamp Bond and reboot the franchise, a move that would necessitate taking control from Cubby Broccoli. Broccoli demurred. He would not support Calley's request to recast James Bond, insisting that Timothy Dalton, a family friend, must remain as 007, despite the poor box-office on his previous two outings. Calley played hardball, telling Broccoli that MGM/UA would no longer fund Bond. In the middle of this furious wrangling Broccoli became ill with congestive heart failure and his daughter, Barbara, together with stepson Michael Wilson, took over the day-to-day runnings of Eon Productions. For many months the subterranean word went out in the industry that the Bond franchise was up for sale to the highest bidder. Having generated billions of earnings and distinguished itself historically as the highest earning movie series ever, a genuine wave of sympathy and support swept through the film world. Even from his sick bed, Broccoli maintained his determination to retain Timothy Dalton and find new backers, but both Barbara and Michael Wilson saw the likelihood of the end of an era and the degeneration of James Bond into a cartoon network sell-off. As it turned out, Calley's tough tactics worked. As Cubby's health faded, Barbara and Wilson conceded to MGM/UA's total creative acquisition of the franchise in a reshaped deal that put Pierce Brosnan – whom Cubby did not want – in the lead role, and replaced director and key creative crews. Bond was relaunched, part-funded in promotion by Germany's BMW (another displacement that hurt Broccoli, causing as it did the loss of the Aston Martin authenticity), starring Brosnan and directed by television's Martin Campbell. From MGM/UA's point of view, the move was canny: $60 million, the biggest amount ever, was spent on the budget, but the nature of the deals with small-time performers meant no back-end profits were sacrificed. With BMW's push, the movie opened well in the summer of 1995, finally grossing $320 million worldwide, potentially saving the studio as a going concern and firmly establishing Brosnan as a Hollywood Bond.

On the face of it, Connery kept away from the mess. Remoulding himself in the mythic embodiment of *Dragonheart* and *First Knight*, ostensibly he didn't need the kind of world-stopping phenomenon-hit of another Bond. Or so the story went. In fact, his competitive and business instincts, so central in his psychological make-up, could not but be roused again by Brosnan and Calley's hit.

It seemed no coincidence, after Brosnan wrapped Bond, that Connery immediately signed with producers Don Simpson and Jerry Bruckheimer for Hollywood Pictures' *The Rock*, to be directed by 32-year-old Michael Bay. Described in *Premiere* magazine as 'a kind of *Die Hard* on Alcatraz', the imprimatur of the producers indicated immediately the competitive territory Connery was targeting. Renowned as mega-macho starmakers since 1986's *Top Gun* put Tom Cruise in the A list, Bruckenheimer and Simpson's hyper-kinetic approach to movie-making itself owed much to the narrative style of the early Bonds. With *The Rock*, they served notice of their intention to out-Bond *GoldenEye* by engaging a young director already notorious for his daring. Michael Bay was a film prodigy from Wesleyan University who had cut his teeth as a product pusher, making controversial commercials for Coke, Nike and Budweiser. In his late 20s his salacious music videos for Tina Turner and Meat Loaf won him the attention of Hollywood studios and *I Touch Myself*, the promo for a band called the Divinyls, garnered MTV award nominations and the admiration of Bruckheimer and Simpson. Connery was obviously keen for the heavyweight bout and many close to him commented on the regime of fitness to which he had recently applied himself. In the 80s, squaring up to Schwartzman's Bond reprise, Connery had crash-coursed a work-out routine. Since *Medicine Man*, Ross Wilson noted, he seemed to intensify his disciplines, 'serving notice that there was a lot of life yet in him'.

It would be hard to conceive of two creative talents as different as Bay and Connery, and it was apparent from the first strenuous days of shooting *The Rock* that conflict would occur. Connery's role as the criminal hero, assisting Nicolas Cage to infiltrate and smash a nuclear-armed terror group ensconced in the prison fortress of Alcatraz island in San Francisco Bay, was his most physically challenging role since *Indiana Jones*. Approaching seventy, one would have expected signs of a slow-down. Comparable elder statesmen of earlier eras – like Richard Harris and Burt Lancaster – emphatically removed themselves from the three-ring circus of actioners in their 50s. Connery, however, undertook the non-stop stunts of Bay's movie like a first-timer. Part of the attraction, he later said, was his desire to work with Cage, an actor of significant versatility who employed the same double-career principles, courting art house films while making blockbusters. Cage reciprocated, generating an on-screen chemistry with Connery reminiscent of Danny and Peachy in *The Man Who Would Be King*, or the Connery–Ford dynamism of *Indiana Jones*. But Bay tested Connery to the extreme. A feisty, impatient director-with-attitude, he didn't so much direct the movie as command it. His debut feature, *Bad Boys*, which grossed $150 million had fuelled his confidence and his angst. 'There,' he said, 'I had a studio that didn't believe in me and a piece of shit script – but I made it work.'

On set in LA Connery's and Bay's filming styles clashed. Bay liked rapid-fire MTV shooting 'from the hip'. Connery liked to rehearse. Seniority won out, and Bay conceded to Connery's insistence on rehearsals and daily walk-throughs of scenes-in-preparation. Since *Thunderball* Connery had complained of the crass indifference of producers and directors to the well-being and health of 'actors who are usually regarded as kind of puppets'. On *The Rock*, this hot issue raised its head again. Much of the action took place in a studio mock-up of the warren drains beneath Alcatraz prison, where Connery's stunt work left Bond in the shade. Bay said: 'One day I had to get [Connery] underwater holding his breath with a fireball coming over him. Apparently he wasn't too happy with the situation. I think the word "fuckhead" came out in the air.'

Connery survived and *The Rock* opened six months after *GoldenEye* with a bang. No movie he had made since *The Untouchables* attracted such unanimously good notices and nothing since Bond grossed so well in the budget-to-box-office ratio. Taking almost $155 million before its ancillary markets distribution, *The Rock* achieved a notable double success for Bay and repositioned Connery as an action player.

In January, before Bay had finished cutting *The Rock*, the Hollywood Foreign Press Association awarded Connery the Cecil B DeMille lifetime achievement award at the Golden Globes. Connery was moved, and he was eloquent, emphasising his continued belief in the edifying substance of ambitious movie-making, while subtly demonstrating his mastery of the industry principles by acknowledging his foundation as an action star. It skipped no one's attention that, while making movies like *The Rock*, he had co-funded and developed the theatrical production of a fringe Parisian play by Yasmina Reza called *Art*, which he took to London and on tour in the US and which was destined to win an Olivier Award, an *Evening Standard* Award and a Tony. 'Truthfully,' Connery told the Golden Globes audience in Beverly Hills, 'it is the stuff in between the shooting and the punches and the car crashes that really counts. The scenes between the men and the women that try to say something about how we really behave, what we really feel, that's ultimately what moves people and sends them into the movie-houses. In other words, I prefer my audiences stirred, not shaken.'

The provocative ghost of James Bond, both *bête noire* and best friend, would not lie down. The week of *The Rock*'s opening Connery told the *Chicago Sun-Times* that he had seen *GoldenEye* and liked it. 'I thought Pierce Brosnan was a good choice. Timothy Dalton never got a handle on the role. He took it too seriously in the wrong way. The secret of 007? The person who plays Bond has to be dangerous. If there isn't a sense of threat, you can't be cool.'

That simple summary comprehensively defined the universe of reasons why Connery personally and in the public's perception, would never fully be free of his best creation. Since the great adversities of his childhood he had naturally courted risk, and been temperamentally suited to deal with it. Money mattered to him, not in the infamous cliché of the penurious Scotsman, but as a measure of his independence and achievement. Competitive energy were bywords for his deepest nature, and his fighting spirit, said his brother Neil, was 'a hard-assed mean spirit'.

It was almost no surprise to see the resurrection yet again of Ian Fleming's nemesis Kevin McClory with another rival Bond movie-in-the-making after *The Rock*. Micheline had once said that Sean always wanted to play Bond 'balding and acting his age'. The virility of *The Rock* awakened echoes and tantalised industry and fans alike.

# 21. FINDING CONNERY

Connery's choice after *The Rock* was a well-intentioned excursion into Bondiana that proved disastrous and scolded him for back-tracking on the promise he'd made to himself in establishing Fountainbridge Films to monitor the creative standards of the work he engaged in. In 1960 *The Avengers* television series was established by Sydney Newman and Leonard White at Britain's ABCTV, creators of *Armchair Theatre*, as a European equivalent of *Alfred Hitchcock Presents*. White wrote the show's manifesto, casting Patrick Macnee as the Edwardian-styled hero John Steed and specifying the key ingredients in a list that read: *Glamour. Unusual and Exciting Locales. An Important Mission. Story Balance. Wit. Humour. Grace. Action.* An acknowledgement of the contemporary literary success of Ian Fleming's Bond novels was made and the series started, with videotaped interiors at ABC's Teddington Studios and location filming around London in December 1960. In June 1962, after a successful 26-week run, Honor Blackman was signed as Macnee's crime-fighting partner, introducing elements of leather-clad fetish to a series distinguished by its accent on good writing. Blackman's popular success, combined with the radical originality of story editors like Richard Bates (the son of novelist HE Bates) and writer Brian Clemens reconfigured *The Avengers* into something unique and far removed from Hitchcock, whose closest parallel in film was James Bond. No overt cadging from the Eon Bond series took place, but a kind of symbiotic union bound the productions all through the 60s. Macnee's John Steed maintained his originality as the anachronistic dandy, but in the women he kept company with and in the Technicolor villainy he encountered, he clearly dwelt in the world of James Bond.

*The Avengers* successfully transferred to the US and became a cult series that lasted long into the 70s, but the compromises of co-production, with French and Canadian finances diluting the formula, effectively killed it in 1977. Thereafter Brian Clemens embarked on a tortuous screenwriting odyssey to reactivate the key concept for the big screen. At various times a movie in 'almost pre-production' was announced and when Clemens moved base to Hollywood there was even gossip of Connery, in the aftermath of *Never Say Never Again*, reviving Steed.

In the honeymoon period after *The Rock* anything seemed possible. On screen, and in casting offices, it appeared as if Connery had turned back the clock. Certainly he had reawoken McClory, who had always longed for yet another reworking of *Thunderball* and now had before him the manifest evidence of Bond's viability in *GoldenEye*. Eric Boehm in *Variety* was first to announce a rival Bond. On 9 October 1996 he wrote that two Bond movies were in the making: 'Bond 18', starring Brosnan, to be directed by Roger Spottiswoode, and *Warhead 2000*. A fortnight later McClory announced from his temporary home in the west of Ireland that the film was cast and ready to go: 'A lot of people wondered where I disappeared to over the last couple of years. I was in Amsterdam writing the script.' Connery would not, however, play Bond. 'But he has said he'd play the villain if the price was right.'

As it had done with *Never Say Never Again*, the threat of legal action against McClory's Spectre Associates company loomed, but the game had changed since the 80s. In June, shortly after the opening of *The Rock*, Cubby Broccoli died in Los Angeles and McClory had lost his chief opponent. Broccoli's passing, aged 87, was a significant marker in many lives, not least Connery's. In the subsequent tribute held on 17 November at the Odeon, Leicester Square, cradle of so many Bond premieres, Dalton, Brosnan and Roger Moore paid respectful attendance, but Connery stayed away. 'They had been close, even devoted, for two decades,' reported the *Daily Express*, 'but their relationship finally soured in the middle eighties.' Connery still harboured 'a deep resentment of what he considers to be the Bond filmmakers' meanness'.

Despite Kevin McClory's entreaties and further showy announcements in the trade papers, Broccoli's passing seemed to trigger an end to Connery's musings on Bond. Instead, early in 1997, he committed to the carbon-copy alternative of *The Avengers*.

Everything about Warners' massively budgeted ($60 million plus) *Avengers* proved diametrically opposite to the template-establishing of *First Knight* and *Dragonheart* and the action-finesse of *The Rock*. Written by Don Macpherson and directed by Jeremiah Chechik, the movie proved a defining model of ineptitude and an unsurpassable example of the artlessness of the modern studio – *viz.* business-led movie. Brian Clemens' great device of supplanting conventional backgrounds with the landscapes of Magritte and Max Ernst was lost in overkill. Ralph Fiennes played Steed with the unplayable approach – parodying parody – and, greatest sin of all, Connery's monumental persona as the villain and vortex in the piece was kilted, primped and filled with bad jokes to present a puffed-up pantomime queen. Throughout the production – long, arduous, bad-weather months at Shepperton – Connery had been bad-tempered and unwell. He and Micheline based themselves at their Belgravia home, from which he commuted, driving himself in the unit Range Rover. During August he took ill, and driving home early one Saturday on the A316 Great Chertsey Road, he was almost killed when a brick lobbed off a pedestrian bridge smashed the front window of the Rover. 'He thought it was a gunshot,' said Neil. 'He was very lucky not to have swerved off the road and done himself in.'

When Connery saw the final cut of *The Avengers* he was outraged. It had seemed all right, he said, as the production unfolded, and he had been constantly reassured about his concerns. But in the end neither Chechik nor the producers knew what they were about. 'It was a complete and utter fuck-up,' he told a close friend. 'Amateur night stuff. If I could get my hands on any of them, I'd kill them.'

It was fortunate, Ian Bannen observed, that there were positive issues to distract him. In May the Film Society of Lincoln Center staged a gala tribute unlike any he'd experienced, that brought together Ursula Andress, Tippi Hedren, Sidney Lumet, George Plimpton, Harrison Ford, Michael Caine and Steven Spielberg to doff their hats – an event he found 'very moving' – and throughout the summer the Scottish National Party's lobbying for a Yes vote in the upcoming devolution referendum drew him back into political activity. 'I felt he was tired,' said Bannen. 'He overextends himself, and he was at the point where he needed the kind of pick-me-up that only a big Scots nationalist victory could give him. And the stars were in perfect alignment for him, because the whole 300-year-old business of whether or not Scotland should have an independent parliament was on the cards.'

Connery had never given a campaigning speech, nor met his political critics face-on in all his years of support for the nationalist party. No one doubted his deep commitment – a commitment made clear in the $50,000 a year he donated to the SNP – but his preference has always been for background action. But in September of 1997 he rose like a phoenix from the previous controversies to share a platform with Scottish Secretary Donald Dewar, Scottish Liberal Democrat leader Jim Wallace and SNP chief Alex Salmond to argue his support for devolution, a key manifesto commitment of the incumbent Labour government. Alex Salmond later wrote that it was a direct appeal by prime minister Tony Blair's close ally Peter Mandelson, not Dewar who was ostensibly heading up Labour's campaign, that persuaded Connery into the campaign. In early September, in spite of the years of aspiration, Scotland itself appeared to hesitate about the desirability of an independent parliament. Polls suggested eleventh hour reconsideration, with the central issue of tax-varying powers the stumbling block. According to the poll appearing in Scotland on Sunday three days before the referendum, 76 per cent of the 1,057 companies questioned believed that a Scottish Parliament with tax-varying powers would harm the business climate. Overall, reported the Sunday Times, a marginal 51 per cent of the population supported a new parliament with control of its own taxation laws.

Connery, to whom the conversational topics of taxes and business models was a daily staple, pulled no punches in letting the world know where he stood. At the time of the referendum the American underwater communications firm, Oceaneering Multiflex, was siting itself at the old Ministry of Defence buildings at the Rosyth Naval Dockyards. With exquisite theatrical timing, Connery embraced the opportunity to appear at a press conference with Chancellor Gordon Brown, announcing this 'major new inward investment' that was 'an undoubted vote of confidence in the future of Scotland's economy'.

The triumph of the Yes vote and the eventual establishment of a Scottish Parliament in the summer of 1999 seemed, from afar, cakewalk victories for the nationalists and smug rewards for Connery personally. In fact, his close friends point out, Connery was bloodied and vexed by the battle, earning the contempt of Dewar and the centrists of the Labour government for his radical edge.

The year that should have been occasion for paramount celebration, 1998, turned into one of his toughest. As payback for his SNP support, according to circulating wisdom, he had lost his chance of a knighthood that even the Conservatives supported. According to the BBC, a Sunday newspaper reported that Dewar had personally vetoed the planned honour. Alex Salmond was outraged and told the BBC that Connery was 'Scotland's most famous son and international ambassador' and that his personal efforts to support Labour's pledge for Scottish devolution were remarkable. Dewar's move, said Salmond, was 'petty, mean-spirited and vindictive'.

At work on yet another American movie, this time a small-budget ensemble piece destined to barely dent the cinema chains, called *Playing by Heart*, Connery called Salmond and left a cool, resigned message on his answering machine, quoting Robbie Burns:

> *A prince can make a belted knight*
> *A marquis, a duke and all that*
> *The man of independent mind*
> *Looks and laughs at all that.*

Nonetheless, the hurt ran deep. As the Educational Trust had borne witness, Connery's objective benevolent support of his homeland was unselfish and true and, despite the brickbats in the summer in the run-up to the release of *The Avengers*, he and Micheline went house-hunting around Edinburgh to mark the auspicious imminence of the new parliament, which he regarded as a step towards inevitable Scottish independence. An elegant Edwardian mansion called Bunkerhill, by the beach in North Berwick, twenty miles east of Edinburgh, was deemed a potential new home base. In July, Micheline formally announced that the twenty-year-plus sojourn in the Costa del Sol was over. 'Sean is now a living legend,' said Micheline, 'and he gets followed everywhere. When I met him, I knew I was taking on the whole package. Everyone wants him and I have to accept and understand that. But there is a limit. We used to be able to walk about in privacy, but now you get people asking for photos all the time and women wanting to talk to him. It's a shame, because the house has become part of our lives ever since we first met. But the privacy issue has become *harder* as he gets older, which is unusual for an actor.' There were other irritants, she said: Sean had never properly learned to speak either Spanish or French, and his patience level in communications challenges had run out. 'About three years ago he said he'd like to move, and we have been thinking about it ever since.'

Weeks after the announcement, the Casa Malibu went on the market, for an asking price of nearly £5.5 million and, according to local estate agents, took months to find a buyer. One British-based real estate agent operating from Marbella said, 'Its problem is its grandeur. Quality British-owned villas change hands every season for half a million. The Connerys built a castle on the coast, and it was hard, in a depressed market, to realise its worth.'

Creatively Connery was in a good mood in the early summer. He had enjoyed working under Willard Carroll and alongside Gena Rowlands in the bittersweet love affair compendium *Playing by Heart*, and been gratified by the Tony honours for the play *Art*. Still high on *The Rock*, he signed on to Fox's like-minded actioner, *Entrapment*, as if, some said, he was taunting MGM's ongoing Brosnan-Bond.

*Entrapment* unfolded as an age- and time-defying phenomenon, brazenly placing Connery, at almost 70, as male sex bait opposite Catherine Zeta-Jones, more than 40 years his junior. Yet another Fountainbridge production, more or less personally managed by

Connery, *Entrapment* comprehensively answered any doubters of the actor's virility or market sense. In director Jon Amiel Connery found perfect partnership and deep rapport. Every bit as physically taxing as *The Rock, Entrapment* spanned the globe, with locations jumping from the Isle of Mull (unmissable proof of the authorship of Fountainbridge), to London, New York and Malaysia, often shooting in extreme conditions. Connery easily weathered it all – hurricane winds in Scotland, monsoons in Kuala Lumpur, endless wire-suspension stunts of the *Diamonds Are Forever* variety – and Amiel found him 'a joy to work with. He *gets it* and he knows exactly what is needed and how to deliver it with maximum economy. Watching him step in front of the cameras is a revelation. And when the cameras turn, you realise exactly why he is an icon.' Zeta-Jones, in the process of emerging as Britain's first truly provocative sex symbol since Joan Collins, and widely in demand, listed her reasons for joining the production simply as 'the script, and Sean'.

The swagger of the production, discernible to all who took part, was vintage-Bondian. Connery portrayed Mac, a mischief-minded master thief hounded by investigator Gin (Zeta-Jones), who is seduced into collaborating in the millennium-eve mega-robbery in Malaysia's twin towers, the world's tallest buildings. Plot, characterisation and action content were all Bond league and Connery's bedside encounters with the semi-nude Zeta-Jones recalled the sexual power of similar scenes with Daniela Bianchi almost forty years before. Pacing MGM's Bond was obviously the richest vein for Connery to mine.

But in late summer the good graces dried up, with the opening of *The Avengers*, followed by *Playing by Heart*, two disastrous box-office performers. *The Avengers* – given the efforts and cash it entailed, easily Connery's most disappointing film – opened with a nervous first week's takings of $13 million, slumping in the second to less than $4 million, parking it, in terms of proportional losses, alongside *Meteor*. *Playing by Heart*, a small film of some nobility distributed by Miramax, opened on only 308 screens across the US (Connery's actioner average was about 2,500 screens), and totted $3.7 million.

*The Avengers* embarrassed all its well-intentioned participants because it became the *Ishtar* of its time, the showcase of 90s' failures. Notorious within the trade long before its August release, Warners 'tried to hide it', according to the *San Francisco Chronicle*, by fiddling and delaying its press screenings. But for Connery, who historically assumed a kind of pride-of-ownership in his recent productions, whether Fountainbridge Films was involved or not, there was no dodging and no forgiving. In a deeply felt rage, his only succour was the progress of *Entrapment*, and his confidence in Jon Amiel whose style, said a friend, was 'close to Guy Hamilton's, which was the sort of "Let's get this shit up and done with" efficiency'.

By November the Connerys had finally bid adieu to Spain and were in the process of rebuilding their domestic lives in New York when another blow fell. While Sean was out of town wrapping *Entrapment*, the family's New York apartment was burgled, with the loss of more than $1 million of Micheline's jewellery, including her Cartier watch, and sentimentally valued Bulgari trinkets. Connery was enraged, but incommunicado, as he remained when the announcement was made of his support for a proposed movie studio complex in Edinburgh, to be co-funded by Sony and a group of undefined Scottish businesses. BBC News reported that the studios would bring 'hundreds of jobs to the city, ranging from security and catering to film technicians and actors, and that as many as twenty native movies could be made in the first five years of production.' John Archer, chief executive of the publicly funded film coordination agency, Scottish Screen, was quoted as saying that Connery was expected to put some of his own money into the studios but, said the BBC, 'dismissed suggestions that [Connery] could be carrying out some sort of revenge by keeping the government at a distance from the project'.

The issue-in-debate of the withheld knighthood – indeed of Connery's place in the political and cultural universe – seemed preposterous and surreal as the end of the millennium approached, though there were comforting historical precedents. In terms of populist phenomena, only the Beatles matched Connery-Bond in money- and esteem-generating contributions to the British economy. The Beatles individually, and their visionary mentor Brian Epstein, had been continually overlooked for significant honours. In 1964 the Beatles (without Epstein) had been granted MBEs – 'just a cardboard thingie on a piece of leather', George Harrison had complained – and though McCartney had finally been knighted in 1998, many felt outraged by the offensive omissions of Lennon, Harrison, Starr and Epstein.

Officially 'annoyed' by Labour's specious blocking of the knighthood – which he regarded anyway as no more than a respectful salute to his Scots contribution – Connery could justifiably burn in resentful rage as he witnessed the frantic legal tugs-of-war over the Bond fortune in the last days of the millennium. What had started with ad hoc creative sparring between Terence Young, the producers and himself had generated £3 billion which now fed greed machines. In the late 90s, as Kevin McClory made a deal with Columbia and its parent company Sony for *Doomsday 2000*, another *Thunderball* remake, Mancuso's MGM had launched a massive lawsuit to scotch any franchise opposition. Sony countersued, claiming McClory's ownership rights not just to *Thunderball* and its outgrowths, but to all of cinematic James Bond.

Wearied by the affronts and by the embarrassment of *The Avengers*, Connery renewed himself in his friendship with Alex Salmond and his determination to maximise nationalist aspirations in the new parliament. In April, days before the first Scottish parliamentary elections, he was galvanised by the SNP's slump in the polls, lagging eighteen points behind Dewar's Labour. Disaffection for many had risen from the SNP's proposed tax-hiking and its opposition to NATO's bombing campaign in the former Yugoslavia, and on 26 April Connery made his first strictly political speech – entirely scripted by himself – to 300 invited business and local political leaders. The keynote was an unapologetic pledge for independence, a concept that comprehensively defined him, and his views for Scotland. Alex Salmond was later to point out in his memoirs, published in 2000, that it had been Connery, and mainly Connery, who fastened the victory for the

Yes-Yes devolution resolution. 'Looking back,' he wrote, 'it doesn't seem credible that one man made the difference between success and failure, given the eventual comfortable margin of victory for the Yes-Yes campaign. However, "Connery Day" was immensely important. It set the tone for the final days of campaigning where the Yes-Yes camp was totally dominant and the No-No rivals were blown away completely.'

In the May elections Connery was rewarded for his input by an improved SNP rating and a better-than-projected footing in the new parliament. On 1 July the Queen presided over the opening ceremony at the parliament's temporary home in the Church of Scotland Assembly Hall, coincidentally while Connery was in town with Catherine Zeta-Jones to promote what one paper called 'his umpteenth triumphant comeback', *Entrapment*.

*Entrapment* – and the historic parliamentary breakthrough – were magical balms to him. The SNP's consolidation, and the new parliament, he regarded 'as matters of personal pride'. But *Entrapment* was his art, and the best of millennial gifts to himself, and to his loyal audience.

In so many ways, in the 45-year span of his career, the wheel had turned full circle. In his boyhood in Edinburgh the passion had been for the wide expanse of far horizons, for the countryside beyond Fife, and escape. Now, like a boomerang, he was back. In the late 50s, Twentieth-Century Fox was the studio that first contracted him, then neglected him. Now he was Fox's salvation. In 1999 Fox rated a poor eighth among distributors. *Entrapment* stopped the slide, with an opening weekend gross of more than $20 million – Connery's best financial return since *The Rock* – and fourth, trailing *The Matrix*, in the year's best earners. *Variety*, like virtually every other journal, ascribed the success of the movie to savvy marketing of a sound product – spiced up with an extra ingredient: 'The sex appeal of [Zeta-Jones and Connery] was the major contributor to *Entrapment*'s success.'

Shortly before his death in 1999, Connery's old friend Ian Bannen had defined 'that loony Scots git' in terms of 'compete and win, and win *and win*'. Through the trials and tribulations of the 90s Connery had repeatedly taken his audience to the high stakes tables, testing himself, as ever, in adventurous ways, this time largely without the safety net of the studio apologia. Now, for all to see, he had acquired the industry clout that raised him to near-auteur status and illuminated the true strengths and weaknesses. After a decade of unremitting creative focus he had reassured himself of his greatest gift: a facility for projecting protean masculinity graced with something amorphous and universal, like the metaphysical luminance in a painting by Picasso. He was not Stallone or Willis or Schwarzenegger or Douglas or Gable or Cooper; or Moore or Dalton or Brosnan. He was unique, and uniquely resonant in the dream lives of those who subscribed to his movie journeys.

It seemed fully appropriate that *The Rock* and *Entrapment* gave *GoldenEye* and *Tomorrow Never Dies* a run for their money. It was even edifying, in context of the cultural reassurance that the 'corporate movie', the horse-designed-by-committee, wasn't the only way. There was still actors with humanity and vision, and still audiences seeking them out.

In December, as the millennium turned, Connery's achievements were marked in Washington when he became a recipient of the Kennedy Center Honors, hosted by President Clinton. The award, among the most significant in American cultural life, was touching for Connery who was, as usual, working on a new and experimental movie, *Finding Forrester*, directed by Gus Van Sant, who had recently scored with the sensitive *Good Will Hunting*. Connery's acceptance speech was short and eloquent but, as ever, he was unavailable to the media, uninterested in reflection, more committed to the future.

The choice of a movie like *Finding Forrester* at this time was of no small significance. Written by first-timer Mike Rich, the story was one of spiritual self-discovery, set within the not-unfamiliar yarn of the gradual fixation of a young urban tearaway, Jamal Wallace, with the reclusive once-famous author Forrester, played by Connery. In the course of the action each of these two main characters becomes a catalyst in the other's life, drawing out their best potential. For Connery, *Finding Forrester* was manifestly a personal journey. In his account of it, the first draft had 'drawn me in totally. I knew it would be difficult – an easy movie to fudge – but the challenge took hold of me from the first reading.' The challenge, to those who knew Connery, was in coming face to face with the personal parallels in Forrester. Like the title character, Connery's fame had been the proverbial double-edged sword that struck him down. Rediscovering his true self required immersion in new waters: in Forrester's case a father–son relationship with an adolescent prodigy; in Connery's a return to the kind of precision psychological essaying of movies like *The Offence*.

Rob Brown, a teenager with no previous acting experience, played Jamal, the gifted black kid who reawakens and realigns the maladjusted Forrester. Connery stood up for Brown's casting because 'he was smart, he had good instincts', and perhaps because, for the first time since *A Fine Madness* he too was playing solely by instinct, cataloguing with extraordinary unselfconsciousness the inner world of the creative temperament. Shot entirely on location in New York, the semi-theatrical parameters of Van Sant's movie satisfied Connery as few movies had ever done and spurred him on, he said, to scouting new projects that would extend him as an actor.

In July he had cause to pause. Against the portentous predictions of the anti-SNP nay-sayers, finally he was knighted in the Queen's birthday list. In his response to the honour, he surprised even himself. Accompanied by Micheline and Neil, he wore Highland dress to the Palace of Holyrood House for the ceremony, kneeling before the Queen and graciously bowing as she placed the red sash over his neck. It was, he said, 'a great honour for Scotland, and one of the proudest days of my life'. The acceptance of the honour, and his pride in it, spoke conclusively of his humanitarian nationalism. Shortly before, while he campaigned for SNP seats in the new parliament, he'd been asked on radio, whom he hoped would win. His answer came pat: 'I hope Scotland wins.' A year later, on the steps of the Capitol in Washington, accepting the Tartan Day award from the new First Minister Henry McLeish, Connery pled for Scottish independence, no less, recalling the 1320 Declaration of Arbroath: 'Scotland is blossoming once again, coming into its own and, I believe, will soon be an equal and independent member of the community of nations.' Alongside him, the First Minister applauded in affirmation: 'I see Scotland as a proud nation within the union that makes up the United Kingdom, and within the larger European union.'

At Christmas *Finding Forrester*, a Fountainbridge production, opened in the US to impressive returns, grossing almost $60 million in its first weeks. The resonance here was the healthy box-office for a movie that was cerebral and calm, as far from *Entrapment* as could be. Connery personally loved the finished movie. It reminded him, he said, of *The Man Who Would Be King*; it was 'a complete picture, one that goes the full cycle. *Variety* endorsed the self-compliment, noting the cultural merits: 'When was the last time a Hollywood movie portrayed the acts of reading and writing in such a gratifying and fulfilling way that it made you want to read a real book rather than an airport bestseller?'

At the end of the 90s Ian Bannen had marvelled at the completeness of Sean Connery's career. As the century changed, with the blessing of a parliament for Scotland, the deeply symbolic knighthood, the outpacing of Bond and the full circle of *Finding Forrester*, it seemed impossible to imagine new peaks or challenges. But Connery found it in returning to the template, in going back to the vortex of hero-creation in signing on for Fox's *The League of Extraordinary Gentlemen*. A few years before, Ian Bannen had prophesied it: 'Sean is organic. He is a born actor. You don't "learn" it. But you grow as a man, as a human being, and your acting evolves. What remains for him is what remains for the rest of us, his audience, till the day he dies. His characters, the people he invents . . .'

In the vast journey of his life Connery has taken his audience from Caribbean beaches to the Arctic, from the absurdity of the human condition, through adrenalin flights of adventure, to the deepest reflection. He has changed modern cinema by adding grace to action, and a subtly political, visionary heart to heroism. Reviewing the misjudged *Avengers*, the *San Francisco Chronicle* wrote that 'Connery's presence is sprinkled throughout and he has the best scenes – solely because Sean Connery is in them'. It is a power like alchemy and, like alchemy, it defies conventions. With seventy-plus years and sixty-plus movies behind him so far one might reasonably interpret a biography as a summary, a curtain-call. In Connery's case, given the substance and the signs, it adds up to a new beginning.

# APPENDIX

**THE FILMS**
No Road Back (1956)
Hell Drivers (1957)
Time Lock (1957)
Action of the Tiger (1957)
Another Time, Another Place (1958)
Darby O'Gill and the Little People (1959)
Tarzan's Greatest Adventure (1959)
The Frightened City (1961)
On the Fiddle (Operation Snafu) (1961)
The Longest Day (1962)
Dr. No (1962)
From Russia with Love (1963)
Woman of Straw (1964)
Marnie (1964)
Goldfinger (1964)
The Hill (1965)
Thunderball (1965)
A Fine Madness (1966)
You Only Live Twice (1967)
Shalako (1968)
The Molly Maguires (1970)
The Red Tent (1971)
The Anderson Tapes (1971)
Diamonds Are Forever (1971)
The Offence (1973)
Zardoz (1974)
Ransom (The Terrorists) (1974)
Murder on the Orient Express (1974)
The Wind and the Lion (1975)
The Man Who Would Be King (1975)
Robin and Marian (1976)

The Next Man (The Arab Conspiracy) (1976)
A Bridge Too Far (1977)
The First Great Train Robbery (1979)
Meteor (1979)
Cuba (1979)
Time Bandits (1980)
Outland (1981)
Wrong is Right (The Man with the Deadly Lens) (1982)
Five Days One Summer (1982)
Sword of the Valiant (1982)
Never Say Never Again (1983)
Highlander (1986)
The Name of the Rose (1986)
The Untouchables (1987)
The Presidio (1988)
Memories of Me (cameo) (1988)
Indiana Jones and the Last Crusade (1989)
Family Business (1989)
The Hunt for Red October (1990)
The Russia House (1990)
Highlander II: The Quickening (1991)
Robin Hood: Prince of Thieves (1991)
Medicine Man (1992)
Rising Sun (1993)
A Good Man in Africa (1994)
Just Cause (1995)
First Knight (1995)
Dragonheart (1996)
The Rock (1996)
The Avengers (1998)
Playing by Heart (1998)
Entrapment (1999)
Finding Forrester (2000)

# ACKNOWLEDGEMENTS AND SOURCES

The generosity of contributors makes good biographies. In this instance I must acknowledge especially John Boorman and Sheamus Smith, whose support started this book more than twenty years ago. I owe a special debt to Neil Connery also, for his warmth and trust. My primary source material was drawn from interviews conducted with the following: Neil Connery, Guy Hamilton, Lewis Gilbert, Michael Caine, Robert Hardy, Robert Henderson, Estelle Winwood, Richard Lester, Dennis Selinger (ICM), Johnny Wallis, Harry Band (UA), Andrew Fyall, Marjorie Bilbow, Paul Higginson (Twentieth-Century Fox), Alfie Bass, Honor Blackman, Zena Marshall, Molly Peters (a special fond hug), Walter Gottel, Celeste Gottel, Craigie Veitch, John Brady, Tom O'Sullivan, Chris Menaul, Michael O'Herlihy, Kieron Moore, Gerry Johnson, Jack Vinestock, Ronald Pickup, Brian Doyle, Ian Bannen, Fred Zinnemann, Richard Brooks, Malcolm Idles, Kevin McClory, David James, Kevan Barker, Ross Wilson, Karen Cook, Michael Hayes, Alvin Rakoff, John Boorman and Sheamus Smith. Eric Sykes, Cyril Cusack, John Clive, Ray McAnally, Donal McCann and John Voort were also hugely helpful. A number of others, encountered incidentally during work in other areas of my career, were tangentially but no less importantly illuminating, among them the writers Anthony Shaffer (whose personal insights on Hitchcock electrified many a Merlot-fuelled evening at my home in Dublin) and John Kruse, and the actors Richard Harris, Bernard Lee, Desmond Llewelyn and Roger Moore, whom I directed in the television series *My Riviera*, made shortly after his retirement from Bond.

The journals consulted are copious, and are referenced within the text. I wish to express my indebtedness for permission to quote from them, and to some very generous journalists – Ivan Waterman, Tony Crawley and Frederic Albert Levy in Paris – who accessed their personal files for me, covering every aspect of Sean Connery's career since the early 60s. I am also grateful to the staff and libraries of the *Edinburgh Evening News*, the *Scotsman*, the *Irish*

*Times*, the *Guardian*, *The Times*, BBC Library, Westminister Central Library, Information Section of the British Film Institute (Pat Perilli), British Actors' Equity (JW Gregson) and the Margaret Herrick Library at the Academy of Motion Picture Arts & Sciences, Los Angeles, California. Also, a special grateful mention to Jeni McConnell and Graham Rye of the James Bond Fan Organisation and Brooke Hauser at *Premiere* magazine in New York, who pulled out the stops to help me beat the clock on this revised work.

A different kind of thank you – for spiritual and creative support – must go to beloved and loyal friends, past and current: to my constant mentor, the writer Dermot Byrne, to my father Michael Callan (who walks the walk), to Gary Goldman and Don Bluth (who never waver), to Shay Hennessy, Antony and Jay Worrall Thompson, Dr John Kelly, Wendy Hopkins and Donna Kail, Lois Smith at PMK, Meg McSweeney at the American Academy of Dramatic Arts in New York, Jeannette Kearney and Jim Kearney, Tricia Mooney (thank you for your patience), Ciara Gibbons and Cathy Boyle at Blue Leaf Art Gallery in Dublin and my personal role models, Moya Doherty, John McColgan and Robert Redford, constant friends through many personal storms. Those who have passed are never forgotten: Mick Harper and Mandy Hakman-Scott, important artists both; and Francis Feighan, Carl Wilson and Margaret Callan, who were there for me.

Warm acknowledgement to my research and support team, spanning twenty years, among them: Samantha Finneran, Anne-Marie Glennon, Helen McGivern, Renee Glennon, Susan O'Neill, Carolann Manahan, Caroline Dunne, Karen Hodge, Susan Deegan, Sue Kinsella, Donna Walsh, J McAuliffe, Sharon Good, Audrey Hanlon, Chiola Swanepoele, Karin O'Reilly, Tricia Hayes. Also to copy typist Emer Ghee; to Ed Victor for his caring advice; to my patient and visionary editors Sally Holloway, Hilary Muray and Susan Hill – and most of all Kirstie Addis at Virgin Books.

Without the wisdom of Ree, Corey Wilson Callan and Paris Callan this revised edition would be a notion floating on a feather on a windy day. Jai guru deva om – as always.

Finally, for the work, and the dreams, and the future, thank you, Sean.

# INDEX